Outsight:
Psychology, politics and social justice

The Midlands Psychology Group
(John Cromby, Bob Diamond, Paul Kelly,
Paul Moloney, Penny Priest)

First published 2022

PCCS Books Ltd
Wyastone Business Park
Wyastone Leys
Monmouth
NP25 3SR
contact@pccs-books.co.uk
www.pccs-books.co.uk

© The Midlands Psychology Group,
John Cromby, Bob Diamond, Paul Kelly, Paul Moloney, Penny Priest

All rights reserved.
No part of this publication may be reproduced, stored in a retrieval system, transmitted or utilised in any form by any means, electronic, mechanical, photocopying or recording or otherwise, without permission in writing from the publishers.

The authors have asserted their right to be identified as the authors
of this work in accordance with the Copyright, Designs and Patents Act 1988.

Outsight: Psychology, politics and social justice

British Library Cataloguing in Publication data: a catalogue record for this book is available from the British Library.

ISBN Paperback 978 1 915220 10 3
ePub 978 1 915220 11 0

Cover design by Jason Anscomb

Typeset in-house by PCCS Books using Minion Pro and Myriad Pro
Printed in the UK by Severn, Gloucester

Endorsements for *Outsight: Psychology, politics and social justice*

This is a delightfully challenging book about why and how psychology has largely failed to fulfil its obvious potential to help us understand and improve our world. The authors map how individualism and positivism are strangling our university psychology departments and the work of many clinical psychologists. They also have great suggestions as to how we might get the blind, bumbling, irrelevant juggernaut that psychology has become to open its eyes and start doing its job. If ever there was a time for that, it is now.

John Read, Professor of Clinical Psychology, University of East London

'We are in a mess' is the starting point for this incisive analysis. In arguing for 'outsight', not just the traditional focus on 'insight', this book shows where psychology has gone wrong and how it can get back on track. The solutions lie not in our heads, but in our lives. The Midlands Psychology Group have synthesised their collective wisdom into a compelling argument.

Lucy Johnstone, clinical psychologist, trainer, speaker, author of *The Straight Talking Introduction to Psychiatric Diagnosis* and *Users and Abusers of Psychiatry* and co-author of *The Power Threat Meaning Framework*

For more than 15 years, the Midlands Psychology Group (MPG) have critiqued taken-for-granted concepts and practices in psychology, proposing what they call a social materialist psychology. The late David Smail, psychologist and MPG member, argued that, instead of promoting 'insight' – seeing the causes of distress as lying within us – we should, instead, aim for 'outsight' by looking for the causes of distress in the ideologies and systems that govern our lives. Extending and developing the MPG's previous work, this book shows how mainstream psychology both reflects and supports neoliberalism, particularly in its promotion of psychological therapies. The authors also examine ways forward, including a focus on communities and on changing the conditions of people's lives. The book is highly recommended to service users, practitioners and trainees and also to the interested lay reader.

David Harper, Professor of Clinical Psychology and Programme Director (Academic) of the Professional Doctorate in Clinical Psychology at the University of East London

What is clinical psychology getting wrong, and why? An overdue, much-needed and scholarly critique of current thinking and practice in clinical psychology, pointing to useful and exciting ways forward. Every trainee and clinical psychologist should read this book.

Anne Cooke, Clinical Director, Doctoral Programme in Clinical Psychology, Canterbury Christ Church University

This is a timely book. The Midlands Psychology Group have created a powerful account of their unique social materialist approach to psychology and distress. Alongside an extensive critique of mainstream psychology and neoliberal economics, the authors offer coherent and compelling theoretical and practical alternatives to individualistic psychology. In explaining how and why context – both social and material – is often neglected in psychological theory and practice, this book offers a more integrated and grounded way to think (or feel) about mental distress. The legacy of David Smail, the founder of the group, is clear, but the book also takes the social materialist perspective in new directions. Smail's work is combined with current theory and practice, including affect theory, community psychology and recent political activism. This book will be of interest to a wide range of academics, students and practitioners as well as those with an interest in mental health.

Laura McGrath, Lecturer in Psychosocial Mental Health, Open University

Contents

	Preface	*ix*
1	We are in a mess	*1*
2	A brief history of the present	*21*
3	The 'state' of psychology	*41*
4	Does therapy work?	*61*
5	The latest technologies of the self	*82*
6	Psychology and the construction of consent	*102*
7	A social materialist psychology	*122*
8	Doing psychology differently	*143*
9	Within and beyond psychology	*162*
10	Postscript: WTF 2020	*181*
	Appendix 1: Draft manifesto for a social materialist psychology of distress	*189*
	Appendix 2: Establishing and maintaining a group	*206*
	References	*209*
	Name index	*233*
	Subject index	*241*

Dedication
For David and Uta

Acknowledgements

This book is immeasurably better thanks to the generosity of our readers who commented on various drafts. Special thanks go to Steve Brown and Rachel Freeth for reading the entire manuscript. Sincere thanks also to Jan Celie, Bill Epstein, David Fryer, Rachel Fyson, Carl Harris, David Harvey, Lucy Johnstone, Keir Milburn, Jim Orford and Wendy Stainton-Rogers. The book would have been immeasurably better still if we had been able to act on all the feedback given.

Finally, we are very grateful to Karen Fraser for 'Burnt Wood – Charcoal', our frontispiece. Karen uses fine art photography techniques, both as an artist and in her teaching at Nottingham Trent University. Her photograph shows the burnt remnant of part of a garden fence, blown down in a freak autumn storm. The ceaseless economic growth demanded by capitalism releases more and more carbon dioxide into the atmosphere, causing global warming and violent, stormy weather. Trees capture carbon dioxide, but they can be cut down for wood, and that wood can then be burned, leaving behind pure carbon. Karen's close-up photograph symbolises the bleak devastation of capitalist-driven global warming, while also – in revealing the burnt wood's fragility, its intricacy, and its subtle, unexpected beauty – suggesting a glimmer of hope.

About the authors

John Cromby is Professor of Psychology at Leicester University UK. His research explores ways in which bodies and social influences interact, focusing particularly on mental health, emotion and feeling. He has published more than 70 academic journal articles, and authored, co-authored or edited academic books including *Psychology, Mental Health and Distress* (2013); *Feeling Bodies: Embodying Psychology* (2015) and *The Handbook of Biology and Society* (2018). He is a contributing author to the Power Threat Meaning Framework, published by the British Psychological Society's Division of Clinical Psychology in 2018.

Bob Diamond is a clinical psychologist with Nottinghamshire Healthcare NHS Trust. Drawing from critical and community psychology perspectives, he has published numerous articles on developing more personal and meaningful services. He has also published several chapters on the importance of a questioning psychology (*Being Human*, PCCS Books, 2008). He co-edited *Madness Contested: Power and practice* (PCCS Books, 2013). As a member of the Midlands Psychology Group, he has contributed to various articles and special editions.

Paul Kelly works in the student counselling service at University College Dublin. He trained as a clinical psychologist in Birmingham, and was involved in setting up the West Midlands Community and Critical Psychology Interest Group and the Midlands Psychology Group. He was also active in the Irish Mental Health Forum.

Paul Moloney is a counselling psychologist based in the Shropshire and Telford NHS Adult Learning Disabilities Team. He has worked in the fields of mental health, social and community work and addictions counselling, and has taught for the Open University. His publications include *The Therapy Industry* (Pluto Press, 2013).

Penny Priest started her working life as a teacher in East London. She first became interested in critical psychology during her own experience of being seen by a clinical psychologist, who mentioned the work of David Smail. During her training as a clinical psychologist at Birmingham University, she made contact with David. He introduced her to the West Midlands Critical and Community Psychology Group, which eventually spawned the Midlands Psychology Group.

Preface

We in the Midlands Psychology Group have sometimes grappled with anxiety, bewilderment or self-doubt. Don't most people face such struggles at points in their lives? Novelists, poets and philosophers would be redundant if this were not so. But it is the scientific discipline of psychology that seems as though it should provide the firmest understanding of who, how and why we are – of our triumphs and our tragedies. Unfortunately, far too many psychology graduates remain disappointed. Despite studying hard, they find themselves none the wiser about their own and other people's troubles. Why should this be so?

For all of us, the circumstances in which we grew up have helped to shape us in ways that are profound, complex and subtle. Some may have had childhoods woven from a web of sunny air, nurtured by a spring of water, pure and fair – to misquote Emily Brontë. Others may have grown up in impoverished neighbourhoods, where hardship and economic struggles were an everyday occurrence, sometimes eased by the kindness and decency of others. Like seedlings, humans need nurturing environments in order to thrive. Yet psychology has preferred to gaze inwards, downplaying the historical, cultural, economic, social and material environments that shape us all and that constrain and damage so many.

If we are to take seriously the despair and anguish suffered by growing multitudes, then we must abandon the temptation to find fault mainly inside the head of each troubled individual. We must look instead to the tangible causes of their distress: an increasingly toxic and turbulent social landscape, delineated by inequality, injustice, and – also increasingly – environmental breakdown. What stops psychology from doing this?

As life begins, our peep holes open, said novelist Kurt Vonnegut. Our professional peep holes were, if not opened, certainly widened by our dear friend David Smail. David's work encouraged, inspired and comforted us. He helped us realise that our unease about many aspects of psychology might have a firm grounding, both in our own experiences and in philosophical and scientific traditions largely ignored by the discipline. David is a fundamental reason for us coming together as a group more than 15 years ago. We want to express our gratitude to him and his family and to note the enduring influence of his work and ideas.

We are a group of counselling, clinical and academic psychologists and this book is written in our collective voice. Despite our differences, we agree on many important questions. This is no accident. For those of us in therapeutic practice, many years of trying to help people whose lives are filled with trauma, hardship and struggle make the limitations of talking therapy hard to deny. It is similar for academic psychology: longstanding familiarity with its favoured methods and preoccupations suggests that – in its current form – it will continue to yield a decontextualised, impoverished image of human experience and suffering.

One of the most complicated and contentious issues that we have grappled with as a group relates to the critical questions we ask about the multiple practices described as the psychological therapies. Most of our group are practising clinicians, and we have long debated our differing and changing views about the theories and methods of therapy. While we have not yet (and may never) reach a complete consensus, we thought it might be helpful for us to articulate some of the questions that have informed our discussions. These include:

- What is therapy, is it helpful, does it work?
- What do we mean by 'work', for whom, and how?
- Can therapy be a form of social solidarity? Can it be radical?

These questions emerged from our own sometimes fraught efforts to both practise therapy and survive professionally, in services that – for the most part – systematically individualise and pathologise the struggles of those who seek their help. We have considered whether we are living in a therapy culture and, if so, what this implies. Our enquiries have led us to the core significance of personal and professional interests and have never allowed us to forget the complexity of the underlying issues – to do with the nature of reality and of what we can ever know of it.

We do not pretend to have definitive answers to all these questions. Nor do we claim that we are the first to have grappled with them. Rather, our continued struggles reflect and illustrate one of the core messages of this book – that the deeds that shape and constitute the lives of all human beings are intricate and multi-determined, and their consequences are often unpredictable. This analysis applies with equal force to the activities called psychological therapy.

Our focus in this book is on the practice of clinical psychology and the psychotherapies it promotes. Our focus is also, simultaneously, on dominant tendencies within academic psychology – the theories and research – that legitimate and support clinical work. There are complex, dense bi-directional relationships between these two bodies of thought and practise. Academic psychology frequently demonstrates its relevance with reference to clinical problems. At the same time, clinical practice frequently legitimates its worth by invoking academic research and theory. So, while we acknowledge the differences between clinical and academic psychology, we also recognise their interdependencies and connections.

When we discuss psychology – both academic and clinical – we will be critical of tendencies toward individualism, and of the way that a particular philosophy of science – positivism – is used. This approach prioritises experimentalism and the apparently context-free evidence that psychology experiments produce (we say 'apparently context-free' because, of course, the experimental situation is itself a particular and unusual context).

Of course, this is not and never has been the only form of psychology. The academic discipline has always contained alternative, contradictory and sometimes even subversive currents – from the connections made by some US cognitivists with Soviet sociocultural psychology and the work of Vygotsky and Luria through to the rise of qualitative research methods in British psychology, and the vocal subdiscipline of critical psychology that began to emerge in the late 1980s. Similarly, clinical psychology includes community, systemic and family therapy approaches as well as the individual psychotherapy that we will particularly critique.

So, we recognise this diversity within both academic and clinical psychology. Indeed, at many points our arguments and evidence draw upon this work. Consistent with our aim of critiquing dominant tendencies within the discipline, though, our primary focus will often be on the way that a particular quantitative approach to psychology both powerfully shapes the discipline and is at the same time aligned with ideological demands.

We are aware that in writing from an explicitly critical perspective we may alienate some who are attached to this kind of psychology. With this in mind, it may be helpful to introduce a distinction that has been made between criticism and critique, and that has informed our work. This can be summed up succinctly as 'criticism is judgemental and focused on finding fault, while critique is descriptive and balanced'.[1]

Our work is not intended as criticism of the well-meaning efforts of colleagues in academic and applied psychology, and certainly not of them as persons. It is meant, in the spirit of academic and social critique, to highlight deficiencies and identify ways of addressing them. Critique is necessary; progress demands it – especially at this fraught and confusing time in human history. We offer our critiques in the hope that they may contribute constructively to a field that we are all part of and working within. And we too, of course, find some of the ideas in this book challenging and see our use of them as a work in progress.

We are equally aware that many other analysts have travelled similar terrain before. We do not claim any particular originality, and acknowledge with humility and gratitude the many whose ideas have infused our work. It has not been possible in this book to discuss the work of all those who might consider themselves fellow critics. Instead, we have of necessity drawn upon a body of writing that we feel closely supports our arguments. We accept that we will have left out more than we have included, and we welcome hearing from those who feel that their ideas align with our own. Equally, we anticipate feedback from those who disagree.

The Midlands Psychology Group is a living, organic entity bound together by shared experiences, values, interests and practices. Its heartbeat consists of our commitment to a tradition of ethical, scientific and rational critique. In our regular meetings over many years, we have found the group a source of comfort and sustenance – especially when returning, isolated, to our respective workplaces. Originally seven, we are now a group of five: David Smail died in 2014, but his ideas and his questioning stance still permeate the group. This book is our attempt to capture years of impassioned conversations and reflective deliberations that have ebbed and flowed between us. In keeping with this we invite you to question what we are saying, take from this book what you find useful, and evolve it with your own ideas and practices.

---

1. **The difference between critique and criticism**
   - Criticism finds fault/Critique looks at structure.
   - Criticism looks for what's lacking/Critique finds what's working.
   - Criticism condemns what it doesn't understand/Critique asks for clarification.
   - Criticism is spoken with a cruel wit and sarcastic tongue/Critique's voice is kind, honest, and objective.
   - Criticism is negative/Critique is positive (even about what isn't working).
   - Criticism is vague and general/Critique is concrete and specific.
   - Criticism has no sense of humor/Critique insists on laughter, too.
   - Criticism looks for flaws in the writer as well as the writing/Critique addresses only what is on the page.

   Taken from Reeves, J. (2002). *Writing alone, writing together: A guide for writers and writing groups*. New World Library.

Our book proposes a social-materialist psychology. This psychology arises not so much from an exhaustive accounting of what is inside of our minds as from a sober and considered outlook on the shared, physical world that surrounds us: on how it might shape everything that we think, feel and do. Hence this book is titled *Outsight* because we believe that looking out at the world, rather than simply inside individuals, is the way to produce a better psychology.

A core element of this endeavour is a critical analysis of the interests that mainstream psychology may be serving. We are far from being alone in believing that we should never forget the marginalised and neglected, and that we should embrace the values associated with a position of compassionate solidarity. However, we contend that mainstream psychology has too often failed to place these values at the core of its theories and practices. We hope that, on reading this book, others will take up some of the resources that we discuss and use them to question, challenge and maybe even change what they do.

Chapter 1

We are in a mess

We are in a mess (Monbiot, 2016). In fact, even before the Covid-19 pandemic threw many thousands of people out of work, even before the government chose to recoup most of the costs of the pandemic from the mass of ordinary working people (rather than from the financial industry, large businesses and the very wealthy) – even before these things happened, we were already in a mess.

Ten years ago, as cuts began to decimate our public services, a friend living abroad asked: 'Is it true that there are food banks at home?' What was unbelievable to her has now been normalised. Yet today, we not only have food banks, we have homeless people living in tents on city streets; zero-hours contracts as standard across whole swathes of the economy; increasing numbers of children being raised in poverty; ever-larger differentials in income and wealth; public land sold off to faceless organisations, and the cherry-picking of health, social care and education services by for-profit organisations. Forty years ago, to predict any of this would have been dismissed as dystopian fearmongering. Yet today, here we are; this is our reality.

This book is about this mess. More specifically, it is about psychology's contribution to the creation of this mess. It is about how psychology responds to the increasing despair the mess creates. It is about the ways that psychology is often complicit in promoting the norms and values that make the mess seem, if not acceptable, at least inevitable. It is also about how a better psychology might play some small part in clearing this mess up.

> *Neville was my neighbour, courteous and considerate. We would pass the time of day in the street, sharing polite conversations, and over time we gained glimpses of one another's private worlds. Typically, Neville would be walking several dogs, but never the same dogs for very long.*

> *Over the years I learnt that Neville had sought paid employment on numerous occasions, but the pressures and occupational demands always overwhelmed him. Eventually he had withdrawn from everyone and everything, finding solace within the four walls of his flat. He felt secure, if a little trapped. Gradually salvaging a semblance of life, Neville found a purpose in life that also enabled him to contribute to his community: providing temporary homes for dogs that belonged to women fleeing domestic violence. Once their owners were safe and back on their feet, Neville returned the dogs. One day, Neville revealed his petrified anguish over an imminent review of his social security payments. Afterwards, he described his utter devastation on hearing the outcome: his support was to be slashed, meaning it would be impossible for him to remain living in the flat where, over the past 15 years, he had come to feel safe.*
>
> *After this, Neville was not seen for some weeks. Then the news came that he had taken a fatal overdose.*

What happened to Neville is tragic, yet unfortunately his story is far from unique. Similar occurrences have significantly increased in the past 10 years as more and more people are forced into financial hardship. Evidence suggests that in the UK between 2008 and 2010 alone there were an extra 1000 suicides by comparison with previous years (McVeigh, 2015). Worsening social and material circumstances, caused by political and economic choices that benefit the already rich and powerful, have devastating psychological consequences. Political and economic decisions have created extremes of inequality unimaginable a generation ago, and this is damaging everyone's health (Dorling, 2017; Wilkinson & Pickett, 2010).

In this chapter, we set the scene for this book by exploring the UK's social and material circumstances: the mess we are in. We outline some of the historical developments that have led to this point and describe how psychology has mostly refrained from commenting on the adverse effects of rising inequality. We recognise that most psychologists, despite their often relatively privileged status, are workers subject to organisational demands, workers with mortgages to pay and mouths to feed. At the same time, we suggest, the individualism that is a defining feature of psychology severely limits its capacity to recognise, let alone redress, the toxic consequences of our current situation. Psychology's individualism combines with workplace practices that stymie critical reflection and action. These practices encourage a focus on narrow organisational imperatives that take wider circumstances as simply given. This leads us to ask whether psychology could do better, and our conclusion is that it could. This conclusion is the starting point for the rest of the book.

Origins of the mess

The last 40 years or so have been dominated by social policies, political agendas and economic directives that neither recognise nor value the interests and needs of society. There has been no place for notions of the common good and the collective betterment of all (Monbiot, 2016). Instead of shared ideals, collective resources and communal effort, there is a relentless focus on the individual. Social inequality is explained in terms of individual differences, rather than the uneven distribution of opportunity and resource. Supposed individual qualities – courage, willpower, resilience, determination, spirit – are invoked to explain why some succeed while most struggle. The individual and their 'inner' qualities are what matters: everything else is mere context.

Over the same period, the market has become the main organising principle of everyday life. We are encouraged to see everything in terms of price, cost and profitability. The economic dimension of our relationships and actions is emphasised. Their moral, ethical, environmental, social, affective, caring and nurturing aspects are either downplayed or commodified to generate profit. Increasingly 'all dimensions of human life are cast in terms of a market rationality' (Brown, 2003). Now that the market dominates everyday life, the self is a commodity to be evaluated, branded, traded, exploited – or, more disturbingly, dismissed. Increasingly, then, there is a critical focus on the attributes, choices and conduct of individuals. The only important social relations, we are told, are those between entrepreneurs and individual consumers.

It is tempting to see social, political and economic changes like these as distant abstractions, always at one remove from the real stuff of everyday life. It is easy to see them as mere context, relevant only to the extent that persons make them so. Achievement comes from hard work, personal commitment and perseverance. Failure is caused by laziness, stupidity and lack of moral fibre. This is a meritocracy, where success is equally available to all who try. It is easy to believe such claims, since this is how we are continuously encouraged to think. But if this is correct, why are today's young adults increasingly described as overly sensitive 'snowflakes' who lack resilience? If it is only individuals who matter, why have they suddenly changed?

To the extent that such claims are accurate, it is probable that social, political and economic changes are the cause. Today's young adults are coping with insecure jobs, low wages, high rents, reduced public services and high levels of debt. They have grown up under the relentless, calculating gaze of an education system that continuously measures their individual worth. They have matured at a time when inequality is growing, opportunities are restricted, selves are commodified, collectivity is demonised, and no alternative way of being seems possible. It is understandable that all this might produce, for some, a habitually increased concern with their own and other's personal qualities. Nor is it surprising that the increased misery and worry these circumstances generate are being cast as manifestations of individual weakness (Friedli & Stearn, 2015).

So the circumstances of young people today are more challenging than those of the previous generation, and this has profound consequences for how they are able to be. In so far as those who are older recognise this, they rarely recall why. After all, memory doesn't just depend on cognitive capacities; what we recall is powerfully shaped by what gets highlighted, rehearsed and repeatedly woven into the fabric of everyday life. Today, there is scant recognition of how government policies during the last century (the Addison (1919), Beveridge (1942), and Butler (1944) reports) laid the groundwork for (respectively) state housing, health and welfare and education provision. These reports instigated reforms that aimed to provide environments and resources hitherto unavailable to most people. The welfare of its citizens became a primary function of the state.

This was widely seen as progress. A more jaundiced view suggests these social reforms were on the back of two world wars, where all families would have known loss and trauma. After World War II, the deprivation and squalor previously endured by many people were widely considered unacceptable. In part, this was because of new-found communal values, which had been central to the war effort and persisted afterwards. Several forces spurred a demand for change, including the strength of the highly unionised[1] workforce and their demands for a better life. Capitalist governments, nervously watching the Soviet Union and fearing revolution at home, sought to appease the masses (Baldwin, 1992).

Social and economic policies that worked to reduce the huge disparities between a wealthy minority and the great majority of ordinary people continued until the 1970s. By this time, the gap between the richest and poorest in Britain was at its narrowest since records have existed. However, at the end of the 1970s, a new policy agenda came to the fore, and that gap has now massively widened again. We must not, however, consider the 1970s as some halcyon bygone time. Even then, inequalities in income, housing, employment, diet and working conditions were still the largest determinants of health outcomes (Townsend & Davidson, 1982). The years that followed, not only under the Thatcher government but also subsequent Tory *and* Labour administrations, saw increasing privatisation of public services and a steady widening of social inequalities.

---

1. This workforce was also to a large extent combat trained and even partially armed, since some soldiers had brought illicit 'souvenir' weapons back from the war.

Then, in 2008, there was a financial crisis, caused by malpractices in the banking system and financial sector. Following Winston Churchill's advice never to let a good crisis go to waste, the UK Conservative-Liberal coalition government took this opportunity to radically cut spending on health, social care and education. Along with some (but by no means all) other countries, the UK introduced massive public funding cuts.

In the wake of these cuts, we have seen the collapse of social care for those requiring support: people with disabilities, the young, older people, any who are vulnerable. We have witnessed the horrific deaths of people in a tower block fire, the residents' concerns about safety having been ignored for many years. Privately owned, profit-based health companies are increasingly undermining the commitment to a National Health Service offering free healthcare to all, from cradle to grave, at the point of delivery. Public transport is becoming disproportionately expensive. According to some estimates, rates of rough sleeping have increased by 141% since 2010 (Homeless Link, n.d.). Meanwhile, housing has become an investment product, further cementing divisions between more and less privileged people. And, unsurprisingly, more and more prescriptions for psychiatric drugs are being dispensed (Iacobucci, 2019).

> *Twenty-five years ago, the then primary school-aged daughter of one of our group was shocked and perturbed at the sight of a rough sleeper in a city underpass. At the time, this was a very unusual sight. Worried for the person's wellbeing, she decided to fundraise for the housing charity Shelter. With rough sleeping now a common sight around our cities, we wonder what sense the young are making of this all too regular sight. We can all too easily become hardened to what is a visible indictment of the failure of a rich, well-resourced society.*
>
> *More recently, another group member was asked for money for something to eat by someone who appeared to be a rough sleeper. With warnings of 'Don't feed drug habits by giving money' ringing in his ears, he cautiously handed over a pound. A few minutes later, he saw the same person in the chip shop queue. Realising the request had been genuine, and feeling miserly over the initial contribution, he offered a more realistic contribution for a hot meal.*

Too often, we no longer see or respond to what's in front of us. The moral compass of society has lost its co-ordinates of compassion, civic good, universal comfort and protection. Self-interest, consumerism and individual responsibility are promoted in their place. And it's not just that we don't see;

we don't *feel*. The sustained barrage of assertions that people's misfortunes are their own fault has deadened our collective empathy. The misuse of language to label vulnerable people as 'skivers', 'scroungers' or 'lazy' has created a blaming culture that furthers the interests of the rich and powerful. Rather than feel anger that there are now so many homeless people in one of the richest countries on the planet, we are encouraged to feel irritated when their presence inconveniences us. Recently, homeless people sleeping in a warm subway near Westminster underground station were moved by the police after the chaplain to the Speaker of the House of Commons complained about the 'ongoing stench' (Chakelian, 2019).

To further illustrate how the rich and powerful respond to the poor, consider what they say about foodbanks. Commenting in 2013 on the reasons for increasing foodbank use, Benefits Minister Lord Freud said it was simply because they offered free food (Morris, 2013). That same year, Conservative MP Michael Gove argued that families turn to foodbanks because of poor financial management (Vale, 2013). In 2014, Conservative peer Lady Jenkin proposed that food poverty was due to poor people not knowing how to cook (Butler et al., 2014). Writing in 2015, right-wing commentator Fraser Nelson argued that increasing foodbank use was caused by a 'cumbersome' benefits system introduced under the previous Labour government (Nelson, 2015). Around this time, too, the idea that foodbank use is simply a 'lifestyle choice' began to be promoted in the right-wing media (Chapman, 2015). In 2017, the then Prime Minister Theresa May was challenged by an NHS nurse who said she had to rely on a foodbank. May replied that there were 'many complex reasons' for foodbank use, before changing the subject to talk about a strong economy for all (Peck, 2017). Then, later that year, Conservative MP Jacob Rees-Mogg described foodbanks as 'rather uplifting' (BBC News, 2017) – could there possibly be anything uplifting about not having enough to eat?

All these commentators failed to acknowledge that the very existence of food banks is a shame on us all. All failed to explain why some who spend their working lives caring for others are left unable to feed themselves. All failed to engage with research demonstrating that welfare cuts and benefit restrictions are significant drivers of foodbank usage (Garthwaite, 2016). Their evasions and denials are also challenged by the growing numbers of children in poverty and the re-emergence of illnesses such as rickets. Until recently consigned to history, or to far away, impoverished places, vitamin D deficiency (the underlying cause of rickets) is 'disturbingly high' (Pearce & Cheetham, 2010) here in the UK, and overall insufficiency is now prevalent. What was once known as 'the English disease' is again increasing.

> *Members of the multidisciplinary team in the adult mental health service where one of us works are spending more and more time assisting clients to complete social security forms. While there was always some support required in this area, the amount of time taken up by this has exponentially increased. This is due to the loss of welfare rights workers posts, the reduction in the outsourced voluntary-funded services that previously took on such functions, and the increasing scrutiny and re-assessing of people using mental health services*
>
> *That adult mental health teams are completing social security forms for their service users is an indicator of a system in collapse. It is not something these workers are trained or paid to do. If mental health workers don't do this, their service users suffer because they cannot survive without the benefits they are entitled to, including referrals to foodbanks. If mental health workers do this, service users suffer in a different way because skilled professionals are distracted from providing personal, meaningful support for their mental distress because of the more urgent concern for their economic survival.*

Since 2008, the social agreements within and between our communities have been unravelled at an alarming pace. The implication is that obtaining a reasonable standard of living is solely down to individual effort and should be achieved without recourse to anything collectively provided. We are very obviously in a mess, and in some ways the necessary response seems equally obvious. Implementing policies to create a more equitable society would do much to counter these problems. So what's stopping us?

Psychology

Clinical psychological practice is, for the most part, based on the individual. While there are some alternatives, in adult work clinical psychology's attention has focused on one-to-one therapeutic interventions. This is so despite overwhelming evidence of the impact on mental health of social factors such as inadequate housing, poorly resourced environments, unemployment and limited access to education (for an overview, see Johnstone & Boyle, 2018). It is alarming, given that we have known for some time the modest effects of psychotherapeutic interventions. In this context, it is unhelpful that trainee practitioners in psychology enter training with pre-ordained ideas about the central importance of the self, or the view that every important influence emerges from, or lies within, the individual. Nevertheless, the practice of psychology remains steadfastly focused on individuals. In part, this is because its evidence base in academic psychology overwhelmingly adopts a similar focus. Yet, judging by the widespread failure of psychological research to generate replicable findings, this focus on isolated individuals works no better for academic purposes than it does in the clinical realm.

Since psychology's intense focus on individuals is unhelpful, both academically and clinically, there must be other reasons why it persists. In large part, we will argue, these reasons are to do with the origins and pursuit of professional interest. In favouring explanations of human behaviour driven by forces purportedly existing within the individual, psychology promotes a reductionist view of human life and experience. This creates a distance between psychology and the more contextually inclusive social sciences. Significantly, it aligns psychology with the other disciplines – psychiatry and neuroscience – whose research it competes with.[2] Western cultural tendencies to emphasise individuals as distinct and separable from their circumstances also contribute, their presence bolstering psychology's claims that its individualistic stance is merely 'scientific'. In this way, the self-interest of psychology is aligned with attempts to promote the scientific status of the discipline.

Having said this, we must immediately say that it is reasonable to expect psychology to promote its own interests. It is also reasonable that individual psychologists should have a vested interest in their discipline. Such is the stuff of life. A central argument of this book is that we are all, *without exception*, influenced by interests, to the extent that interest should be seen as an important psychological concept.

So, when we say that psychology is acting in its own interest, this is in many ways nothing more than a statement of fact. Of itself, it does not necessarily imply any moral or ethical judgement. However, when promoting interest includes ignoring evidence that challenges what is being promoted, psychology undermines its own integrity. Rather than shedding light on the sources and causes of inequalities and ill health, both mental and physical, psychology exists more like a barnacle on the shipwreck of life.

So we all have interests, and for all of us these interests shape what we do, feel and think. As will become clear, throughout this book we will state our own interests. We consider that the wider profession of psychology would be more robust for being similarly open. Yet it is not just that the role of interests in our professional world is rarely acknowledged. It is also that there is very little consideration of public, shared or social interests. This is especially clear

---

2. In the Research Excellence Framework, the cyclical and competitive assessment of research quality by which government funding for universities is distributed, psychology research is assessed by the same 'panel' as research in psychiatry and neuroscience. Over time, this has led many psychology departments to de-emphasise social psychology and invest resources in neuroscience and biological psychology.

with regard to clinical psychology's promotion of psychotherapy, which we will discuss at some length. Here it is not just a case of acknowledging the interests behind our own work but also of identifying interests that are being overlooked.

> *A frequent request from staff in adult mental health services is for trauma-informed services (Sweeney et al., 2016). This framework for care makes a lot of sense if we look carefully at its key principles: respect, recognition of historical abuse, recognition that services can re-traumatise, collaborative practice, ultimately possible referral to specialist trauma services. So this approach respects personal histories that include past abuse and experience of oppressive practice; it encourages the values promoted by the service user movement; it recognises the potentially damaging effects of psychiatry, and it is not aligned to any specific psychotherapeutic model but instead draws on non-specific factors in therapeutic relationships.*
>
> *The one exception is the final principle, which suggests a referral to a specialist trauma therapy service. Unfortunately, this principle – which seems to be rooted primarily in interest – could potentially contradict all of the others. Recognising and respecting that, when damaging things happen to us, we are likely to feel damaged; avoiding retraumatising; taking seriously historical cultural contexts; being trustworthy and transparent; working collaboratively and with mutuality; encouraging safety; if possible, enabling empowerment, choice and control and developing survivor partnerships – these are all very important values informing practice. But are they really new? And do they really need a dedicated specialist service to deliver them? Moreover, is the 'recognition that services can re-traumatise' being deliberately overlooked because to do otherwise would not be in the interests of those who work in mental health services?*

Psychology has been quick to take up the seductive invitation to comment on topical facets of contemporary life. When the social psychologist Kurt Lewin declared that there is nothing more practical than a good theory (Lewin, 1951), his intentions were more innocent than those of the mass media and the psychologists they (the media) court. Today, it is common to see psychologists on TV shows, quoted in news articles, or interviewed in documentaries. We have *Psychologies*, a glossy 'monthly women's magazine dedicated to personal development and well-being', and we have so-called cultural and political gurus like the Canadian psychologist Jordan Peterson, with his cultural musings and questionable self-help advice.[3]

Yet psychology has been careful, measured, indeed almost silent in commenting on the divisive policies that are adversely affecting our health. Again, it seems that interests are at play here: those of the handful of billionaires who own and control the great majority of our media, as well as those of psychologists themselves. The interplay between interests and power and the values, ideas and practices of psychology is a core theme of this book. We recognise that it is inaccurate and partial to consider psychology as simply neutral and scientific – as though it were wholly detached from, and unaffected by, cultural and historical circumstances. The dominance of this naïve view means that relatively little has been said about the effects of power on and in the mainstream of psychology, and even less about the impact of interests.[4]

In the relative absence of such analyses, new clinical psychology trainees bring with them a set of values and beliefs that echo those of their education and upbringing. Typically, this means that they think of selves as isolated individuals. All too frequently this leads them to consider human suffering and distress as an internal process: dislocated from the norms and values of culture, disconnected from socio-economic policies and structures, and somehow separate from the combinations of toxic or adverse social and material circumstances that many clients continue to endure.

Not so long ago, the 'scientist-practitioner' was a high-profile concept in clinical psychology. It involves clinical psychologists in 'integrating these two functions in their professional work by making a laboratory of their applied settings and studying scientifically both the phenomena that are the focus of their services and the results of those services (APA, n.d.). Simply put, scientific evidence improves practice while practice generates new scientific evidence. On the face of it, this is a laudable aim, but this approach effectively precludes wider questions about what should count as evidence; about the social and material environments in which findings are interpreted and applied, and about the relevance of perspectives and concerns that are missing or downplayed. More recently, the notion of the 'reflective scientist practitioner' has begun to be promoted instead; even so, thorough critical reflection is still, for the most part, absent from the discipline.

Without such critical reflection, it is impossible to know the extent to which the cycle of enquiry is inclusive. This, in turn, makes it impossible to

---

3. For an insightful discussion of Peterson's work see https://www.currentaffairs.org/2018/03/the-intellectual-we-deserve

4. The subdiscipline of critical psychology often engages with power but barely mentions interests. In the work of David Smail, this concept is developed at some length.

strike an effective balance between looking out for interests and maintaining professional integrity. In other words, a critical analysis of the mess we are in could contribute to the integrity of our discipline. Yet, all too often, merely suggesting such critical questioning prompts accusations of professional heresy. The notion that we should open up professional practice to a critical gaze is commonly met with a series of rebuttals or accusations: of failing to understand the evidence; of being disloyal to the profession; of not appreciating how hard people are already working; of gratuitously bringing politics into psychology; of lacking in care and compassion; of stoking needless conflict with psychiatry; of being more interested in troublemaking than helping.

> *It used to be possible, when teaching clinical psychology trainees, to talk about the value and functional applications of community and critical psychology. Occasionally some trainees would even seek out such a placement. Now, with trainees often based in private/independent placements, they increasingly regard community and critical perspectives as anachronistic. Private (for-profit) services and state health service provision are now so entwined that the values of free health provision from cradle to grave are threatened, not least by the poaching of qualified staff.*
>
> *All health professions are vulnerable to this effect. Like clinical psychology trainees, student nurses also frequently undertake placements in private residential settings. It is now common practice that managers of such establishments identify the students who appear most committed to their work and, well before the end of their training, offer these soon-to-be qualified staff attractive opportunities in the private sector. In this way, public services lose much-needed professional staff.*

How have we got to this position? Where is our professional discerning voice? To answer these questions, we must step into the present-day culture of psychology, to appreciate how dominant beliefs and values get communicated and reinforced. Awaydays and training courses succinctly illustrate how ideologically infused satire meets reality in everyday working life. Here are two examples.

Ethereal balls

Jonathan, the facilitator of this NHS workshop for therapists, began by describing his journey: from therapist to successful educator, administrator, personal coach, entrepreneur, and now motivational speaker and consultant in managing organisational change for the public and corporate sectors. Over the decades, Jonathan had flown across the globe many times. Yet, like many who invoke spiritual and green credentials, he did not seem to glimpse the irony.

Jonathan first told the assembled group of about 60 NHS therapists that they were to adopt a 'solution-focused framework'. Features of the workplace that could hinder and frustrate were to be identified, and practical answers sought. Earnest discussion ensued, and responses included improved communication with managers, in-house educational seminars, increased support for specialisms in psychology and requests for mindfulness.

The striking thing about these suggestions was the near-complete avoidance of everything that really mattered. No one remarked on the lack of clinical rooms in which to see clients and give and receive clinical supervision, nor on the new mandatory policy of hot-desking, under which everyone but managers had to conduct administrative tasks on the hoof. No one referred to the recent downgrading in salaries, or the intensified regime of surveillance. The ever-growing demands for data entry and audit – an increasingly fraught requirement, owing to reliance on a clunky and capricious computer system – similarly went unmentioned. And there was only very limited discussion of how many mental health crises might have been prevented had the therapists not been compromised by widespread demoralisation, chronic staff shortages, and a poorly planned relocation to wholly inadequate premises. The handful of participants who broached such issues were firmly told that the purpose of the day was not to dwell upon large-scale changes over which they had little control, but to forge practicable 'take-away' answers, suitable for 'cascading' to colleagues.

In the afternoon, Jonathan guided them through concentration and breathing exercises designed to help them build their own spiritual refuge, their inner temple. This was followed by some more dynamic Tai Chi-based exercises. Following Jonathan's instructions, the large group of therapists began acting as one to gather the power of the universe in their cupped hands. Once they were deemed to have stored a sufficient motherlode of this vitality, Jonathan urged them to each seek another participant and gently toss them the gift of their individual sphere of Chi. The outcome, Jonathan said, would be good karma and positive feelings all round. While many beaming faces broadcast what seemed to be fun-filled camaraderie, other participants appeared to be just as determined to avoid eye contact, each grimly hurling their ethereal balls into empty space.

Extinction penguins

Elsewhere, 10 senior members of an organisation were learning about 'Managing Change'. In the morning they took part in exercises where they shared their experiences. They were told that the *reasons* for change were less important than the process, and in particular the feelings that change creates. The facilitator presented a way of understanding these feelings, based on research by Elisabeth Kubler-Ross. Her sensitive studies of death and dying have given rise to the 'Kubler-Ross Change Curve'[5] in business studies. When organisations change, it is claimed, those within them go through the same stages as people confronting death: denial, anger, bargaining, depression, acceptance.

In the ensuing discussion, someone said that accepting organisational change is quite different from accepting a death. The point was acknowledged, but not explored. Someone else commented that common reactions to organisational change – for example, anger – were being portrayed as irrational. But perhaps it is entirely rational to be angry if, say, you are made to re-apply for your own job on a more insecure basis? The facilitator agreed, but stressed that the important thing is to realise that people subject to organisational change need opportunities to *grieve* for what they are losing.

In the afternoon, they were introduced to a model of change developed by John P. Kotter, Professor of Leadership at Harvard Business School. It describes eight stages said to be necessary if organisational change is to succeed, including 'create urgency', 'create a vision', and 'create short-term wins'. To illustrate, they were shown a 10-minute animated film about penguins.

One penguin, Fred, noticed that the ice floe where the penguins lived was cracking and could shear away. The entire colony could be wiped out! Fred presented evidence about the cracks to the Chief Penguin. This created urgency. The Chief Penguin then led the colony through the other stages of Kotter's model, and the penguins moved to a new ice floe. More than this, they recognised that they were now in a new, fast-moving world, so in future they must be flexible and move ice floes every year. In this way, in Kotter's terms, change became *institutionalised* in the penguin colony.

The film ended, and a lacklustre discussion ensued. As two people at the back whispered together, the words 'flexible' and 'precarious' were overheard. Then someone said that presumably the cracks in the ice floe were caused by climate change: why did the film not consider this? The facilitator smiled. When leading organisational change, he said, it is important to focus only upon those things we can influence or control: everything else, we must simply accept.

* * *

Awaydays at work are often seen as entirely harmless, if largely useless. Yet it would be wrong to infer from this that they are 'not political'. Rather, they are profoundly so – but their political agenda is that of the organisation and its managers, not its workers. Both of these examples describe superficially open and democratic events, replete with opportunities to share experience, pose

---

5. See www.change-management-coach.com/kubler-ross.html

questions and engage in discussions. Nevertheless, critical questions were met with friendly but firm rebuttals, and both were infused with a banality that seemed almost designed to deaden critical reflection.

In both examples, too, something more manipulative was also revealed by the use of deflection, diversion and displacement. The focus on 'take-away solutions' diverted participants away from fundamental problems and towards trivial ones. Gathering and sharing the ethereal power of the universe displaced consideration of the very real difficulties that workers faced. Discussion of hypothetical penguins deflected the wider questions about organisational change that would have accompanied any actual human example. The existence of negative feelings about organisational change was acknowledged, and their importance was even emphasised. At the same time, their dynamics were restrictively described within a model of grieving that positioned them as understandable, yet also irrational.

In both cases, the away day was set up as an occasion to affirm, rehearse and support dominant values and practices. Changing organisational contexts were a given; the collective task of both sets of participants was adjustment. What was crucially missing was any kind of political perspective on the potential misuse of evidence to create pacified, inward-looking employees, unable or unwilling to recognise the workplace as one of the sources of their personal ills.

In this sense, awaydays are a microcosm of life in general. Their dynamics and functions illustrate how, more generally, the value of dissent at work is frequently overlooked. While seemingly inclusive, often what lies behind the rhetoric of participation during awaydays is a subtle form of control over what can and cannot be discussed – a pervasive, coercive dismantling of open participation. Such organisational practices eviscerate and discredit any morality not closely aligned with the market – any ethical concerns that run counter to the financial bottom line. To this extent, albeit in a small way, they ultimately begin to erode the very roots of democracy (Brown, 2003). Faced with such practices, it is hard to see things as they are and, when faced with duplicity, to speak out.

Could psychology do better?

Some time around the US presidential election of 2016 and the ultimate crowning of Donald Trump as victor, the idea of fake news became widely spoken about. Some analysts suggest that the spread of fake news is bound up with the free and easy exchange of information via social networking. Information flows today are massively multiple, so that laborious, time-intensive fact-checking struggles to keep pace. Once an 'alternative fact' is published, it can easily get established as truth. For example, President Trump's press team invented the 'fact' that his inauguration ceremony was attended by more people than that of any previous president. Likewise, the 2016 Brexit campaign invented the 'fact' that the NHS would be better off by £350 million each week should the UK leave the European Union. In the 2019 election, the Conservative Party resurrected this claim alongside another that, if elected, they would 'get Brexit done' within weeks. All of these claims were demonstrably false.

Whether we call it fake news, misinformation, alternative facts or lies, clinical psychology is not immune. The profession is at least passively complicit in the dissemination of what are, at best, partial truths. Clinical psychologists, then, could do better. They could acknowledge the business influences and market pressures that inject an unsettling sense of competition into services. They could initiate dialogues that set experience and activity meaningfully within their circumstances – dialogues that address traumas and adversities, historical and current. They could speak of the damaging effects on wellbeing of social and material deprivation, and how people require opportunities beyond the confines of the clinic to build rewarding, purposeful lives. This is not rocket science, and nor does it depend on mysterious therapeutic rituals only accessible to the initiated. It is speaking truth to power, and while this happens occasionally, it is still the exception, not the norm.

Psychologists more generally could also do better. We could develop more sophisticated explanations of what it is to be human, explanations that include the ways we are intrinsically and inextricably locked into our social and material circumstances. We could recognise that people are accountable to each other within specific material settings and relationships, upon which the particulars of their experience are sensitively dependent. We could acknowledge that this, in turn, means that explanations of conduct that begin and end within the person are only ever partial, and that the individual level of explanation is not necessarily the most helpful (Harré, 2002). Human experience is fundamentally social, so to understand ourselves and each other, we must hold up a mirror to society. Instead of focusing solely on internal dynamics, we should also consider social processes and material resources. Instead of emphasising unhelpful habits of thought and behaviour, we should emphasise the circumstances that forged them.

> *How often do psychologists discuss with the people to whom we are offering psychological help the known modest outcome effects of psychotherapies? How often do we initiate conversations about the effects of psychotropic medications, some of which are core to people's sense of who they are, affecting weight, libido, physical health? How frequently do we consider this?*

> *Many staff in mental health services are scrambling to seek further training, for example in cognitive behaviour therapy for psychosis (CBTp), the latest model of CBT for this particular client group. This is not necessarily because they believe it to be effective, since they have most likely not engaged in detail with the evidence. It is more commonly because they fear being left behind, trapped with a CV that does not include the latest therapeutic box of tricks. Such fears are understandable, but how many are honest about this motivation?*
>
> *At the same time, there is a lack of honesty about the sources of seemingly fresh approaches to understanding distress. Services regularly colonise and subsume initiatives proposed by service users. This has now occurred with the recovery movement, just as it did with the hearing voices movement of 20 years ago. But once corporatised, sanitised and controlled by services rather than service users, such initiatives lose many of their original strengths.*

Another way of saying all this is that, rather than insight, we need *outsight*. The distinction between insight and outsight comes from the work of David Smail. Whereas mainstream psychology mostly encourages the kind of insight that allows the person to see the error of their ways and adjust their conduct accordingly, our aim is more or less completely the opposite: to help the person achieve outsight, such that the causes of distress can be demystified and the extent of their own responsibility for their condition put into its proper perspective, (Smail, 2005). As this book's title suggests, the cultivation of outsight is one of our main goals.

This book

In this book, then, we recognise that something is profoundly wrong with the way we live today. Over the past 40 years, it has become habitual to feel that the only viable route to a better life is through competitive individual striving. This habit of feeling has not arisen accidentally. It has been encouraged and rewarded by media narratives, political and economic policies and material changes to the organisation of work, public services and everyday life. As a result, we have made a virtue of pursuing material self-interest. This pursuit now constitutes what remains of our sense of collective purpose (Judt, 2010). This selfish bias is also present within psychology, which can seem to provide evidence that this state of affairs is somehow 'natural' – evidence that may then serve as a self-fulfilling prophecy (Bregman, 2020).

Rejecting this pessimistic conclusion, in this book we argue for a social materialist psychology. What this means will become clearer as the book unfolds. For now, it is enough to say that by this we mean a psychology where social and material influences are continuously integral to psychological experiences, capacities and functions – rather than merely contextual. Social and material influences do not just provide the backdrop to psychology, they shape, guide and constitute it.

As a result, our social materialist psychology recognises the value and importance of the collective good. It promotes what David Smail called 'compassionate solidarity'. With regard to clinical work, it centrally recognises the value of clarifying our concerns in trusted conversations. It acknowledges that we all require comfort and encouragement sometimes (Smail, 2005). And with regard to both academic and clinical psychology, it recognises that we all need access to resources in order to wield influence over our lives, together with social and emotional connections to give our lives value and purpose. As will become clear, this means that the psychological concepts and explanations we develop will sometimes differ from those of mainstream psychology.

Importantly, we don't pretend to have found the solution to all of today's ills. Nor do we think that we have a finished account of an alternative psychology. What we will present is a beginning, a provisional outline. It is an attempt to recognise injustices and inequalities and to foster respect, dignity and honesty. We know that our psychology is partial and incomplete, but we are clear that it would reduce the harms associated with some current practices, and confident that it identifies some initial elements of a better understanding of what it is to be human.

Terminology

We describe our approach to psychology as social materialist, but the word 'materialist' has two different widely accepted meanings. It can be used to describe a greedy person, someone concerned primarily with the acquisition of wealth and material goods. It can also be used to describe the philosophical stance that our world consists only of material things. Throughout this book, we will consistently use 'materialist' only in this second, philosophical sense.

Frequently, this book will focus on the phenomena variously described as mental illness, mental ill health, mental health difficulties, distress and distressing behaviour, emotional distress, or problems in living. Taking this focus also means that we will also sometimes talk about the people who experience these phenomena: the patients, the clients, the service users, the psychiatric system survivors.

As the diversity of these terms suggests, there is no ideal or universally acceptable terminology available here. This perhaps reflects the observation that these phenomena are 'essentially contested' – that they are inherently troubling of sociocultural norms and expectations, to the extent that the very language we use to discuss them will always be controversial. This means that to speak of these phenomena inevitably risks potentially alienating or offending some people and groups.

Since we have no principled solution to this problem, we have addressed it pragmatically. In relation to the phenomena themselves, we will mostly use the terms 'distress' and 'mental health/mental health difficulty'. In terms of the people who have these experiences, we will mostly use the term 'service users'.

We recognise that these terms bring problems of their own: for example, not all those who encounter services are experiencing distress (but they may be distressing to others); euphemisms such as 'mental health difficulty' still individualise and medicalise (though arguably less so than the term 'mental illness'), and describing people as 'service users' downplays the extent to which, at one extreme, some are coerced into receiving interventions, and at the other, services may be actively harmful rather than helpful.

Nevertheless, it is necessary to adopt *some* language for these phenomena in order to be able to discuss them. In our view, the terms we favour are for the most part sufficiently precise, relatively understandable, reasonably widely used, and not as offensive as some of the alternatives. We recognise, though, that others may disagree.

Concepts

The social materialist approach to psychology that this book describes includes a small set of what we see as fundamental psychological concepts. These are feeling, language, memory, habit, interest and power. In Chapter 7, we focus in detail on these concepts and offer detailed discussions of each. In the preceding chapters, however, we will be already using these concepts in our discussions because (for most purposes) their everyday meanings are close enough to the definitions and discussions we provide later. We have done this so that, by the time readers encounter the more formal discussion in Chapter 7, they will already have some sense of how these concepts are used in practice, and this should aid understanding.

Vignettes and examples

Throughout the book we present anonymised[6] examples of the kinds of distress that people experience, the situations and circumstances within which their distress arises, and the kinds of interventions they receive. These examples are primarily drawn from the clinical practice and professional experience of the authors in health service and academic settings. They describe experiences and interventions that are relatively recent, typically occurring within the last

---

6. A few of the examples are already in the public realm.

five years. Indeed some – including, for example, the awaydays we describe in this chapter – are very recent. We have included these vignettes and examples in order to illustrate and ground our arguments by demonstrating their relevance to people's lives and experiences.

At the same time, the funding cuts, marketisation and privatisation to which our health and social care services have been subjected in recent years – while unprecedented in scale – have varied in their extent from place to place, and have impacted unevenly. They have produced what is commonly described as a 'postcode lottery' in service provision (although it is a peculiarly biased lottery, since the already wealthy frequently have the best chance of winning (Butler, 2019)). Moreover, the effects of these processes have become more noticeable over time as their consequences have accumulated. Overall, the general trend has been to make sensitive, creative and thoughtful interventions of the kind that we favour both less likely and more difficult.

As a result, it is likely that some of the examples we describe may seem at odds with some readers' experience or knowledge of their local services. We would emphasise, then, that our rationale for choosing these particular examples was not that they represent experiences or service contexts that we presume to be universal. Instead, we chose them for their value in illustrating and exemplifying the points we want to make.

Overview

We have argued in this chapter that the last 40 years have been dominated by a particular policy and economic agenda. This agenda is associated with an ideology called neoliberalism. In Chapter 2, we describe neoliberalism in more detail, showing how its imposition created both a new culture and new ways of living and being. Drawing on evidence from a range of disciplines, we describe how neoliberalism was imposed, identify its main characteristics and begin to sketch some of its adverse consequences.

Chapter 3 extends this analysis by showing how certain aspects of psychology both reflect and support neoliberal ideology. We argue that two defining aspects of the discipline of psychology – its claim to be a positivist science and its individualism – closely align it with certain ideas and practices of neoliberalism. Then, using the examples of stress, resilience and optimism, we demonstrate some of the inadequacies and flaws of this mainstream approach.

With this critique of mainstream psychology established, in Chapters 4 and 5 we turn our gaze to psychological therapy – probably the highest-profile and most widely prevalent application of the discipline. Chapter 4 addresses a series of questions related to therapeutic efficacy, presents a critical analysis of the clinical outcomes literature, and concludes that, overall, the positive effects of psychotherapy are difficult to demonstrate. Given this less than encouraging conclusion, we wanted to consider more recent therapeutic endeavours, and so Chapter 5 assesses the evidence for four newer psychological interventions: mindfulness, dialectical behaviour therapy, eye movement desensitisation and reprocessing, and cognitive behaviour therapy for psychosis. Again, our analysis suggests that, overall, evidence for positive outcomes is lacking. This leads us to propose that the current cultural and psychological prominence of therapy might owe as much to ideology as it does to scientifically demonstrable efficacy. Given such modest outcomes, we suggest, one reason for the continued high profile of psychotherapy may be the support it provides for the consoling myth that, if only people try hard enough, they can remake themselves through deliberate effort.

Chapter 6 focuses on contemporary issues, including so-called austerity, the nature of work and the seductions of consumerism, and discusses the role of mainstream psychology in relation to these. One feature of contemporary culture under neoliberalism is the way that alternatives to these social and economic arrangements have been made to seem largely unthinkable. While we take this difficulty seriously, we conclude the chapter by suggesting that this might now be changing, and that a new, progressive generation of young people seems to have emerged.

The relatively optimistic conclusion to this chapter heralds a change in tone. Until now we have been largely critical of current social and economic arrangements, of growing inequality and injustice, and of mainstream psychology. In the remaining chapters of the book, by contrast, we present and evaluate ideas and initiatives that, in our view, have some potential to overcome the problems we have identified. As explained above, Chapter 7 formalises some initial conceptual elements of a social materialist psychology (feeling, language, memory, habit, interest and power). Chapter 8 then discusses some organisational and institutional initiatives from three areas of applied psychological practice (criminal justice, adult learning disabilities and mental health). Broadly speaking, these initiatives are compatible with a social materialist approach because they locate the origins of psychological difficulties not simply inside people's heads but in the shared world they occupy. Then, in Chapter 9, we present some suggestions for both mental health work and social change. Just as some psychologists have managed to foster helpful organisational and institutional initiatives, so certain ways of working psychologically – rooted in the social materialist psychology we have begun to describe – can potentially ameliorate people's distress and support struggles for a better world.

And that was going to be the end of our book when, at the end of 2019 the Covid-19 pandemic emerged and the economy was largely paralysed. Since the effect of the pandemic will shape social and material circumstances for many years to come, we added a postscript (Chapter 10) reflecting on it.

Chapter 2

A brief history of the present

The previous chapter explained that recent decades have seen the imposition of a new form of capitalism: neoliberalism. Neoliberalism is associated with steep increases in inequality and with changes to the nature of work. It involves drastic cuts to welfare, health and education. At the same time, public services are privatised, so that they can generate profits for shareholders. Where these services aren't fully sold to private companies, markets are imposed in other ways. This is the form of capitalism that dominated when the Covid-19 pandemic began, and that strongly shaped the government's response to the virus.

Neoliberalism is an economic model, but its imposition also involved radical changes in how people should understand themselves – changes in culture, and associated changes in selfhood or subjectivity.[1] Welfare, health and education cuts require people increasingly to take individual responsibility for their circumstances; surviving on insecure, poorly paid work demands flexibility, adaptiveness and resilience. Former UK Prime Minister Margaret Thatcher, who first implemented large-scale neoliberal policies in this country, was quite clear about her ambition to forge these new subjectivities (which is why neoliberalism in the UK is often known as 'Thatcherism'). Interviewed in the *Sunday Times* in 1981, Thatcher said: 'Economics are the method; the object is to change the heart and soul' (Butt, 1981).

To have outsight means to have a clearer understanding of how social and material circumstances are configured. Accordingly, in this chapter, we first briefly describe neoliberalism. We then discuss some of the cultural changes associated with its imposition. We focus specifically on changes to working-

---

1. The term 'subjectivity' is used in social science to refer jointly to the phenomena that psychologists refer to as consciousness and as selfhood (see Blackman et al., 2008).

class culture because people allied with this culture are most numerous in terms of societal functioning and politics, and are also most adversely affected by neoliberalism in terms of mental health. Our discussion emphasises the rise of information technology and changes to the nature of work, employment and social security, and draws on economics, cultural studies, history and politics. We show how these changes were imposed using both seduction and coercion, and how they were also shaped by the collective resistance of working people. We conclude with a brief discussion of the toxic consequences of neoliberalism for individuals and communities.

Neoliberalism

In an influential book about neoliberalism, the British anthropologist and geographer David Harvey described its main features:

> Neoliberalism is in the first instance a theory of political economic practices that proposes that human well-being can best be advanced by liberating individual entrepreneurial freedoms and skills within an institutional framework characterized by strong private property rights, free markets and free trade. The role of the state is to create and preserve an institutional framework appropriate to such practices.
> (Harvey, 2005, p.2)

Here, Harvey highlights how neoliberalism fundamentally changed the relationship between the individual and the state. Following World War II, it was widely agreed in Western democracies that states should provide protection and security to their citizens. Social goods – healthcare, education, housing, social welfare, and an aspiration to full employment – were treated as human rights and states were often seen as 'welfare' states (Barr, 2004).

With the rise of neoliberalism from the early 1980s, the role of the state was radically transformed. Previously the provider of security, the state now became a facilitator of competitive markets that would, increasingly, provide the social goods the state used to supply. The market was now to be central. Social goods were no longer human rights but private products to be purchased by individual consumers. This involved creating artificial markets where none previously existed, including within healthcare and education. There were also mass privatisations – of public utilities such as water and electricity (Meeks, 2015), and of bus and railway services.

These changes were justified in economic terms: markets were claimed to be more efficient than states at meeting people's needs, and competition would supposedly drive up standards. Moral justifications were also given: it was said that those who worked harder and were more successful would be suitably rewarded – the so called 'meritocracy' (Verhaeghe, 2014). It was also argued that these changes would free individuals from the demands and obligations of an oppressive state. This would unleash creative and entrepreneurial potential, producing both personal and economic benefits (Harvey, 2005).

By contrast, many critics of neoliberalism viewed it as little more than an invigorated form of the capitalism that was previously dominant: a greedier, hungrier, more aggressive twist to an already exploitative set of social relations – capitalism, with fewer fringe benefits for the masses. They argued that it would inevitably lead to the increasing accumulation of wealth and resources by powerful companies and individuals, at the expense of the less powerful majority (see, for example, Harvey, 2005; Rutherford, 2008).

Certainly, economic inequalities have increased spectacularly under neoliberalism when compared with the era of the welfare state (Dorling, 2004). A common phrase used during times of economic growth is that 'a rising tide lifts all boats' (Stiglitz, 2002). This evokes the idea that neoliberal policies have generated unprecedented global wealth, which spreads from the top to rich and poor alike; therefore, these policies contribute to social justice (Whelan & Layte, 2007). Similarly, neoliberalism endorses claims of 'trickle-down economics' (Stiglitz, 2013), where it is claimed that everyone benefits from increasing wealth.

In fact, neoliberal policies have actually led to what some call 'trickle-up' economics (James, 2008), where income is increasingly transferred to the already wealthy. Before neoliberalism, the income of the richest was steadily decreasing, as a result of policies geared towards wealth redistribution. However, this has now been radically reversed (Marsh, 2011). While the average citizen's relative income has not increased at all since the 1970s, there has been significant income growth for those at the top, and 8.1% of the global population now owns 84.6% of global wealth (Inequality.org, n.d.).

The injustice of this is sometimes acknowledged even by those who benefit from it. In a 2006 interview, when asked to comment on the fact that he pays proportionately less tax than his low-paid employees, billionaire businessman Warren Buffet said: 'There's class warfare, all right… but it's my class, the rich class, that's making war, and we're winning' (Stein, 2006).

Making neoliberal culture

Neoliberalism adversely affects the majority of people in this country. Yet not only have they put up with it, in some cases they seem to have welcomed it. This can only be because neoliberal economic policies were accompanied by changes in culture. And these changes, just as Margaret Thatcher foresaw, have transformed how people understand themselves and their worlds: they have changed their very hearts and souls.

In what follows, we discuss how working-class culture in this country has been changed in recent decades. In particular, we describe how formerly prominent values of community, trust and solidarity have been weakened. But not all of the changes we discuss began in the Thatcher years, and we trace some of their origins back to the 1960s. This allows us to show that, despite appearances, the rich and powerful haven't had it all their own way.

Caution is necessary when discussing such issues. When we critique the culture of the present, we must be careful not to romanticise the past. False contrasts between a miserable present and an idealised past can only mislead. Our focus is on the working-class culture that predominated in the UK until the 1980s. Yet this culture, at least as we consider it here, was a relatively recent accomplishment.

Importantly, too, this culture was never homogeneous. It proscribed different expectations and norms for men and women. Ethnically predominantly white, it was cross-cut by subcultures associated with black, Asian, lesbian, gay and other minority groups. These subcultures had their own styles, tastes and preferences that continuously modified, and sometimes contested, what it meant to be working class. So working-class culture was never a monoculture, and the tendencies we emphasise were always filtered through the sensibilities of different subcultural groups.

Working-class culture was not only heterogeneous; like other cultures, it contained internal contradictions. For example, it prized solidarity and mutual aid, yet it simultaneously distrusted difference. It had overt sexist, racist and homophobic elements, and could mock those who were different or 'got above themselves'. Respectability was a key aspirational value (Hanley, 2016), associated with progressive activities aimed at self-betterment – education, for example. Yet these same activities could open up routes toward a more middle-class existence. In these ways, progressive notions of personal betterment could also be associated with snobbery and disdain.

The need for caution when making arguments about changes in culture was demonstrated in an article by cultural studies scholar Jeremy Gilbert, published on the Open Democracy UK website in July 2016 (Gilbert, 2016). He was responding to another piece, by journalist and activist Paul Mason, that appeared in the *Guardian* (Mason, 2016). We will now outline both articles, since the debate between them neatly summarises many relevant issues.

Paul Mason was commenting on a 2016 report showing that white working-class students were now the worst-performing group in British schools. He offered an explanation for this, based primarily on the systematic destruction of working-class culture under Thatcher:

... a specific part of their culture has been destroyed. A culture based on work, rising wages, strict unspoken rules against disorder, obligatory collaboration and mutual aid. It all had to go, and the means of destroying it was the long-term unemployment millions of people had to suffer in the 1980s. (Mason, 2016)

This assault was not conducted for its own sake: its goal was to neutralise the living basis of working-class politics in Britain. Mason argued that it left poor white people in particular without the means to tell a forward-looking 'story' about themselves.[2] Such a story is needed, Mason proposed, if disadvantaged individuals are to motivate and organise sustained efforts at learning.

Although Jeremy Gilbert (2016) broadly agreed with Mason, he also highlighted other issues. One was the New Labour argument that, by the 1980s, working class people had already largely rejected the security and social equality of post-war Britain. Instead, they were said to desire a more technicolour world of instant gratification and consumerism. According to this argument, people voted for Thatcher, and then Tony Blair, because they were no longer motivated to defend socialism and the welfare state. New Labour claimed to believe that everyone now was, or wanted to be, middle class. Socialism and other left-wing ideas were behind the times, and could never in future command substantial support.

Stated this way, the New Labour argument presumes that people actually realised that they were facing a choice: they could have either consumerism or welfare and security, but not both. It also overlooks how the seductive offer of being able to buy your council home at a greatly discounted price (a flagship policy of the Thatcher era) powerfully recruited the interests of many. But according to Jeremy Gilbert, it omits something more significant still: working-class resistance to capitalism. Gilbert argues that this resistance was already destabilising working class culture – the culture that Thatcher attacked and New Labour denigrated – long before Thatcher was elected.

Gilbert explains how the mid-1900s were dominated by an era of mass production and consumption that analysts call 'Fordism'. Named after the car manufacturer, Fordism describes an economic model where repetitive labour on production lines was paid well enough to enable mass consumption – for example, of (cheaper models of) the cars produced. So Fordism was not confined to the automobile industry. It describes a more general style of mass production, and associated mass consumption, that spread across the industrialised world from the 1920s onwards.

---

2. Mason argues that this is because ethnic minority groups could attribute their difficulties to racial prejudice and discrimination – an option not available to poor white people.

Fordism required a different kind of worker to the traditional models of either unskilled labour or highly skilled craft labour. It needed individuals who were highly disciplined, relatively docile and not especially emotionally invested in their efforts. And these workers, exhausted by their long, repetitive hours, needed supportive wives (for wives they almost exclusively were) to meet their domestic needs. In these ways, Gilbert argues (following the theorist Gramsci), Fordism cemented a new gender division of labour. It paved the way for the 'nuclear family', the 2.2 children, the capturing of aspiration by modest dreams of a nice house in the suburbs, a serviceable car in the driveway and an annual fortnight in the sun.

Fordism greatly increased profits. Nevertheless, from the perspective of the rich and powerful, it had significant downsides. The problem was that Fordism itself did much to *sustain* working-class culture, including its potential to challenge the interests of the wealthy. Its aspiration to full employment gave workers confidence that they could always find another job, making it easier to drop out or move around. This flexibility, in turn, helped facilitate the growing resistance to Fordism that Gilbert identifies as important.

At the same time, by bringing masses of workers together, Fordism facilitated unionisation and was particularly vulnerable to strikes. Large factories, located alongside relatively settled communities of workers who laboured there, fostered feelings of community and solidarity. These feelings could potentially bolster resistance, and it was precisely to destroy these potentials that the Thatcher government attacked working-class culture. To this extent, says Gilbert, Mason's account is accurate.

But, Gilbert says, a whole other strand of resistance is missing from Mason's article. From the 1960s onwards, working people themselves were rebelling against the conformity and uniformity that Fordism required. Young people refused expectations of convention, hierarchy, deference and tradition. Women refused the limitations associated with their gender role. Ethnic minorities refused demands to assimilate to 'British' ways of living, and gay and lesbian people refused to be ashamed of their own desires. The 'anti-psychiatry' movement initiated widespread questioning of notions of mental illness, sowing the seeds of today's service user movement. Taken together, this diverse wave of resistance is often called the 'counterculture'.

So Gilbert agrees that the Thatcher government systematically assaulted working-class culture. At the same time, he argues, this culture was being powerfully destabilised long before Thatcher came to power. It was already being eroded by a growing counterculture, shaped, to a considerable extent, by working people themselves. In 1978, in their song 'End Result', the punk band Crass described factory workers as the living dead, whose only purpose in life was to work for 'that big blue sign' – a reference to the Ford Motor Company and its blue logo; the name tellingly rhymes with 'bored':

> I hate the living dead and their work in factories
> They go like sheep to their production lines
> They live on illusions, don't face realities
> All they live for is that big blue sign, it says
> 'I'm bored, bored, bored, bored.'[3]

So by the late 1970s, many people were already rejecting the conventions and expectations of Fordism. They may not have anticipated or desired the neoliberalism they ended up getting, but nor did they want the culture of their parents. Many nevertheless supported the miners in their doomed strike of 1984–85 (including Crass, who played benefit gigs). Arguably, though, this only underlines how:

> The elements of the industrial working class who Thatcher assaulted in the early 80s were already residual, and their leaderships realised far too late what the New Left had been trying to tell them since the early 60s: that without a radical democratisation of their aims and their practices, without an embrace of feminism and cosmopolitanism, without an understanding of the technological revolutions which were already well under way – they would be doomed. (Gilbert, 2016)

Nevertheless, the unequal social and material circumstances created by capitalism are always creating potentials for rebellion. Inequality and injustice continuously give rise to anger and resentment. The rich and powerful live in constant fear that these feelings will proliferate and grow, breeding discontent and sparking new progressive movements. This means that these feelings have to be continuously managed, suppressed, diverted or displaced.

This is why, under Thatcher, there were attempts to transform working-class culture by seductive appeals to self-interest: the right to buy for council house tenants, the promotion of share dealing and owning to the masses ('Tell Sid!'[4]). These inducements were accompanied by coercive measures: changes to the benefits system and employment laws, and new legislation to constrain trades unions.

---

3. Crass. (1978). End result. In *Feeding of the 5000*. Small Wonder. https://crass.live/remix-project

4. 'Tell Sid!' was the advertising slogan coined to promote the privatisation of British Gas (see Saunders & Harris, 1990).

But in implementing this mixture of seduction and coercion, the Thatcher government was far from unique. Neoliberalism, which has informed the policies of successive governments since the 1980s, often favours temporary rather than permanent employment. Rather than settled communities with long-term jobs, neoliberalism encourages transient, fragmented communities. It creates precarious workers with little or no job security (e.g. those on zero hours contracts) who must develop diverse employment portfolios. By these means, neoliberalism obstructs opportunities for solidarity and collectivity to flourish.

To be clear, we are not suggesting that all of the technological, social, material and policy changes of recent years were *deliberately* designed to fragment communities, neutralise collective power and promote individualism. At the same time, it does seem that – as they have come together – they have had these effects. To illustrate, we will now briefly survey some of the major cultural changes of recent decades, focusing on three related areas. First, we will consider technological change, and particularly the massive impact of the so-called digital revolution. Second, we will discuss changes in the availability, nature and organisation of work. Third, we will consider changes in how those out of work are treated by the benefits system and portrayed by politicians and in the media.

The digital revolution

Probably the most significant material driver of cultural change in recent decades is the digital revolution. By this we mean our increasing reliance on electronic devices such as computers, tablets and mobile phones. Not only are these devices cheaper and more powerful than ever; they are connected in ever faster, more comprehensive networks. The combined influence of these and related technologies is so profound and far-reaching that some say we are currently experiencing a fourth industrial revolution (Federal Ministry for Economic Affairs and Climate Action, 2022).

The information technologies within these devices did not develop spontaneously. They were initiated and funded by governments, the military, multinational corporations and venture capitalists. This means that the technologies developed in ways that reflect the interests of these groups, and this often gives them a double-edged character. Smartphones, for example, are incredibly versatile and convenient. But they also constantly record and transmit massive amounts of data, making everyday movements and activities continuously visible to commercial, security and other agencies.

So, on the one hand, communication is easier than ever, and expert knowledge is increasingly accessible. On the other, everyday life is more scrutinised – and more monetised – than ever before. New business models have emerged based on the appropriation of 'free' personal information and the ability to uniquely dominate its exploitation (Srnicek, 2016; Zuboff, 2019). Friendship networks, bank accounts, shopping habits and movements and activities inside and outside of work are all analysed for patterns that might yield marketing opportunities. They are also continuously monitored by police and security forces, and the data from CCTV and number plate recognition cameras used to help maintain the status quo and identify 'extremists'. Evidence suggests that people experience this surveillance in contradictory ways: as reassuring, but also as threatening (Ellis et al., 2013).

Information technologies have facilitated new forms of collective action. In the wake of the 2008 financial crisis, protest groups including Occupy and UK Uncut were supported by the hacker group 'Anonymous' (Kazmi, 2011). The WikiLeaks website exposed American war crimes and the frightening potentials of the security services to spy on all of us. In Egypt, the Arab Spring uprising of 2011 made extensive use of mobile phones, the internet and social media (again, supported by Anonymous (Allagui & Kebler, 2011)). More recently, the 2017 socialist renewal of the UK Labour Party was attributed, in part, to young people using the internet and social media to bypass conventional communication channels.

At the same time, the digital revolution has supplied powerful new weapons of mass distraction: online shopping, computer gaming, streaming video. And, as the Cambridge Analytica data misuse scandal illustrated, it offers disturbing potentials to subvert fundamental democratic processes (*The Guardian*, n.d.). Electronic communication is easy, and almost instantaneous, but these strengths are also weaknesses. Once communication requires almost no effort, it can matter less. Social media may encourage superficial 'clicktivism' that can displace more sustained or deliberate engagement (White, 2010). In any case, online communication alone seems unlikely to build the trust and solidarity that determined political action requires. Moreover, governments routinely monitor all electronic communications. When the Arab Spring first threatened the balance of power, the Egyptian government responded by disabling the country's internet (Eltantawy & Wiest, 2011).

Overall, the consequences of the digital revolution are mixed. Its technologies have made communication, information sharing and organising easier than ever, while also making all of these more open to surveillance. Politics, of all stripes, is booming online – but the extent to which that translates into real-world activism is variable. Meanwhile, the digital revolution has enhanced the ability of mass entertainment to displace, divert and manage feelings that might foster resistance to neoliberalism. The recent growth in online psychotherapy, accelerated by the Covid-19 pandemic, could be seen as one aspect of this process.

Work and employment

Changes in the availability, nature and organisation of work have also encouraged shifts in culture. Some of these changes are facilitated by digital technologies. For example, many employers using zero-hours contracts depend on employees being contactable at short notice by phone. This is a particularly iniquitous example of the more general phenomenon of information technology obliterating the distinction between work and leisure (e.g. Hilbrecht et al., 2008). We have all been at meetings where participants spend the entire coffee break checking their phones, and anyone who uses public transport during rush hour knows that commuting time is now 'read your emails' time.

Going further, some companies have introduced 'wellbeing' schemes that require employees to wear electronic monitoring devices. These devices are worn 24/7, at home and at work. They upload data on eating, sleep and exercise patterns, with the aim of showing employees 'how they can improve their work through better personal habits' (Finley, 2013). In other words, increased productivity – rather than improved wellbeing – is the primary goal.

Meanwhile, in the massive warehouses that distribute the goods we buy online, workers wear armband devices that track movements, allocate jobs, forecast completion times and record performance. Workers who exceed the targets these devices set can earn small bonuses, but only with considerable effort. One study found that 'the guys who made the scores were sweating buckets and throwing stuff all over the place' – and that the armbands reduced the company's need for full-time employees by 18% (Moore & Robinson, 2016).

Taking a broader perspective, some argue that the digital revolution is implicated in changing patterns of work more generally. The 'jobless recovery' that has occurred since the 2008 slump has been attributed, in part, to the availability of new technologies. When the recession hit, companies reduced their workforces. But when it ended, many did not create new jobs. Instead, they invested to mechanise and automate jobs that, previously, were performed by humans. This is why conversations at the supermarket checkout increasingly concern only the unexpected item in the bagging area. Profits have recovered, but jobs have been destroyed (Ford, 2016).

Vitally, new technologies are not driving these changes of their own accord. They are doing so because of their coincidence with neoliberalism (Brown, 2006). Like Fordism, neoliberalism requires a new kind of worker – one with a transformed heart and soul. This is why you are being told that there are no longer 'jobs for life', that you are in a race to remain relevant, that your primary competitor is the person sitting beside you (Read, 2009). You must be continuously flexible, always looking out for new opportunities, always developing your personal brand (Hearn, 2008). Going forward, you must enhance your skills portfolio to leverage your human capital in a task-focused, results-driven fashion, synergising holistic capacities with strategic capabilities to constantly push the envelope of individual achievement.

If these seductive exhortations do not appeal, the neoliberal message also gets communicated coercively. Some employed on permanent contracts now feel compelled to work longer hours than before (Crowley et al, 2010). Others juggle two or more fractional contracts, but still struggle to get by (Walsh et al., 2016). Related to this, increasingly harsh anti-trades union legislation has made it harder for unions to organise and defend workers (Wintour, 2015). At the same time, in the UK, massive cuts to legal aid have effectively made the courts inaccessible to many (Bowcott, 2016). The net result of these changes has been to tilt the balance of power further away from employees and further towards employers.

So neoliberalism includes changes in the nature of work, which has become more precarious and exploitative. This, in turn, implies corresponding changes in how workers should understand their rights, their obligations and themselves. But, as we have mentioned, neoliberalism also includes changes in the nature and function of the state – changes characterised by some as a shift from 'welfare' to 'workfare' (Jessop, 2002).

Welfare benefits and the media

This brings us to our third topic: the way successive changes to the benefits system since the 1980s have made life considerably harder for those out of work. Over this period, rates of unemployment benefit – now either Jobseeker's Allowance or an element within Universal Credit – have been greatly reduced as a proportion of average income (Rutherford, 2013). Simultaneously, access to benefits has been made more difficult and more conditional on efforts to present oneself as an active 'jobseeker' (Daguerre & Etherington, 2014). Conditionality now operates to such an extent that even being terminally ill does not remove the obligation to seek work (Ryan, 2017).

These changes have been made to appear more reasonable by a massive, sustained effort to transform perceptions of claimants – in other words, to effect a cultural shift. This effort has considerably intensified since the 2008 economic crisis. We have been told that cuts are necessary because we can no longer afford 'profligate' welfare spending (Clarke & Newman, 2012). Ministers have made speeches that distinguish between 'strivers' and 'skivers' (Valentine & Harris, 2014), and talked of families where three entire generations have never worked. They imply that all who claim benefits are cheats, living dishonestly off the hard work of others. And these efforts have had an impact: a 2012 survey found that people believed 27% of the benefits budget was fraudulently claimed, when the government's own estimate was around 0.7% (TUC, 2012).

> *In June 2018 the body of 57-year-old grandfather Errol Graham was discovered in his Nottingham flat. Errol, described as suffering with severe social anxiety and other longstanding mental health difficulties, had cut himself off from family and friends. Some months before his death, Errol's benefits had been stopped after two visits by DWP officials went unanswered. His body was discovered when bailiffs chasing rent arrears broke down his door. There was no gas or electric supply in his flat, and the only food was two tins of fish that were four years out of date. The coroner conducting the inquest concluded that Errol had starved to death. When he was found, his emaciated body weighed just four and a half stone. (Butler, 2020).*

Elements of the media have contributed to this sustained attempt to change cultural perceptions of the workless. The right-wing tabloids, in particular, have been vociferous in whipping up anger, resentment and disgust against benefit claimants. The 2008 case of Shannon Matthews – a little girl from Dewsbury, Yorkshire – was a particularly high-profile example. Shannon was the victim of a fake kidnapping orchestrated by her mother, Karen, with the aim of collecting the reward money.

When her deception was revealed, the tabloids enthusiastically reported how Karen Matthews did not work and that her seven children had five different fathers. They hinted at the 'suffering' Shannon might have endured during her captivity by 39-year-old Michael Donovan, a relative of Karen's partner. The *Daily Mail* described the toothless Donovan as a 'misfit' and 'weird loner' (Sims et al., 2008), while the *Sun* called him a 'bug-eyed beast', a 'freak' and an 'oddball' (Hanley, 2016, p.172). The incident:

> became a useful case study into Britain's indulgence of an amoral class. 'Her background, a scenario that encompasses the awful, dispiriting and undisciplined face of Britain, should be read as a lesson in failure,' one columnist wrote in the *Birmingham Mail*. 'Karen Matthews, 32 but looking 60, glib hair falling across a greasy face, is the product of a society which rewards fecklessness.' (Jones, 2011, p.18)

The same media largely failed to report how the Matthews family were so poor they sometimes used Morrison's carrier bags instead of children's nappies. Nor did they appreciate that, when a 40-year-old British man, in 2008, has no teeth, it 'suggests a sickness in the society rather than in the person' (Hanley, 2016, p.172). Instead, these indicators of material desperation were largely ignored. The media ratcheted up reasonable moral judgement into foaming outrage and disgust. At the same time, they implied, Karen Matthews' behaviour was not unusual: it was entirely typical of the dangerous 'underclass' from which she came.

Television contributes to this cultural warfare. Recent years have seen a new genre of so-called documentaries focused on the lives of the poor that critics describe as 'poverty porn' (Jensen, 2014) – programmes such as 'We Pay Your Benefits', 'Shoplifters and Proud', 'Britain on the Fiddle' and 'Benefits Street'. Like the tabloid coverage, these programmes are not merely lurid voyeurism; they are profoundly ideological.[5] They translate densely tangled webs of ignorance and presumption about welfare and poverty (webs constructed by powerful interests (Slater, 2012)) into everyday language. They try to embed these presumptions as a new common sense: Britain is 'broken', there are high levels of benefit fraud, those without work lack aspiration, make the wrong choices, and are members of an underclass who expect something for nothing. Poverty porn:

> ... presents the 'others' on the screen as dysfunctional in their choices and behavior, *as well as* presenting a dysfunctional welfare state which rewards such 'lifestyles'. In such a framework, the poverty-porn viewer is compelled to understand social insecurity (her own and that of others) as a problem of self-discipline, resilience and responsibility, rather than as a consequence of the extensions and excesses of neoliberalism. (Jensen 2014, italics in original)

Changing hearts and souls

So, attacks upon working class culture neither began nor ended under Thatcher. In the decades since the 1980s, they have continued, largely unabated, and gained in persistence and shrillness since 2008. Over this period, the digital revolution profoundly transformed how we work and live. But, in so doing, it was shaped by the requirements of neoliberalism and the interests of the rich and powerful. We are more connected than previous generations, but many of those connections are now mediated electronically. We remain physically

---

5. The definition of ideology is contested and has been much debated. In this book we follow literary theorist Terry Eagleton in treating ideology as 'false or deceptive beliefs [...] arising not from the interests of a dominant class but from the material structure of society as a whole'. Because thoughts and ideas are the product of external material and social realities, in order to explain why certain ideas predominate in a society, we must relate them to the ways in which that society is structured (Eagleton, 1991, p.30).

alone with our phones and computers, even as we chat with others. It is relatedness, but of a new sort: a relatedness that physically individualises.

Over this time, the working-class culture of the 1980s has had its material and economic basis coercively ripped away. We are now encouraged to see ourselves, not as workers, or even citizens, but as individual buyers and sellers. We are all quite literally *in the business*: the business of 'selling' ourselves in the jobs market and 'buying' what little welfare and security the state still provides.

In place of solidarity and community, neoliberalism promotes a seductive culture of hyper-consumerism driven by practices of sales and marketing. It celebrates the devious manipulation of people and the presentation of a fake, superficial charm. Previously these practices were largely restricted to the advertising industry and aimed at selling consumer goods; now they extend into public services such as health and education. Just a cursory look at any major university website, for example, will show how its stories of academic and sporting excellence are designed to entice new customers (especially those from abroad, who pay the most fees).

This helps explain why notions of choice and user consultation have proliferated across public services. Their spread has not been driven by compassion but by the presumption that customers have the right – the need, indeed the obligation – to choose (Schwartz, 2005). Choice and consultation foster the illusion that public service recipients are actually *consumers*, in the economic sense that they 'purchase' these services in an open market. Of course, rather than being forced to choose a surgeon, say, you might prefer to simply be confident that any surgeon in any hospital will do a good job. But such expectations are inconsistent with neoliberalism.

This is also how we should understand the 2010 imposition of student fees of more than £9,000 per year in England. The policy makes no financial sense – projections show that much of the money loaned will never be recovered. But it makes *ideological* sense to compel students to see themselves as customers, just as it does to train them into the habit of taking on debt. Higher education is then no longer an opportunity to broaden horizons, absorb new perspectives and have novel experiences. Instead, it becomes dominated by the financial imperative to receive value for money by acquiring skills, forging networks and learning how to polish and market oneself (Collini, 2012). Little wonder that student rebellion against austerity was muted by comparison with the activism of previous generations. Today's students are forced to be both customers and (precarious) workers-in-training – social positions that afford precious little space for political protest.

Under neoliberalism, we are expected to understand ourselves through the business logic of consumption and competition. This is why it is increasingly impossible to use any kind of service without being asked to 'rate' your experience. The customer is always right and has an opinion that must be requested: not just because it provides valuable sales information but because it facilitates the appearance of marketisation. Consequently, an audit culture has been imposed across many public services – school league tables, hospital waiting time targets, and so on (Power, 1999). This is justified on the basis that the public has a right to information about the quality or value of services. However, such ratings can conceal more complex and often problematic realities. For example, funding for some US domestic violence programmes now depends on simplistic outcome measures, such as numbers of women who leave abusive partners (Fine, 2012). While this may be seen as one measure of success, women in these situations frequently talk about multiple difficulties in leaving violent relationships, not least the increased risk to their lives that this entails.

Neoliberalism and distress

Unsurprisingly, the economic and cultural changes of neoliberalism are associated with adverse effects on mental health. Here, we briefly outline some reasons for this. First, we discuss the connections between an increased emphasis on competition and experiences such as anxiety and low mood. Second, we highlight the effects of increased social inequality. Finally, we consider the corrosive effects of neoliberalism on the shared interests and values that constitute communities.

Competition

Psychologist Oliver James uses the term 'selfish capitalism' to describe what he sees as the four dominant characteristics of modern neoliberal societies: business success being judged on share price; privatisation of public utilities; limited regulation of business with low taxes for the rich, and the conviction that markets can meet almost all human needs (James, 2008). Researching the links between selfish capitalism and personal distress, James interviewed people who were successful and wealthy in seven countries (New Zealand, Australia, Singapore, China, Russia, Denmark, the USA). He discovered that many of them were deeply unhappy, with often significant levels of anxiety, low mood and substance abuse. James used the term 'Affluenza Virus' to describe how modern culture places 'a high value on money, possessions, appearances (physical and social) and fame' (James, 2008, p.xi), leading to a serious rise in levels of emotional distress over the past four decades.

In a similar vein, others identify the 'universal principle of competition' as the core value of neoliberal societies (Dardot & Laval, 2013). As previously mentioned, this is justified on the basis that competition will supposedly improve standards. However, a relentless focus on competition ultimately harms our deepest desires for a sense of belonging, equality, solidarity, cooperation, care and love. Competition, by its very nature, produces 'winners' who take the spoils and 'losers' who are shamed, humiliated and led to blame themselves for their misfortunes.

Clinical psychologist David Smail was working in the 1980s when neoliberalism was first widely implemented in the UK. He recalls how middle-class professionals such as accountants, who had rarely before attended psychological services, began presenting with anxiety and panic. Smail related this to the relentless pressure brought to bear on those he often found to be sensitive and gentle individuals to become cut-throat salespeople in a world that was increasingly becoming an aggressively competitive marketplace (Smail, 1993).

Three decades later, with neoliberal ideology firmly entrenched, psychoanalyst Paul Verhaeghe described how we are currently witnessing 'an avalanche of depression and anxiety disorders among adults, and ADHD and autism among children' (Verhaeghe, 2014, p.193). In a society obsessed with image and 'measurements' of success, social anxiety will inevitably become more prevalent. Similarly, workers are now expected to be flexible, mobile and adaptive, to move from one precarious, short-term job to another. This profound uncertainty is, of course, especially difficult for those who favour predictability and routine. No surprise, then, that diagnoses of autism appear to have sky-rocketed in recent years.[6]

Inequality

Neoliberalism increases inequality, which leads to more human suffering. The late American sociologist Eric Olin Wright (2010) discussed how capitalism is inherently based on the competitive pursuit of profit. Workers are treated as exploitable and dispensable resources, and this generates 'vulnerability, poverty, deprivation and marginalization' (Wright, 2010, p.44). Wright described how class inequality is a defining feature of capitalism,[7] in an analysis that speaks to the substantial empirical evidence for the relationships between the social inequalities of neoliberalism and the prevalence of physical and mental health problems (Rogers & Pilgrim, 2003). It is well established that, in areas of high unemployment, rates of depression diagnoses (and other health problems) are significantly higher than in more privileged areas (Meltzer et al., 2004). Social class is one of the strongest predictors of physical and mental

---

6. This boom in diagnoses has also been facilitated by the increasing elasticity of the diagnostic criteria, which has transformed autism into something quite different from Kanner's initial 1940s conceptualisation.

7. While there has been some debate within sociology about the significance of the relationship between social class and inequality (see Savage, 2000), the damaging effects of class-based inequality are well evidenced.

ill health and there is a clear gradient in the relationship, with the worst off experiencing the poorest health outcomes (Rogers & Pilgrim, 2005).

Exploring this gradient, epidemiologists Kate Pickett and Richard Wilkinson have extensively researched the links between social inequalities and health outcomes (Wilkinson, 2005; Wilkinson & Pickett, 2010). Their findings show that the types of relative social inequalities found in developed capitalist economies have profoundly negative effects on the health of citizens. A key psychological component in their analyses is the way in which social inequality induces people to constantly compare themselves negatively with those in situations of greater advantage, so internalising a sense of social inferiority associated with their relative position in the social hierarchy (Wilkinson & Pickett, 2010). These constant negative comparisons are a source of chronic stress that can have severe effects on health (Sapolsky, 2004).

The destabilising effects of neoliberalism are such that its policies are creating a new social condition of 'precarity', which afflicts people who are often well educated and qualified but have no prospects of secure employment or income and frequently work for free (Foti & Romano, 2004; Mute, 2005). A 2017 report described how, in the London borough of Harrow, '37% of employees are working in low-paid jobs, and 42% of jobs in the area pay less than the London living wage [...] Last year, on average, twice every day, Harrow's food bank gave out three-day emergency food supplies for children' (Younge, 2017).

In societies characterised by growing economic inequalities, poverty has an unrelentingly toxic nature because it is:

> not a certain small amount of goods, nor is it just a relation between means and ends; above all it is a relation between people. Poverty is a social status [...] It has grown with civilization [...] as an invidious distinction between classes. (Sahlins, 1975, cited in Wilkinson, 2005, p.66)

So social class indexes both one's position in society and how such positions are intimately associated with judgements of moral worth (Sayer, 2005). Research shows that low social status is deeply damaging to mental health and is an important psychosocial pathway to mental health problems, such as chronic feelings of anxiety and low mood (Gilbert, 1992).

The corrosion of community

In addition to its negative effects on wellbeing, neoliberalism erodes community cohesion because of its focus on competition, deregulation and privatisation (Wright, 2010). These dominant values are toxic influences that impede shared human needs for security, community, feeling competent and being autonomous and authentic (James, 2008). Indeed, there is empirical evidence suggesting that social inequalities break down trust in communities, with corresponding increases in hostility (Wilkinson & Pickett, 2010). In a particularly powerful study, geographer Danny Dorling analysed murder statistics in Britain since Margaret Thatcher came to power in the late 1970s. He suggested that the dramatic increase in murder rates that he found are intimately related to the changes wrought by neoliberal policies, which resulted in growing social inequalities that 'have bred fear, violence and murder' (Dorling, 2004, p.190).

> Mark was a 32-year-old white man from a deprived area of a big city. He grew up on a housing estate made up of almost exclusively white working-class families. His father left when he was three years old, and his mother struggled to make ends meet. She was diagnosed with chronic depression and he remembers her often spending weeks at a time in bed. During his teenage years, Mark became involved in an organisation that claimed the 'indigenous' white population of the UK was under threat of annihilation from non-white immigrants. He began to attribute problems of poverty and community breakdown almost exclusively to immigration. Throughout his 20s, he became increasingly attached to this organisation and was involved in violent confrontations with groups of Asian men.
>
> One time he was arrested for assault, which resulted in his being referred to a psychology service for 'anger problems'. During his sessions, he talked about how his parents had told him his neighbourhood used to be safe, with a strong sense of community, but this had all changed when the 'foreigners' moved in, in the late 1970s. He had grown up hearing constant derogatory language regarding black and Asian people, and did not question this.
>
> Despite attempts by the psychologist to suggest that perhaps his anger related to wider social injustices shared across all deprived communities, Mark held to his beliefs. Unsurprisingly, he stopped attending the psychology service after only three appointments. Although he did not state his reason for withdrawing, it appears likely that challenges to his views did not fit with what he had learned to habitually think and feel about minority groups. He had learned not to see the relevance of the distal socio-political context to his personal situation, but rather to locate the reasons for his problems in his proximal circumstances.

The current global expansion of neoliberalism is characterised by the constant geographical mobility of resources – including workers, who can no longer rely on being part of stable communities with secure employment. This leads to an understandable lack of emotional and practical investment in those communities (Sennett, 2006). This corrosion of community undermines the sense of shared purpose and solidarity that can provide a platform for political challenge and change. It creates feelings of loss, resentment and anger that racist or reactionary political groups can exploit.

Previously, stable, secure and long-term employment within communities enabled individuals to develop useful skills or crafts, often honed over a lifetime, and a corresponding sense of emotional stability. However, the neoliberal transition to flexible, short-term, mobile and ever-changing employment undermines both skill specialisation and emotional stability. In the terminology of cultural critic Richard Sennett, the corrosion of community produces a 'corrosion of character' (Sennett, 1998).

Conclusion

Neoliberalism has both accelerated the demise of working-class culture since the 1980s and been facilitated by it. It has been assisted by technological developments and by changes in law and policy. Its imposition involved both seduction and coercion, with the balance between these depending in part on status, and the already disadvantaged frequently being more coerced than seduced. As a result, important sources of collectivity and solidarity – large workforces, relatively settled communities, stable conditions of employment, trades unions – have been weakened.

At the same time, the 1960s counterculture produced an increased emphasis on the needs and rights of different groups and challenged the post-war consensus around the importance of the common good (Judt, 2010). Neoliberals exploited this, using it to cast as outdated class identities and values of solidarity and collectivity. Consequently, many radical potentials of the counterculture have been lost or subverted. Overall, there is now a renewed emphasis on the individual, with all the pressures and strains that brings. Among other things, this seems to have created a cultural space for psychology, and its applied arm, psychotherapy, to flourish. All of this illustrates how subjectivity cannot be meaningfully understood separately from the social and material circumstances where it arises, and shows why outsight is essential.

Vitally, none of this is simply in the past, entirely finished, already settled. As we will describe in Chapter 6, it is also *now*. It involves ongoing seduction, ongoing coercion and continuous work – work of marketing goods and brands and promoting mass (and niche) distractions; work of pacifying, consoling and concealing, of sapping energy and filling time; work of circulating negative stereotypes to channel anger and sow mistrust; work of diverting attention from complex realities and towards auditable ratings – indeed, the work of audit itself; work of persuading us, over and again, that the only significant relationships are economic, wealth is the most important accomplishment, inequality is inevitable, the rich and powerful have everyone's best interests at heart, and in any case, *there is no alternative*.[8]

If none of this is simply in the past, this is not the end of the story. Despite the efforts of the very wealthy, neoliberalism continues to produce opposition and resistance. It is so profoundly exploitative it cannot do otherwise. For those concerned about mental health, this social and material actuality should be a source of grave concern. Somewhat perversely, perhaps, the resistance it creates is simultaneously a source of hope.

---

8. Margaret Thatcher was sometimes called 'Tina' because of her association with this phrase.

Chapter 3

The 'state' of psychology

The previous chapter described how the ideology of neoliberalism came to dominate our economic, social, cultural, and political landscape, and discussed some of the harmful effects that this is having. In this chapter, we extend that analysis to consider how some aspects of psychology reflect and support neoliberal ideology. We intend to argue that:

> Rather than a disinterested bystander, hegemonic forms of psychological science are thoroughly implicated in the neoliberal project. (Adams et al., 2019)

As we explained in the Preface, psychology (both clinical and academic) contains diverse perspectives and approaches, some of which avoid, or at least minimise, the problems we will identify in this chapter. However, our primary focus in what follows is on dominant tendencies within academic work. Accordingly, we will begin with a brief description of two fundamental principles underlying what we will call 'mainstream' or orthodox psychology – two core principles that strongly characterise this dominant approach: first, psychology as a (particular version of) science; second, the emphasis within psychology on the study of individuals. This will be followed by a critical look at how these two principles relate to certain ideas and practices of neoliberalism.

Mainstream psychology

By 'mainstream psychology' we mean psychology as it is predominantly taught on most undergraduate and postgraduate degree courses.[1] For the most part,

---

[1]. We are aware that there are a number of sub-disciplines (or counter movements) within the wider field of psychology that do not reflect, and in some cases overtly challenge, the core tenets of mainstream psychology. These include community psychology, critical psychology, cultural psychology, liberation…

on these courses, psychology is presented as a science. The British Psychology Society's website, for example, defines psychology as 'the scientific study of the mind and how it dictates and influences behaviour, from communication and memory to thought and emotion'.[2] This description gives the impression that psychology, as an academic discipline, involves the steady accumulation of incontrovertible facts about the human mind that are gathered using scientific methods.

A similar impression is gained from the descriptions of psychology in textbooks recommended for university degree courses. One best-selling undergraduate psychology textbook, which is illustrative of many others, defines psychology as the 'scientific study of behavior and mental processes' (Gleitman et al., 2010, p.1). The authors go on to explain how psychology is primarily about developing an understanding of the individual, and then how individuals act in groups. From the outset, then, two principles of this orthodoxy are crystal clear: first, psychology is a *science*; second, this science predominantly studies human beings as *individuals*.

The textbook's authors ensure that the reader is left in no doubt about the scientific orientation of psychology by dedicating the opening chapter to the topic of research methods. Here, they outline the tenets of an approach to scientific investigation known as positivism. The chapter presents information about how to systematically collect data, form and test hypotheses, draw conclusions, and use experiments to establish cause and effect relationships. Perhaps unsurprisingly, the research methods described are exclusively quantitative in character. Psychology is portrayed as akin to other experimental sciences, such as chemistry or physics, in its aim to discover empirically verifiable facts about individual human beings. Driving this point home, the authors confidently conclude that:

> The commitment to scientific inquiry has served psychology remarkably well. Psychologists know an enormous amount about human behaviors, feelings, and thoughts, and we know how humans differ from other species as well as how we resemble them. Moreover, we're quite certain about these things – our claims are not matters of conjecture or opinion, but assertions rooted in well-established facts. (Gleitman et al., 2010, p.45)

The second fundamental principle of mainstream psychology is the study

---

… psychology, some traditions within social psychology, and even (to a more limited extent) some more sophisticated cognitive psychological work that tries to include situated activity and embodiment. While significant, however, these approaches are all outwith the dominant mainstream. We discuss some of the work and ideas within these fields later in the book.

2. www.bps.org.uk/public/what-is-psychology

of humans as individuals. This is clearly reflected in the textbook's chapter titles, which include all of the familiar individual psychological constructs: perception, memory, intelligence, motivation, learning, personality, emotion and so on.

As suggested by the earlier reference to the study of humans in groups, however, there is one chapter devoted to social psychology. Someone studying this book sequentially would have to read more than 500 pages of text before reaching this chapter. Having done so, they might reasonably expect some examination of the complex, multi-layered, intertwining connections between human minds and the social, material, political, historical and cultural environments in which they exist. They might anticipate detailed discussion of the ways in which experience is forged in social relations, and of the connections between experience and subjectivity.

Unfortunately, these expectations would be quickly dashed. Instead, the reader is informed that social psychology is about how individual human beings are influenced by other individuals, and that 'how we respond to other people depends on how we think about and interpret their actions' (Gleitman et al., 2010, p.507). While there are some references to wider cultural influences, the vast bulk of the chapter is dedicated to individual processes of 'social cognition' and to micro-relational factors such as attitudes, conformity, altruism and love.

Notably, too, this chapter on social psychology frequently portrays social influence in largely negative terms. It includes discussions of Zimbardo's notorious Stanford Prison experiment, the notion of de-individuation among crowds (rooted in Le Bon's work), Asch's studies of conformity, Milgram's studies of obedience, Janis's concept of groupthink and Latane's experiments on 'social loafing' (which found that the presence of others reduces individual productivity). In these examples, social influence has largely negative effects: encouraging brutal or sadistic behaviour; unleashing collective violence; promoting errors of judgement, reasoning or decision making, and encouraging laziness.

As if sensing a threat to psychology as the study of the individual, the chapter concludes with a statement of how, in the face of social factors that may influence us, we maintain our individual agency to both actively interpret and to act on the social world, and that, 'through our interpretations we create the realities with which we contend' (Gleitman et al., 2010, p.541). So rather than reality consisting of enduring configurations of actual social and material circumstances, reality is created by individuals. More specifically, it is created by their individual interpretations: in other words, their cognitive processes. Psychologist Edward Sampson calls this tendency 'subjectivism', and as we will see, it is a feature of many psychological explanations (Sampson, 1981).

In our view, the treatment of social psychology in the textbook exemplifies how social influence mostly appears in this kind of psychology more generally. First, both the position and the relative extent of its coverage strongly suggest that it is less important than a host of (what are presumed to be) individual processes and characteristics. Second, its content is largely restricted to interpersonal or micro-relational factors. To the limited extent that politics, economics, history and culture appear at all, they are treated abstractly, as separable contexts. For example, the way in which the work of Polish social psychologist Henri Tajfel on social identity foregrounded the links between psychology and culture is ignored (Tajfel, 1982). Third, social influence is frequently cast as negative or unhelpful, as causing individuals to fall below accepted moral standards or to perform or decide sub-optimally. Fourth, and somewhat paradoxically, social influence is also presented as largely a matter of interpretations or cognitions (subjectivism). And fifth, social influence is portrayed as impacting from the outside on individuals, who might consequently alter their behaviour but whose psychological processes remain almost entirely individual in character. The overriding impression is that individuals are to be understood as separate from, and to a large degree independent of, social influences.

Some challenges to mainstream psychology

It is beyond the scope of this chapter to provide a comprehensive account of the many critiques of mainstream psychology that have emerged over the past century.[3] Instead, we will focus on some of the challenges to the two fundamental principles outlined above: that psychology is a positivist science, and that its proper focus is the study of individuals.

Psychology as a positivist science

As we have seen, psychologists sometimes describe their approach to science as positivist. What this means, simply put, is that they believe that it is possible to gather objective facts about human psychology. These facts are morally, ethically and politically neutral. They are true independently of the methods used to derive them or the theories used to interpret them. Their identification presumes a world characterised by observable and measurable objects that have law-like, causal relationships with each other. Once these causal relations have been discovered, researchers can develop new testable hypotheses. These hypotheses can then be checked through further experimentation, leading to the identification of further objective facts. In this way, the steady accumulation of objective, value-neutral facts, identified using rigorous methods, will – of itself – lead to progress and enlightenment.

---

3. For a general introduction see, for example Fox et al., 2009; Cherry, 1995; Rose, 1996, 1999.

As a philosophy of science, positivism is somewhat dated. It is now almost 100 years since it first appeared in its modern incarnation (and considerably longer since its antecedents were proposed).[4] In that time, we have found out much more about the potentials and capacities of science, about the strengths and weaknesses of scientific methods, and about the processes by which scientists produce facts and theories. There is now even an entire discipline – science and technology studies, or STS – that empirically investigates the complex processes of scientific knowledge production. At the same time, initiatives in philosophy have shed new light on what we can know about human psychology, and indeed on the limits of knowledge more generally. These initiatives include the rise of phenomenology and of process philosophy, the development of poststructuralist and social constructionist approaches, and the emergence of critical realism.

Superficially, it seems odd that an avowedly evidence-led discipline like psychology should endorse a dated philosophy not informed by the latest evidence and debate. We would suggest, though, that the endorsement of positivism serves mainstream psychological interests. It allows psychologists to describe their research findings as objective, value free and immune from bias. It helps them to imagine themselves as contributing to an intrinsically progressive project of bettering society through the provision of more accurate knowledge about individuals. It allows them to claim that methodological rigour, by itself, will guarantee sound knowledge. Overall, it functions to bolster the claim that quantitative, experimental research is *necessarily* superior to other ways of knowing – for example, those emanating from the humanities or that use qualitative psychological methods.

Ironically enough, in furthering these interests, the mainstream's endorsement of positivism is itself value laden. It promotes the interests of quantitative, experimental psychologists over those of others. It conceals issues of morality and politics within debates about research design, operationalisation and statistics. It makes psychology's emphasis on individuals, as opposed to their circumstances, appear more reasonable. Clearly, the soundness of all of this is debatable.

Going further, we can question whether this kind of psychology could ever, in fact, provide value-free or ideologically neutral knowledge. After all, its very focus – the individual conceived as wholly separate from her or his circumstances – is a culture bound and, in many ways, *ideological* concept. This was recognised as long ago as 1944, when Nobel award-winning economist Gunnar Myrdal described how:

---

4. An older version of positivism associated with Comte can be traced back to the 1800s, but even the more recent version – often called logical positivism – originated in the early 1920s.

> Cultural influences have set up the assumptions about the mind, the body and the universe with which we begin; pose the questions we ask; influence the facts we seek; determine the interpretation we give to these facts; and direct our reaction to these interpretations and conclusions.
> (Quoted in Gould, 1981, p.23)

Later in this chapter, we discuss psychological research into stress and resilience, showing how this research is both culture bound and ideologically influenced. For now, our conclusion is that claims that psychology is a positivist science are rhetorically useful for some psychologists. However, they do not mean that psychology can be understood as an objective, value free science.

This leaves open the question of what kind of enterprise orthodox psychology represents. The poststructuralist theorist Michel Foucault argued that the human sciences, psychology included, operate on a fluid plane between 'a priori'[5] sciences, such as mathematics, 'a posteriori'[6] sciences, such as geology, and philosophical reflection (Pilgrim, 2008a). By this, Foucault meant that psychology consists of reasoning, evidence and theories that do not consistently hang together. Each of these elements get emphasised at different times or for different purposes, but overall the relations between them are somewhat inconsistent.[7]

Overall, Foucault saw both psychology and psychiatry as simultaneously reflecting and transmitting the power of the state. Psychological knowledge – produced in hospitals, clinics, schools and prisons, as well as laboratories – is organised into discourses that operate in the service of power. Broadly speaking, this happens in two kinds of ways. First, these discourses legitimate forms of social action that might otherwise appear unacceptable. The discourse of intelligence as an individual psychological capacity, for example, helped usher in the 11-plus test – which, in turn, filtered many children into secondary modern schools with lower educational standards. Second, as we use these discourses to understand our own experience, we construct our self-understandings in ways that align with dominant power relations. This, in turn, means that it is relatively easy for us to be misled by powerful others,

---

5. Knowledge 'relating to or derived by reasoning from self-evident propositions' – see www.merriam-webster.com/dictionary/a%20priori

6. Knowledge 'relating to or derived by reasoning from observed facts' – see www.merriam-webster.com/dictionary/a%20posteriori

7. See Canguilhem, 2016. In this paper Georges Canguilhem fundamentally questions the existence of the field of psychology as a unified discipline, summing up its inconsistencies in the statement that 'for psychology, the question of its essence, or more modestly of its concept, also brings into question the very existence of the psychologist since, lacking the ability to explain what he is, he has difficulty explaining what he does' (pp.200–201).

because our very beliefs and values, our habits of feeling and arguing, are ultimately not wholly our own.

This view that psychology is not a positivist science is also supported by its history, which shows a distinct lack of the progressive knowledge accumulation seen in the physical and biological sciences (Pilgrim, 2008a). In these other disciplines, scientific truth or validity is said to gradually emerge through what appears to be a broadly democratic process whereby theories are developed over time.[8] Their soundness is assessed with reference to established and emerging facts, and they are tested and challenged by other scientists until – ideally, at least – it becomes evident that one theory robustly explains the facts under observation (Charlton, 2000). A good example is the discovery of the double helix structure for DNA (typically attributed solely to Francis Crick and James Watson, despite the central contribution and insights of researcher Rosalind Franklin (Elkin, 2003)). That DNA has this structure is now widely accepted by the scientific community as scientifically valid or true. Once accepted as true in this way, such claims form a base upon which further theories can be tested, leading to an increasingly comprehensive field of progressively valid knowledge.

Consistent with their endorsement of positivism, mainstream psychologists tend to present their field as operating in a similar way, by producing 'assertions rooted in well-established facts' (Gleitman et al., 2010, p.45). However, even a cursory examination of any branch of psychology reveals a very different picture. As Foucault suggested, what could best be described as fragmented, confused and sometimes contradictory sets of evidence, concepts and theories are not the exception but the rule. It is difficult to find any meaningful theoretical claim that the whole of psychology broadly accepts as valid or true, in the way that the double-helix structure is accepted as true in biology and genetics.

This can be illustrated with reference to psychotherapy, one of the key applied areas of psychology. Psychotherapy has become so ubiquitous that some argue we now live in a 'therapy culture' (Furedi, 2003). We hear frequent claims that psychotherapy is, in the currently popular jargon, 'evidence-based'. Clinical or counselling psychologists are said to conduct their therapeutic practices according to coherent theories based on a foundation of *well-established facts*.

Unfortunately, however, the field of psychotherapy is riven with deep disagreements and confusions. Consider, for example, the process of

---

8. Empirical research conducted by science and technology studies scholars demonstrates that, in actuality, the processes of knowledge production and verification are often far messier and more contingent than those suggested by public narratives of scientific progress.

formulation. A formulation is 'a hypothesis about a person's difficulties, which draws from psychological theory' (Johnstone & Dallos, 2013, p.4). It is widely accepted that the problems of a client presenting for help with psychological distress can be formulated from within a number of vastly different theoretical perspectives, including cognitive-behavioural (CBT), psychodynamic, systemic, social constructionist, social inequalities and integrative.

That many of these perspectives are so radically different in their underlying assumptions demonstrates the lack of any coherent and agreed theory of psychotherapy. Notwithstanding the incompatibility of these different approaches, however, one would at minimum expect theoretical coherence within a single approach. Unfortunately, even this does not appear to be the case – not least in respect of CBT, currently the most prominent approach. Rather than representing a coherent scientific theory based on well-established facts, CBT has been described as a 'form of eclecticism or syncretism, at best it is a "tradition" and at worst an inconsistent mish-mash' (Pilgrim, 2009). The recent ascendency of CBT, supported in no small part by the political establishment, is perhaps less to do with theoretical integrity and a sound evidence base and more due to how it fits with the dominant cultural or ideological paradigm. We will have much more to say about psychotherapy in the next two chapters.

Anthony, a 29-year-old trainee clinical psychologist, was confused. He had been taught that, based on sound, scientific research, CBT was the approach of choice for individuals said to have anxiety and depressive disorders. However, when he tried to deliver CBT to a range of clients in an adult psychiatric outpatient clinic, he found that it seemed to be of very limited benefit. His confusion was compounded by attending multidisciplinary team meetings where reference was frequently made to the often-appalling conditions in which clients lived, yet this was given scant attention in the CBT literature. When he spoke to his supervisor about this, he was told that the job of the psychologist is to deliver 'evidence-based' psychological interventions. In his attempts to become a more successful practitioner, he attended further CBT training workshops – to no great avail. He eventually became disillusioned with an approach that encouraged him to view his clients' problems as internally generated rather than as an understandable outcome of their real social worlds. His disillusionment was supported by a subsequent critical reading of the 'evidence base' for CBT, which he found to be flawed in the extreme.

The replication crisis

Whether or not one believes that psychology has the potential to be scientific, at present it cannot even be said to consistently meet one of the most essential criteria of science: the ability to replicate studies. In a collaborative project published in 2015, researchers attempted replications of 100 studies published in three leading psychology journals. In the original studies, 97% reported statistically significant findings, but in the attempts at replication, only 36% achieved similar results. The authors conclude:

> This project provides accumulating evidence for many findings in psychological research and suggests that there is still more work to do to verify whether we know what we think we know. (Open Science Collaboration, 2015).

Their appropriately cautious conclusion contrasts strongly with the aforementioned statement that, in psychology 'our claims are not matters of conjecture or opinion, but assertions rooted in well-established facts' (Gleitman et al, 2010, p.45).

The failure to replicate results is only one of a series of far-reaching concerns associated with psychological research that, at best, throw serious doubt on many of its findings (Spellman, 2015). Others include questionable research practices, such as not reporting all the variables in a study; statistical issues, including failures to correct significance levels for multiple testing, and the all-but ubiquitous use of statistical rather than clinical significance criteria (Jacobson & Truax, 1991); the inability to gain access to data of studies; fraudulent practices, and the 'file drawer' phenomenon, whereby studies that are unfavourable to the researchers aims are not published (a practice that has been identified as a problem with outcome research in psychotherapy (Epstein, 1995)). These concerns are compounded (and, to some extent, camouflaged) by the convention of reporting only group means and the probability levels associated with the differences between them. This practice 'depopulates' psychology by concealing exactly how many people within each group differed, and to what extent (Billig, 2013).

However, rather than acknowledging that these concerns reflect fundamental problems with the claimed scientific status of psychology, we are told instead that we are witnessing a revolution that will rectify errors and lead to a situation where 'we will (finally) have the seat at the table that our science deserves' (Spellman, 2015). This aspiration reflects how large parts of psychology remain wedded to the view that 'methodological rigour in and of itself ensures bona fide knowledge' (Pilgrim, 2008a). It shows, again, how the mainstream favours methods of research based on natural science approaches, and how it aspires to be seen as a positivist field of enquiry.

Critical realism

The shortcomings of positivism can also be highlighted by contrast with critical realist philosophy. Critical realists endorse both ontological realism (there is a real world out there) and epistemological relativism (we can never have complete or perfect knowledge of that world). Reality is constituted by open, contextually sensitive, historically contingent and emergent properties. This means that the relationships between objects and events are not necessarily empirically observable and measurable (Bhaskar, 2008). Because the objects of enquiry in psychology and other social sciences are 'always open and usually complex and messy', it is simply not possible to meaningfully isolate individual components and examine them in controlled conditions, such as the laboratory (Sayer, 2000, p.19).

This helps explain the failure to replicate some psychological studies, since the nature of what is being studied is open to change over time. The experimental practice of controlling for multiple extrinsic variables in order to isolate the effects of other variables in a laboratory has contributed to developments in fields such as physics and chemistry. When it comes to the study of what it is to be human, though, this practice is not only insufficient and potentially misleading, it is practically impossible. In the study of distress, for example, it is simply not feasible to conduct research that simultaneously assesses every variable known to be potentially relevant. Moreover, some variables – for example historical and biographical meanings, cultural mores or personal values – are not straightforwardly empirically observable and quantifiable, even in retrospect. Besides, any attempt to actually assess such a raft of variables would be incredibly intrusive, and would inevitably influence the measures obtained.

Another concern raised by critical realists is that social sciences, including psychology, mostly deal in abstractions – such as 'personality' – rather than observable physical entities. Critical realists describe this as an 'epistemic fallacy', where we unwittingly confuse our conceptual map with the actual territory it is said to represent. The possibility of doing this makes the task of carefully conceptualising concepts critical to any empirical study. There is no benefit in studying something unless we can agree on the existence and nature of what is being studied. This might involve, for example, a historical analysis of when the concept of 'personality' first emerged, why it might have done so at that time, how its use and definition have changed over time, the relationships between these changes and relevant evidence, and so on. Unfortunately this type of analysis rarely takes place, suggesting that much research is at best inconclusive, or at worst misleading – another possible reason why so many studies failed to replicate.

Applying critical realist ideas to mental health, Pilgrim (2015) identifies psychiatric diagnosis as an example of the epistemic fallacy. Informed throughout by what he describes as 'judgmental rationality', Pilgrim presents an account of distress and distressing behaviour that interrogates the 'demi-regularities' that psychiatric diagnostic categories imperfectly represent. Across cultures, 'People *are* anxious, sad, unintelligible, recurrently dysfunctional, and so on at times' (2015, p.129, original italics), and these experiences are contingently associated with rule transgressions and role failures. Pilgrim identifies a series of possible 'generative mechanisms' that can contribute to such experiences, most obviously early childhood trauma, adversity and abuse, while also emphasising that a complete account of causality is beyond our current grasp.

It is important to emphasise that rejecting positivism in favour of another philosophy – for example, critical realism – certainly does not have to mean rejecting the gathering and synthesis of evidence.[9] Rather, it means advocating a much broader psychology that also includes theories and evidence from disciplines such as politics, economics and sociology. This psychology would include a thorough critique of sole reliance on quantitative experimental methods within psychology, and the introduction of more recent philosophical perspectives that shed the pretence of straightforward ethical, moral and political neutrality. Far from rejecting the gathering and synthesis of evidence, then, rejecting positivism in psychology means having a more sophisticated understanding of its character and status. It also means taking seriously whole swathes of good evidence and sound theorising that – currently, and for no good reason – mainstream psychology largely ignores.

Individualism in psychology

Try to describe an experience you have had – just one – that was entirely free of social and cultural influence. Difficult, isn't it? One of us has been posing this question to large groups of students for more than a decade now. So far, of the hundreds of students asked, none has managed to identify any experience that clearly bears no trace of social relations, cultural norms or technological, material or economic resources. If this were not telling enough, the examples proposed by the students are almost without exception trivial: blinking, sneezing, the precise moment of catching a wave while surfing, and so on. But from an orthodox psychological perspective, where individuals are supposedly separate from their social and cultural contexts, it seems there should be a boundless pool of such experiences.

---

9. An example of this misunderstanding appears in www.nationalelfservice.net/mental-health/power-threat-meaning-framework-innovative-and-important-ptmframework/

By focusing on individuals, psychology has carved out a distinct conceptual space. This space contains a variety of psychological concepts, including self-concept, self-esteem, stress, resilience, personality traits, beliefs, attitudes, motivation, attention, memory and willpower. Most of these concepts were either invented by psychologists or were co-opted by them from the folk psychology of everyday life (see, for example, Harré, 2002). As a result, although many of these concepts reflect everyday concerns, their scientific status is sometimes unclear.[10] In order to illustrate how such concepts relate to psychology's emphasis on individuals, we will now briefly examine two examples: first, the related concepts of resilience and stress; and second, the concept of optimism.

Resilience/stress

A prominent strand of recent media commentary frequently characterises the current generation of young people as emotionally fragile and as having an overinflated sense of entitlement (Fox, 2016). Explanations for this are said to include over-protective parenting, alarmist child-protection agencies and policies, and the anti-bullying industry – and not, as we observed in Chapter 1, the actual social and material circumstances facing our young people. Together, these influences are said to have contributed to the creation of 'our very own overanxious, easily offended, censoriously thin-skinned Frankenstein monster' (Fox, 2016).

Such arguments hark back to an era when children were allowed to climb trees, walk to school and play leapfrog, marbles and conkers, and weren't banned from playing British Bulldog in the school playground: all activities said to foster the 'resilience-building freedoms' enjoyed by past generations. The implication is that, if we could encourage parents to allow their children more freedom, and rein back those over-zealous child protection institutions, our children would acquire the emotional resilience to deal with most of the stress of life. The problem for today's young people, in other words, is their acquired shortfall of individual resilience – and not the oppressive nature of the wider structures of the society in which we live.

The argument for inculcating resilience in individuals is predicated on the notion that some people appear to be better able to cope with stress and adversity. This implies that they possess some personal qualities or attributes that perhaps could be taught to those who don't have them. However, even if this were true, it ignores social influences, such as class, gender, ethnicity, that frequently bestow distinct advantages upon those deemed resilient (Smail, 2005). Furthermore, the focus on individual factors conceals the social

---

10. The concepts of belief and 'self-esteem' are good examples (see Cromby, 2012a; Scheff & Fearon, 2004).

causes of stress. Poverty and inequality – which as we have seen are endemic to neoliberal societies – if referred to at all, are individualised through psychological notions such as resilience, as opposed to 'political' notions such as access to power and resources (Harper & Speed, 2012; Epstein, 2013).

Interest in resilience is not just a media phenomenon. It is also reflective of a wider movement within the mental health field that jointly emphasises the concepts of resilience and recovery (see Friedli, 2009; Pilgrim, 2008b). Recovery was initially associated with the service user movement, where it was a positive challenge to a medical model that deemed people to be suffering from incurable, life-long mental illnesses. However, concepts of recovery and resilience have since been taken up with gusto by a mental health industry that largely promotes individualised approaches to distress, as opposed to challenging the abuses and inequalities that cause suffering in the first place. Divorced from its radical origins, recovery is now described as individuals finding ways of changing their 'attitudes, values, feelings, goals, skills and roles, in a deeply personal way, in order to effect change within their own life' (Harper & Speed, 2012). Here, mental health is predicated on fostering a socially acceptable set of attitudes and values – self-reliance, competitiveness, taking responsibility for your own problems – that would not go amiss in a neoliberal society.

It is perhaps also no coincidence that these notions have been promoted by a psychology industry that benefits massively, in terms of power, status and financial interest, from offering depoliticised, individualised models of therapy, such as CBT, that fit neatly with neoliberal priorities (Moloney, 2013). At least in part, CBT's dominance is a function of how it reflects dominant social values of heroic individualism, much like its 19th-century mystical faith-healing predecessor, Christian Science (Epstein, 2006). The central role of mainstream psychology in supporting these values is illustrated by the part played by psychologists in designing and implementing resilience training programmes for the US military. These programmes are supposed to equip soldiers to cope with the traumas of warfare, rather than articulating the destructive effects of violence (Becker, 2013). Again, then, in deflecting attention from the actual causes of distress, these initiatives reinforce an individualised, competitive, neoliberal status quo (Harper & Speed, 2012).

One hotbed of neoliberal ideology is the modern university. Students are now encouraged to foster personal resilience – along with flexibility, adaptiveness and creativity – to boost their employability. These imperatives promote the ideal of the successful, productive, competitive self that fits with the demand for 'a skilled, flexible and productive labour force characteristic of capitalist economies under neoliberal governance' (Aubrecht, 2012). As students are encouraged to develop so-called resilience, they are simultaneously 'educated' to downplay or ignore structural causes of distress – including how the interests of the powerful are tied up with an increasingly toxic competitive culture of corporate education (Ball, 2009).

> *Shayla, a 20-year-old university student doing an undergraduate business degree, presented to the college GP with experiences of low mood and panic attacks. She could not identify any specific triggers to her sometimes overwhelming distress, but expressed the view that she often felt inadequate and worried about how she was seen by her peers. She experienced some improvement over the next few weeks, following a diagnosis of mild depression and a prescription of medication. However, she said that she now felt a bit numb and detached from people who she had previously felt close to. Although she did not now feel as acutely distressed, she often felt lonely and unhappy. At this point, she was referred to a counsellor. She talked about how she had attended an average secondary school that was not overly academic and where she had good friends. During these years, she remembered feeling some anxiety around exams but it was when she started university that this intensified to a level requiring professional help. She said that most of her university classmates were from wealthier backgrounds and many had attended private secondary schools. She found the pressure to compete socially and academically at university very intense. However, despite being able to talk about the negative impact that this highly competitive environment was having on her, she firmly believed that the core problem lay within herself and that she needed to learn psychological techniques to 'cope' better.*

A similar argument can be made in relation to the stress that resilience is said to help people deal with, since:

> The stress concept draws the outside in – and in such a way that we end up believing that we need to change ourselves so that we can adjust to societal conditions, rather than changing the conditions themselves.
> And the chameleon-like nature of the stress concept makes it possible to obscure or conceal social problems by individualizing them in ways that most disadvantage those who have the least to gain from the status quo – among them, women and the poor. (Becker, 2013, p.3)

Most obviously, understandable responses to traumatic events and circumstances frequently get medicalised and psychologised. Their subsequent description as symptoms of post-traumatic stress disorder (PTSD) deflects attention from the frequently avoidable social and material conditions that gave rise to the initial traumas. Instead, attention gets focused on the subjective reactions of the victim. Consequently, gender differences in reactions to traumas are hypothesised to result from psychological differences in the ways in which men and women express and experience emotions. However, an alternative environmental explanation is that women are disproportionately affected negatively by traumas because, on average, they have access to fewer material resources to assist coping. At the same time, women's resource losses as a result of stressful events tend to be proportionately greater (Hobfall, 2001; Hobfall & Lilly, 1993).

This individualisation of resilience and stress is not inevitable. Some psychologists have long recognised that stress is a reductive and individualising concept (Brown, 1996). Likewise, in a 2009 WHO report, the concept of resilience is expanded beyond an individual attribute to a structural feature of families, communities and society as a whole (Friedli, 2009). The report refers to resilient places, resilient communities and resilient social policies. It summarises research showing that people living in communities that offer opportunities for social support and participation and reduced social isolation appear to have a decreased risk of developing mental health problems. However, it also points out that social support and participation do not remove the effects of material deprivation – in other words, absolute poverty operates as a high-risk factor in relation to mental health. Where the report does refer to resilient individuals – such as children with high levels of cognitive ability or emotional adjustment – it is made clear both that these individual characteristics are related to socio-economic status and that these early individual differences are usually wiped out by differences in material advantage. For example, at 'age 16, children from economically disadvantaged backgrounds with above-average reading skills early in life do worse in their exams than economically privileged children who had lower reading skills at age 5' (Friedli, 2009, p.28).

Optimism

The rise of positive psychology and its self-serving bias to always look on the bright side of life[11] is linked, conceptually, to a recent upsurge of interest in optimism. In psychological research, optimism has been defined by one set of authors as 'an individual difference variable that reflects the extent to which people hold generalized favorable expectancies for their future' (Carver et al., 2010). Individuals with higher levels of optimism, it is claimed, tend to fare

---

11. See www.youtube.com/watch?v=SJUhlRoBL8M

better in relation to health, education, income and relationships, compared with those with higher levels of pessimism. In their review of the literature, these authors describe research linking the development of an optimistic disposition to social background resources such as parental warmth and financial security. They also comment on how people become more optimistic in response to increasing stability in their lives, such as job security.

The inclusion of this important research linking adverse social and material circumstances to subjective experience could have led the authors to recommend that changing these circumstances would improve mental and physical health outcomes. However, their interest is in optimism as an *individual difference variable.* Consequently, they go on to cite research indicating that optimism, as a psychological trait, is associated with a reduced likelihood of dropping out of university. Here, the primary causal pathway is from the individual to the social. While they again refer briefly to evidence that poor socio-economic status as a child is linked to the development of pessimism, they then focus almost exclusively on how optimists tend to have better relationships. No further reference is made to the impact on individuals of wider social and material resources. Tellingly, the paper concludes with a call to discover how individuals can be changed so that they approach the world as optimists, rather than as pessimists.

The message from this type of review is loud and clear: we need to find ways for individuals to be transformed from within, using the technology of psychology, in order to adapt to the world as it is: we should cultivate insight, not outsight. This review also exemplifies how psychology frequently promotes this message by making only glancing reference to the actual circumstances of the people it purports to research. The psychological impact of lives of grinding poverty and biographies scarred with despair and desperation gets fleetingly acknowledged, then quickly subordinated to (supposedly) more powerful individual psychological traits. Hence, very little reference is made to what people might actually be optimistic or pessimistic about. Such 'traits' seemingly exist in some sort of vacuum inside people's heads, where they are almost completely disconnected from life circumstances, past, present and future.

This tendency is particularly pernicious in the way it minimises, or deflects attention away from, a wealth of research linking psychological distress to real world abuses such as poverty, social inequality and physical and sexual abuse (e.g. Bruce et al, 1991; Friedli, 2009; Goodman et al., 1997; Marmot, 2010; Repper & Perkins, 2003; Wilkinson & Pickett, 2010; Williams & Watson, 1996). Despite this overwhelming evidence, psychotherapy models such as CBT presume that it is not the experience of such abuses that lead to distress, but rather our so-called negative beliefs about them (see Beck, 1995; Beck & Weishaar, 1989). Here, beliefs are constructed as simply existing inside individual's heads, rather than arising from and being about real-world situations and circumstances. They are also constructed as purely cognitive, and as having primacy over the embodied feelings – themselves reflective of actual circumstances, both past and present, that are actually integral to lived experiences of believing (Cromby, 2012a). Yet again, then, the emphasis is firmly placed on the private and the individual over the social and the material.

In contrast, commentators not blinkered by mainstream psychology make frequent reference to how subjective experience links to real world issues. In this regard, recently there has been considerable interest in – and some critique of – the ideas and writings of a loose grouping of academics and commentators who have been referred to as the 'New Optimists' (Burkeman, 2017). In recent years, we have experienced profound political turmoil and uncertainty, with inter-related issues such as Brexit, the war in Syria, the deaths of migrants in the Mediterranean and elsewhere, North Korean missile tests, terrorism, Covid-19, Russia's invasion of Ukraine, and human-driven climate change. Faced with such circumstances, profound pessimism tempered by cynical humour may, in fact, be the only approach that makes sense.

However, according to the New Optimists, this pessimism is misplaced and we are in fact living in the best time in the history of humanity. For example, economist Max Roser claims that, on average, between 1990 and 2015, the number of people living in extreme poverty fell by 128,000 a day (Roser & Ortiz-Ospina, 2013). Journalist Oliver Burkeman (2017) accepts this, but still challenges the idea that, just because some things may have improved, we should feel optimistic about the world as it is. We already have the capacity to completely eliminate extreme poverty, end famines and ameliorate or even reverse climate change, but have so far failed to do so; in this context, pessimism about those failures is arguably more appropriate. So New Optimism is not simply about the accuracy of individual attitudes to the world, as psychology might view it: it is an ideological position based on its proponents' advocacy for the free markets of neoliberal capitalism.

The important point here is that what psychology construes as individual psychological attributes, such as optimism or resilience, cannot in fact be separated from the social and material circumstances in which they arise and develop. They are the products of personal biographies, lived in real-world situations, whose effects cannot simply be wished away. Consequently, optimism or resilience cannot be adequately understood as value free, objective, politically neutral psychological traits. Their acquisition, their promotion and their effects are all inextricably bound up with actual circumstances, shaped by enduring power relations and have wide-reaching, profound and sometimes toxic consequences.

Once this is understood, it becomes impossible to construct psychology as a wholly quantitative and experimental science of individuals. Ultimately, it means understanding psychology itself as a contextually (historically, ethically, socially, politically) situated body of ideas, evidence and practices. With this shift comes the requirement to ask not only whether psychological constructs are valid, but also whose interests they best serve.

How does this matter?

The quantitative, experimental and individualist focus of mainstream psychology is not merely an academic concern. How a discipline defines and orients itself powerfully shapes how it operates in and on people's lives. For example, psychological theories fundamentally shape and guide the content and delivery of psychological practices such as psychotherapy. Similarly, psychological evidence and research get taken up within other disciplines (marketing, management, human relations) and are used to inform policy debates and to selectively reinforce certain political values. In these ways, psychology not only misleads us about other people, it also – when it returns, innocuously embedded as taken-for-granted truth within other theories and practices – misleads us about ourselves.

Individualism, for example, both reflects and supports how self-interest has become a dominant value within rich neoliberal societies over the past four decades. The indulged western world increasingly attributes ultimate value to all things individual, private and competitive, as opposed to communal, social and co-operative. In recent years, individualist values have manifested in ways that have sometimes garnered popular support: in the previous chapter we mentioned the 'right to buy' council homes, for example, which remains one of Thatcherism's most popular policies.

However, over ensuing decades, the subsequent lack of investment in building new affordable homes, alongside a deregulated private rental sector, has made housing one of the most divisively toxic elements in British society. Increasing differentials between rich and poor communities have emerged as property prices, fueled for many years by easily accessed mortgage loans, have rocketed beyond the reach of most average-income citizens. Further damaging and divisive consequences have also occurred in relation to residency-based access to those schools identified as more successful.

In recent years, policies based on competitive individual values have resulted in public funding and provision of community-based services and projects being slashed, and state and publicly owned assets being stripped and sold off, in almost all sectors – including the National Health Service (NHS). The public is no longer able to access a high-quality NHS, free at the point of delivery. Rather, they must navigate so-called 'menus' of service treatment choices and site preferences, increasingly provided by private (for-profit) companies. And, exemplifying the idea of the sovereign individual as all-important, the wellbeing of the nation – which seemingly equates, somehow, to health – is now assessed using individual and deeply flawed 'happiness' scales (Cromby, 2011). Meanwhile, the stripping of funding for social, community initiatives and the covert privatisation of the NHS and other public services continue apace.

The values associated with individualism were also played out on an international scale with the referendum decision of the UK to leave the European Union. The reasons why so many British people voted to leave the EU are multiple, complex, varied, and to a considerable extent themselves a product of the effects of neoliberal policies (Cromby, 2019). Nevertheless, with respect to individualism, appeals to the electorate were made on two issues that clearly embody individualist tendencies: first, a fear of otherness, in the case of immigration; second, the withdrawal of shared control, in the case of national sovereignty.

Relatedly, the 2016 election of Donald Trump in the USA also mobilised individualist, selfish and self-centred values. The Trump campaign slogan 'Make America great again' placed USA national interests above shared humanitarian global issues such as world poverty and hunger. This call understandably appealed to those threatened by the fear of losing some of their wealth and privilege and also to those already oppressed and living in relative poverty. However, it is not an element of a dynamic, creative framework that can accommodate sustainable and ethical global development, and so ultimately can only foster destruction and suffering. The level of personal riches in the minority Western world has never been so great and possessed by so few. Equally, the divide between rich and poor has never been so wide (see Wilkinson, 2005; Wilkinson & Pickett, 2010). Individualism, then, supports a new status quo whereby a starkly divided society is increasingly run by and for those at the top of the pyramid.

As this book progresses, we will outline an approach to psychology that incorporates the social and material aspects of subjectivity into every facet of psychological theory and practice – a social materialist psychology. Importantly, this does not mean that we ignore individuals. It simply means that we do not systematically ignore the evidence of outsight that social and material influences continuously shape their experiences. Nor does it mean that we *only* consider these influences, at the expense (for example) of biological or bodily influences. It means that we do not simply assume, as most of psychiatry does,[12] that biological influences are necessarily the most

---

12. The growing numbers of psychiatrists aligned with the Critical Psychiatry Network frequently question this simplistic assumption (see Double, 2019).

important. It also means creating and endorsing psychological concepts that can incorporate such ideas, values and practices as uncertainty in subjectivity, unfamiliarity, interdependence, diversity, political consciousness, constructive critical discourse and action, relatedness and the importance of the other.

Our social materialist psychology contrasts with mainstream psychology, which is built on and promulgates the ideology of the individualist, autonomous, choosing self of neoliberalism (Rose, 1996). In recent years, the close relationships between psychology and the neoliberal state have enabled the discipline to thrive as never before. This may be seen as akin to the mutually beneficial relationships seen between the 'cleaner fish' and their much bigger hosts – relationships that always have the potential to develop parasitic tendencies![13] In this regard, the relative silence of the psychological establishment with regard to these relationships is noteworthy in itself.

The next section of this book further extends our analysis of the relationships between mainstream psychology and neoliberalism. In Chapters 4 and 5 we move on from discussing psychology as an academic discipline to focus on psychological therapies. This reflects the fact that this field arguably represents the most visible and prevalent application of psychology in the real world, and therefore increasingly impacts on the lives of many citizens in the UK and elsewhere. In these two chapters we will summarise evidence to show that psychotherapy cannot support the strength of its own claims for clinical effectiveness. We will suggest, instead, that it has proliferated precisely because many facets of it act in support of neoliberalism.

---

13. https://en.wikipedia.org/wiki/Cleaner_fish

Chapter 4

Does therapy work?

Previously, we described how neoliberalism was imposed in this country and briefly summarised some of its damaging consequences. We then explained how two related aspects of mainstream psychology – individualism and the claim that psychology is a positivist science – align it with neoliberalism. In this chapter and the next, we scrutinise psychological therapy – probably the most high-profile and most prevalent application of the discipline. We show that what is widely regarded as some of the best positivist research in this area – supposedly upholding the high effectiveness of talking treatment – is in fact deeply flawed, even on its own terms. The field suffers from systematic but largely ignored biases and failings that, together, undermine the confident claims of practitioners.

For the most part, psychological therapy individualises distress. There are exceptions, of course, some of which we will discuss later in the book. But, to a large extent, therapy involves working with individuals (sometimes in small groups) to formulate and address their suffering. This work tends to treat the distress as interior to the person, so that they need 'insight' to recognise its influence. The idea that they might benefit more from a measure of outsight that could absolve them of personal responsibility is far less prominent. Therapy also tends to rely, at least implicitly, on notions of willpower. It implies that, if only people committed themselves with diligence to these exercises, to the practising of these techniques, or to doing this homework, then their distress would recede.

Psychological therapy – and again, there are exceptions – tends to implicitly make individuals responsible for their own distress. And neoliberalism, of course, is often characterised by the idea of our being made individually responsible: for our health, our diet, our wellbeing, our social care needs, our careers. Now that there are no jobs for life, now that we can no longer expect the state to provide welfare, healthcare or education, we must take responsibility for meeting these needs ourselves (which would be great, actually – if we only had the necessary resources and freedoms).[1]

Psychological therapy also has the gloss of science. It presents itself as having specialist techniques, wielded by experts who have undergone years of professional training. It is frequently described as evidence based – as providing treatments and interventions that have scientifically been shown to work. Indeed, for the well-established therapies that are the focus of this chapter, the literature is replete with sophisticated studies that mostly seem to show therapeutic efficacy.

Only a generation ago, however, talking therapy practitioners were struggling to prove their claims (see, for example, Pilgrim & Treacher, 1982; Smail, 1983). The speed and scope of this turnaround should raise some obvious questions. After all, to listen to the distraught, to give them comfort and advice, are tasks familiar to many. And if these practices reliably bring succour and relief to those experiencing distress, then maybe their ideological dimensions can be overlooked. However, if this is not the case and therapies do not reliably relieve distress, then their ideological aspects necessarily become more of a concern.

The next chapter will examine newer brands of therapy, such as eye movement desensitisation reprogramming (EMDR). This chapter will examine the evidence base for the established psychological therapies, much of it dealing with variants of cognitive behavioural therapy (CBT) – the brand most favoured in the rationalised public healthcare systems of the UK (see, for instance, Iliffe, 2008).[2] Whatever their affiliation, the vast majority of talking therapists base their claim to expertise on their ability to wield specialist knowledge and skills, and with results that are benign and effective. Indeed, the leaders of the field assert that the quality and quantity of supportive research has flourished enormously in the last 30 years – enough to raise the widespread practice and promulgation of talking therapy beyond all dispute (Cooper, 2008; Wampold & Imel, 2015). This is the 'common sense' not just of the thousands of psychological therapists in the UK but of many government advisors and influential thinktanks, not to mention the mainstream media and popular opinion (Davies, 2015; Moloney, 2013). But sometimes it is the things that are right in front of our noses that are the hardest to see, and science is nothing if it is not about our readiness to keep our eyes open. Accordingly, the rest of this chapter is impelled by a series of questions:

---

1. As Chapter 2 explained, the idea that it will unleash creative potential is one of the most seductive allures of neoliberalism. The brute fact remains that, without social and material resources with which to be creative, this will always be an empty promise.

2. On the rise and ubiquity of CBT as a mechanised form treatment, see, for instance, Loewenthal & Proctor (2018) and Jackson & Rizq (2019).

- Can people be trained to be professional therapists?
- How important are therapeutic theories and techniques?
- Is there good evidence that some therapies are more effective than others?
- Can therapy do more harm than good?
- Has there in fact been a revolutionary expansion of evidence in favour of psychotherapy in recent years?

And, finally, gathering all of these themes together into the ultimate question… Can psychological therapy be shown to *work at all* as a reliable technology of personal change?

However, before we can address these questions, we must briefly set the scene.

In the early decades of the 20th century, most professionals refused to discuss details of their practice, much less allow direct observation of their work. It was not until the late 1940s, more than 30 years after the introduction of psychoanalysis to the US, that Carl Rogers published a transcript of a therapeutic encounter (despite opposition from his colleagues). At this time, assessments focused on the apparent helpfulness of therapy. Two-thirds of clients were typically reported to find significant and lasting relief from their distress (Frank, 1961) – close to currently accepted ratios (Orlinksy, 2010).

However, therapist testimonials are not the same as systematically collected evidence. The first attempts to compare groups of treated patients with counterparts who remained on a waiting list for therapy caused something of a panic for the practitioners, because the two groups seemed to recover from their problems at the same pace. This implied that psychotherapy was just another hollow placebo ritual. Perhaps – as in the case of many mild physical illnesses – the moderately distressed would improve after a while, regardless of whatever health care they might receive. These conclusions were later challenged on grounds of the early researchers' selective choice of data. Nevertheless, a fundamental question had been raised: how can we tell that a given therapy is genuinely helpful?

For a growing number of researchers from the late 1960s onwards, the answer lies in the randomised controlled trial (RCT): an experiment intended to measure the effectiveness of a given therapy by creating a situation in which every alternative explanation for the results, including chance events, can be discounted. In a well-designed RCT, one group of participants will receive the focal therapy, while another might get a different but proven variety, or a placebo designed to look genuine but minus the presumed active ingredients. The treatment will be scripted: a set of procedures (interventions or techniques) deployed under the guidance of a therapy manual. To avoid unfair bias, each client should be allocated randomly to their respective group and kept ignorant, or 'blind', as to which is the focal therapy. This 'blinding' should also hold for those who assess each client's progress, to ensure that their judgements are impartial (Bausell, 2007).

Since the late 1970s, thousands of RCTs have been performed to test the effectiveness of psychological interventions. Results have been favourable on the whole, but too varied to allow definitive claims. Seeking a way out of the muddle, investigators have turned increasingly to the method of meta-analysis. Here, many published RCTs are culled from the literature, and their findings blended and distilled in order to reveal salient trends (Wampold & Imel, 2015).

The first meta-analysis, in 1977, took 475 studies and found that the typical treated client was likely to feel better than 85% of their untreated counterparts. Statistically speaking, this 'effect size' for therapy could be regarded as very high (Smith & Glass, 1977). But the meta-analytic method is itself contentious. The outcome depends heavily on the quality of the studies that are chosen and the clinical experience of the researchers. Also, not everyone agrees that it even makes sense to lump together the results of disparate clinical trials that may use divergent, and perhaps incompatible, measurements of therapeutic change (see, for example, Smith et al., 1980). Over the years, researchers have tried to become more rigorous in their selection of RCTs. They have developed statistical techniques that are said to check for sampling bias and other issues (Wampold et al., 1997; Wampold & Imel, 2015), although some critics remain unconvinced (Charlton, 2000; Epstein, 2019; Stegenga, 2018). With more cautious usage over the years, the typical effect size has been gradually whittled down to around 65%. Nevertheless, this is enough to uphold a consensus that talking therapy, delivered by trained professionals, is as clinically helpful as many commonplace medical interventions (Lambert & Bergin, 1994).

Every year, dozens of new RCTs and meta-analyses are published. Their findings are central both to the international evidence-based therapy movement and to the fiscally driven managed care regimes that dominate North American and, increasingly, British health services (Rogers & Pilgrim, 2015). The UK's National Institute for Health and Care Excellence (NICE) strongly relies on meta-analyses to create its recommendations for psychotherapies for various disorders (NICE, 2017). For most researchers and practitioners, then, the fundamental questions have already been answered, and the remainder – notably, which therapies work best for whom – will be soon be settled (e.g. Roth & Fonagy, 2005). Nevertheless, we have some fundamental questions of our own.

Can people be trained to be professional therapists?

Very few studies have shown that psychotherapy training fosters better clinical relationships or rates of cure. Rather, multiple investigations have shown that trainees, or even paraprofessionals chosen for their compassion and common sense, can do as well as their fully licensed, highly experienced counterparts (even when the latter group include 'superstar' clinicians like Carl Rogers and Rollo May (Strupp & Hadley, 1979).

Perturbed by such unwelcome findings, researchers crafted clever arguments to prove the superficiality and transience of what the amateur therapists seemed to have achieved. But, for many onlookers, this always sounded like special pleading (Howard, 1998). More to the point, the early findings have withstood the test of repeated replication, as demonstrated by a landmark meta-analysis conducted in the 1980s (Durlak, 1979; Hattie et al., 1984; Berman & Norton, 1985). In the following decades, attention turned to the question of whether gains in therapist accreditation and clinical experience might nurture improved performance. Occasional studies found this to be so, but they were the exception. The general trend of this literature implies that practice does not make perfect, and that long-serving clinicians may even become less helpful to clients with the passage of time (Goldberg et al., 2016; Tallman & Bohart, 1999; Watkins, 2011, p.235).

What distinguishes a professional from a lay person is the ownership of proven intellectual and clinical skills and the willingness to scrutinise and refine them – usually with the aid of mentorship from a more experienced or knowledgeable colleague. Most counsellors and psychotherapists believe that such guidance enhances their power to attend to clients and restore wellbeing; indeed, regular clinical supervision is a mandatory requirement for training and practice (Rousmaniere, 2016). Once again, however, the research literature on this topic is far less sanguine. While some isolated studies have implied that supervision makes therapists more helpful, most of this material, including three large and recent reviews, suggests otherwise. In the words of one researcher: 'We do not seem to be any more able now, as opposed to 30 years ago, to say that supervision leads to better outcomes for clients' (Watkins, 2011).

How important are theories and techniques for achieving therapeutic change?

Almost all of the 500 or more talking treatments currently in existence boast their own repertoire of concepts and methods by which therapist expertise is justified and personal change is said to be achieved. However, clients usually report the most gains in the early stages of talking treatment, well before any specific therapeutic techniques have had time to work (Wampold & Imel, 2015).

More importantly, when researchers take pains to isolate the active ingredients of therapy in order to study their effects, then the more elusive and feeble these influences become. In so-called component studies, for instance, researchers create an RCT in which they either remove a putatively critical part of a given therapy or add an element that should boost its power. At least one clinical study has sought to excise or minimise the exposure element from cognitive therapy for trauma, by ensuring that therapeutic conversations did not dwell on recollections of the event that had fomented distress. Instead, the researchers focused on how the original traumatic event had disrupted clients' understanding of themselves, and how they might seek to modify their problematic thoughts. This approach was found to be just as helpful as the traditional exposure-based therapy, on seven separate clinical outcome measures (Tarrier et al., 1999). A similar finding emerged from a well-conducted study that carefully excised the 'negative thought-challenging' elements of CBT for people given a diagnosis of depression – but with no apparent dent in the measured helpfulness of the treatment (see, for instance, Longmore & Worrell, 2006).[3] Of course, these are merely individual clinical trials among the thousands that are published each year, and their results could be flukes of chance.

Enter the meta-analytic studies: two large-scale summaries of substitution-based RCTs for those described as having depression and anxiety problems have likewise found zero or clinically minor differences between whole treatments and those from which presumptive key ingredients had been amputated, including the internal 'thought-control' exercises that are one of the hallmarks of CBT (Ahn & Wampold, 2001; Bell et al., 2013). While one of these analyses found that the *addition* of a therapeutic component to an existing treatment *did* improve the potency of that therapy, the gain was small, and it was only for scores on narrow symptom- and behaviour-specific checklists, which did not always reflect improvements in each client's overall wellbeing (Bell et al., 2013).[4]

Another study supplied an early and inclusive summary of treatments for people labelled with post-traumatic stress disorder (PTSD), including CBT, behavioural therapy, anger management, EMDR, psychodynamic, hypnotherapy and psychodrama. When combined into an aggregate score, the main outcomes for all of the treatments (which included levels of 'avoidance', 'depression' and 'anxiety') were the same, apart from 'agitation', which in itself

---

3. It is worth noting that this can be a tricky procedure, because therapies seldom have completely distinct elements. For instance, methods that seem purely behavioural, such as getting the phobic person to face their fears or the miserable to become more physically active, might have an indirect bearing on how the patient thinks about themselves and their problems.

4. This phenomenon also raises the suspicion that the 'improvement' seen in many forms of therapy may be a reflection of how the patient – in completing that treatment school's signature questionnaire at the end of each therapy session – is progressively coached to adopt the conceptual language and upbeat narrative favoured by the therapy. Critics as diverse as William Epstein (2019) and Bruce Wampold and Zac Imel (2015) have suggested that the Beck Depression Inventory – one of the most widely used instruments in the CBT field – may have exactly this property.

said little, owing to the bewildering number of ways in which this construct had been measured (Sherman, 1998).

Another way to address the relative importance of clinical techniques is to compare a legitimate psychotherapy with a placebo version. In a psychotherapy trial, however, it is challenging to blind the participants as to whether they are receiving a genuine treatment or a fake created for the RCT. Where the placebos used are suspect or patently unconvincing, unsurprisingly, the familiar bona fide therapies do best by a wide margin. However, when placebos are thoughtfully constructed and delivered with care, by empathic practitioners who themselves appear to have some belief in them, then the outcomes will approach, and often equal, those of the genuine therapy (see the discussion in Wampold & Imel, 2015).

In one study, researchers developed a credible placebo to be used in the investigation of exposure-based treatments for PTSD. Their control therapy lacked the traditional confrontational elements of CBT as far as traumatic memories and situations are concerned. 'Present-centered therapy', as they called it, offered a cogent rationale and therapeutic rituals for clients to perform, including active learning about the effects of trauma and using problem-solving skills to identify and change maladaptive thoughts and actions (Frost et al., 2014). So compelling and effective did it prove that, perhaps to the embarrassment of its creators, it has since become a manualised approach for helping people labelled with PTSD, and is backed by the American Society of Clinical Psychology[5] (Wampold & Imel, 2015).

Finally, the power of techniques can also be judged by scrutinising how closely the practitioner follows a manual for a given treatment; how well they display signs of technical competence, and to what extent their proficiency in doing these things adds up to treatment success. None of this is easy to assess, because therapy is a supremely personal encounter. Clients are not standardised, so few therapists can cleave as fully to the treatment guidelines as instructed. Moreover, competence is to some extent in the eye of the beholder, dependent on how the client perceives and behaves toward their therapist. Evidence to date suggests that treatment fidelity and apparent competence have a small but in general non-significant bearing upon the outcome (Rousmaniere, 2016).

Overall then, there are few grounds for believing that the techniques deployed by psychologists and counsellors are any more than minor ingredients in whatever results they achieve.

---

5. The Society of Clinical Psychology is Division 12 of the American Psychological Association, which describes itself as 'the leading scientific and professional organization representing psychology in the United States'. For their endorsement of PCT therapy, see www.div12.org/PsychologicalTreatments/disorders/ptsd_main.php

Lucy was referred to adult mental health services when she was finding it increasingly difficult to manage compulsive behaviours associated with longstanding fears of contamination. These fears had been developing since childhood and seemed related to incidents of ill health within her family. She had developed increasingly elaborate physical and mental rituals in response to the risks she perceived. These were now getting in the way of her studies at university and led to her taking breaks from her academic work.

Earlier in her life, Lucy had been referred by her GP to child and adolescent mental health services, where she had undergone a course of CBT, but this had not helped. When I saw her, in my capacity as an adult mental health services psychologist, I tried at first to work with her and her family as a whole – since it seemed that Lucy's difficulties might owe something to longstanding but unacknowledged conflicts and to the shared feelings and beliefs that sustained them. However, the family was beleaguered by housing problems, money worries, and health issues – all of which made it hard for them to find the time and space to create new ways of getting along together and helping Lucy. After about 18 months of roughly fortnightly psychology sessions, this young woman was accepted as an inpatient at the national service specialising in anxiety disorders, the Anxiety Disorders Residential Unit (ADRU). I thought that maybe the lack of progress was because I was simply not good enough at delivering CBT, the treatment recommended by NICE for obsessive compulsive disorder.

Lucy spent three months receiving treatment from the ADRU. She made some very small gains, such as being able to tolerate getting out and about a bit more. But on her return, despite my continuing to work with her, she slipped back towards her usual ways of coping. Eventually, after just over 100 sessions, I discharged her and suggested that she might find it helpful to receive support with moving out of the family home and into a different environment. She was duly referred to social care services, only to be re-referred to psychology about a year later, to begin work with another practitioner who specialised in CBT. More than 60 sessions later, this psychologist is at the point of discharging her, having tried further CBT and, in addition, EMDR, neither of which has led to any significant change.

Is there good evidence that some therapies are more effective than others?

Some large-scale reviews have suggested that CBT might be superior to other approaches in the management of panic and for people labelled with anxiety disorders. However, the clinical (as opposed to statistical) superiority is questionable, and the former declines in proportion to the quality of the study. One well-regarded meta-analysis, for instance, summarised 108 studies across all the anxiety disorder diagnoses and showed three different treatment varieties, cognitive, behavioural and CBT, to be equally helpful (Norton & Price, 2007). Likewise, an examination of treatments for people given PTSD diagnoses showed a broad similarity of outcomes across different forms of treatment (Benish et al., 2008).

Several meta-analyses in the mid 2000s likewise gave similar effect sizes for a range of treatments, including CBT. However, control therapies that offered comfort and listening, or were poorly described, did no better than waiting list or treatment-as-usual groups. These finding were taken as support for the principle of confrontation in therapy. But doubts remain because the results were based on comparisons across separate studies, rather than comparisons of treatment within the same study – rather like setting out to compare apples and oranges in the belief that they are the same kind of fruit. Some of these analyses were also compromised by the small scale of the trials on which they were based, a perennial problem within the meta-analytic literature (Wampold & Imel, 2015, p.156).

Similar issues arise with treatments for other forms of anxiety, such as obsessional states and panic. The efficacy literature for these is vast and quite often contradictory, not least because the relevant psychiatric diagnostic categories are neither valid nor reliable and seldom speak to the causes or nature of distress from the standpoint of the sufferer. Nevertheless, as far as therapy is concerned, key trends emerge when the evidence is examined carefully, and at the present time there seem to be 'no substantial differences in efficacy between bona fide psychotherapies for anxiety disorders' and claims to the contrary 'are overblown and in need of further testing'. So say the well-known American researchers Bruce Wampold and Zac Imel, in their book *The Great Psychotherapy Debate* (Wampold & Imel, 2015), which offers an exhaustive analysis of some of the main psychological outcome evaluation literature of the last 30 years, encompassing more than 500 studies and publications. Indeed, this principle appears to apply for every kind of psychological problem: large scale analyses that suggest the pre-eminence of a particular therapy, often CBT, become less compelling when the all-too-commonplace design and sampling issues are taken into account (Wampold et al., 2017; Dalal, 2018).

So far, then, there are few grounds for thinking that therapist training or particular techniques make any real difference to the outcome of therapy, or even that one treatment variety is best. But other questions must also be considered.

Can therapy do more harm than good?

The widespread belief in the value of counselling and psychotherapy suggests an equally widespread notion that, at worst, they can be ineffective. In truth, between one in 10 and one in four clients will say that they have gained nothing from therapy, and others will say that they feel worse because of it.

This issue of client deterioration is poorly researched, but the evidence suggests many potential causes. One is the therapist's exploitation of clients for emotional, sexual or financial purposes. Jeffrey Masson, the one-time psychoanalyst and director of The Freud Archives, documented many such cases, some perpetrated by renowned practitioners (Masson, 1985). A penumbra of shame and silence makes this a difficult topic to study. However, surveys and accounts by former clients suggest that it is more prevalent than was once believed (Bates, 2005).

By contrast, the issue of the possible toxicity of psychological treatments carried out in good faith has received less attention. In the last decade or two, it has been reluctantly recognised that certain therapies can, in particular circumstances, do more harm than good. Grief counselling for ordinary bereavement, punitive 'boot camp' interventions for people described as personality disordered, and critical incident debriefing in the wake of trauma can all deepen distress. Intensive exposure therapy can add to the woes of those described as suffering from panic disorder. For some, CBT can fuel self-harm and suicide; applied relaxation training and exposure treatment can generate anxiety, and group therapy sends some people into a state of dread (see, for example, Hallam, 2018; Barlow, 2010; Lilienfeld, 2007). Even more worryingly, clients with few outward signs of severe distress can become intensely disturbed, and in the worst instances homicidal, as a result of counselling or mindfulness training (Farias & Wikholm, 2015).

Considerable mystery surrounds the true extent of client deterioration. Clients may often be reluctant to admit that they are not profiting from treatment; therapists, even when they observe problems, may be equally reluctant to report them, even in anonymised studies. This reluctance may also extend to the publication of studies that report harmful effects (Barlow, 2010). However, bearing all these caveats in mind, surveys suggest that between five and 10% of the recipients of therapy experience an intensification of their problems (or a set of fresh ones) as a result of psychological therapy (Curran et al., 2019). It is possible that the deterioration rate may be higher still in some services and client populations where therapists, owing to their training and background as middle-class professionals, may struggle to acknowledge their clients' experiences of chronic social adversity (Davies, 1997; Reeve, 2000; Saeromi & Cardemil, 2012).

In the psychotherapy research literature, vigilance in respect of potential harm should be high. In fact, though, clinical trials dealing with medications are up to 20 times more likely to mention adverse reactions than those that deal with talking treatments. In a review of 132 trials of psychological interventions for adults and children described as having behavioural and mental disorders, only a fifth asked participants about adverse effects or deterioration in treatment. And just four of these, or 3%, gave a description of such problems and of the methods used for ascertaining them. Not surprisingly, these practices were far more common for investigations of therapies aimed at traumatised clients, where there is more sensitivity to participant safety. Overall, it seems that pharmacological researchers are more vigilant than their psychotherapy colleagues when it comes to detrimental treatment effects (Jonsson et al., 2014).

Has there been a revolutionary expansion of the evidence in favour of psychotherapy?

In so many areas of life, affiliations count. Few who investigate the value of psychological therapies are disinterested. Most are committed to a particular approach, to its superiority as a treatment and as a set of theories that purport to explain how distress comes about. Psychotherapy research was probably one of the first fields to raise questions about how far the professional allegiance of researchers might shape their actions and how they report their studies (Norcross et al., 2011), because there are many ways in which subtle biases might happen within an RCT. Where two or more treatments are being compared, there might, for instance, be systematic differences in the selection of therapists, in the quality of their training, in the enthusiasm of practitioners and researchers for one treatment against another, and in how well the effects are recorded and assessed.

One review examined 29 studies that had compared cognitive, behavioural and psychodynamic therapy. The author concluded that more than two thirds of the differences in treatment effectiveness could be attributed to the allegiance of the researchers alone, almost enough to swamp claims for the clinical pre-eminence of any one type of therapy (Tolin, 2007). As is so often the way with meta-analyses, however, this study was later questioned regarding the clarity, completeness and relevance of the chosen outcome data. In the ensuing decade, subsequent analyses gave somewhat mixed results, though with an overall tendency suggesting that allegiance effects are present (Anderson et al., 2010; Wampold & Imel, 2015).

Another impressively large study surveyed 30 meta-analyses, using benchmarks designed to overcome the limitations of the previous work (Munder et al., 2013). The results endorsed earlier findings of bias, and the authors recommended that future researchers guard against their own partiality by ensuring that comparative studies are done by teams with mixed allegiances; that every therapist is equally motivated to learn and deliver the treatment, and that all meta-analyses check for researcher affiliation as a rival explanation of apparent efficacy. At present, it is probably correct to regard researcher allegiance as 'a very strong determinant of outcome in clinical trials' (Wampold, 2001) and 'one of the greatest threats to the internal validity of findings from RCTs' (Westen et al., 2004, quoted in Munder et al., 2013, p.508).

The issue of researcher affiliation is also a problem for those large-scale meta-analyses that set the standard for evidence-based practice and guide the whole field of talking treatment. But no such analysis can rise above the quality of the individual studies selected for inclusion. It is therefore worrying that meta-analyses for psychotherapy yield much larger effect sizes than are found in many fields of clinical medicine. For some, this suggests that researchers are not choosy enough. They have allowed their field to drift in a direction that consistently flatters the outcomes.

Meta-analysts are required to follow broad guidelines for the evaluation of bias in the work they examine. However, there are none that tackle the problem of their own commitments. Surprisingly, there were no attempts to gauge the severity of this potential issue until 2017, when a study looked at how often investigators disclose their allegiance and then take steps to rectify it (Dragioti et al., 2015). This was a large study, embracing 146 meta-analyses and nearly 1200 published RCTs, comprising a wide range of psychological and physical distress, treatments and outcomes. The results were not encouraging: the vast majority of studies failed to give any of the desired details. A mere 25 meta-analyses mentioned the topic, and a total of six, or just over four per cent, used valid statistical and other procedures to control for its effects. It was worse for the individual RCTs. Only three per cent gave the affiliations of researchers, and only one study described an attempt by the authors to compensate for this potential source of bias.

In the absence of a strict disclosure policy, investigator allegiance is unlikely to be reported in these studies. This has consequences for the whole field, where the quality of research lags behind current standards for the pharmaceutical industry.

And yet this is not the only source of systematic distortion in the research literature for talking therapy that we need to consider. 'Publication bias' is the tendency for authors to submit, or for editors to accept, manuscripts for publication based on the direction or strength of the study's findings. In recent years, it has become increasingly clear that this phenomenon is widespread in the field of pharmaceutical treatments for people labelled with depression, psychosis and other mental health problems. Critics argue that negative or inconclusive trials are under-reported by drug company-funded researchers, meaning that the safety and strength of their products are over-rated (Healy, 2013; Moncrieff, 2013, 2020).

The same may be true for psychological treatments: positive results are five times more common in psychology than in the physical sciences, such as astronomy (Staddon, 2017) – a strong hint of publication bias. When sleight of hand becomes routine within a research field, its traces can nonetheless be detected with some authority via statistical methods designed to probe for likely gaps in the publication record. One high-profile investigation considered trials dealing with outpatient CBT for people described as having depression (Cuijpers et al., 2010a). The authors selected 117 studies spanning 30 years and with almost 10,000 participants. Their definition of bias was conservative: they focused only on published studies and ignored the selective reporting of outcomes, which is an equally common practice. Nevertheless, they highlighted a 'considerable and significant risk' of such distortion, including evidence for 51 'missing' studies. When the results of these were included, the general effect size dropped by more than a third. Overall, this area of clinical science did 'not seem to be any freer from publication bias than research on medication treatment'.

Despite its scale, this meta-analysis is purely inferential and mathematical; the gun is smoking, but no projectile is in evidence. However, at least one sizeable bullet has been found. An analysis of 55 clinical trials funded by the US National Institute of Health (NIH) between 1972 and 2008, all testing psychological therapies for people described as having major depressive disorder, used NIH archives to trace the progress of each trial. A total of 13 trials failed to publish – almost a quarter of the total. This figure resembles the rate for industry-funded trials of so-called antidepressant drugs (Healy, 2013; Burstow, 2015). When these 'lost' findings were combined with the published ones, the estimated clinical power of the therapies dropped from highly effective to moderate (Driessen et al., 2015).

There is yet a subtler form of bias associated with the passage to publication. This happens when researchers decide, at an early stage of a trial, in light of what they have seen so far, to reprioritise or change the stated outcomes. In pharmaceutical research, this has always been regarded as a dubious practice. It is far less common than it once was, owing to statutory requirements that full protocols for industry-funded drug trials be publicly registered from the outset. In many countries, this does not apply for talking treatments. Consequently, there is no precise estimate of how often the results of psychotherapy studies might be manipulated or concealed in this way. However, a survey of clinical research protocols from Canada implies that the practice is common (Chan et al., 2004, Goldacre, 2019). For all types of clinical research, just two thirds of trials were found to be prospectively registered. The vast majority of these focused on drug or biological interventions, rather than psychotherapeutic ones. Even for these publicly registered studies, nearly a quarter changed their primary outcomes at the earliest opportunity. Some argue that this practice surely happens more often for the many dozens of unregistered psychotherapy trials that go ahead without hindrance of oversight.

Overall, does therapy actually work?

Turning then to the ultimate question: the best quality evidence available suggests that talking treatment is less potent than many imagine. At least one reason for this is straightforward: most people are never counted in the evidence base. In a typical RCT, roughly two thirds of clients are excluded at the outset, usually because they have been given multiple psychiatric diagnoses or are judged to be at risk of self-harm. Of the remainder – the ones who manage to get into the treatment set – around half will show some improvement at the end. Of these people, about two thirds will report that they have recovered, and of this group, less than half will maintain their recovery beyond a year or two. Not surprisingly, few practitioners can bear to publicly unpack all of these Russian dolls, since the final cured manikin cuts a diminutive figure, representing only a 20th of the original client pool (Dalal, 2015; Shedler, 2015).

> *Angela is 61 years old and has been a patient of mental health services on and off for more than 30 years. Her latest episode of care from a community mental health team started around 12 years ago. Prior to that, she had had various admissions to psychiatric facilities. She was referred to me in 2015, as she was being discharged from intensive treatment for eating distress and self-harm at a private psychiatric hospital. Commissioners in her area agreed to fund the out-of-county private placement because it was felt that she could not be managed or undertake psychological work safely in the community.*
>
> *Angela discharged herself from the hospital before the treatment had finished, when her friend was diagnosed with cancer. She wanted to spend time with them and didn't feel there would be much benefit from staying in the hospital. Five years on, she continues to meet with me and there is no plan for discharge any time soon. She manages to*

> keep herself relatively safe, which could be seen as the one clear merit of her treatment. However, Angela has not yet managed to reach a point where either she or the people working with her believe that she can resist her urges for very serious self-harm.

The US National Institute of Mental Health Collaborative Research Program (MHCRP) on people labelled with depression exemplified these tendencies. Back in the 1980s, this was the first large, multi-site research project to compare three active treatments, all of which did slightly better than the standard outpatient care dispensed by medical practitioners. However, only a relatively small percentage of people stayed in treatment – a number so minute that, for many commentators, it raised questions about the over-selling of evidence-based treatments (Elkin et al., 1989).[6] None of this has prevented this study from being widely cited down the years as a 'classic' – bolstering the value of talking therapy in general, and of CBT in particular, as a remedy for depression.[7] While it has been succeeded by many new trials and meta-analyses of psychotherapy for severe low mood over the decades, the kinds of issues that quietly dogged the MHCRP study have not gone away. If anything, they continue, concealed in plain sight. Take, for instance, the well-known Dutch psychologist Pim Cuijpers' assay of 500 trials of talking treatment, in which he acknowledged how many of these studies were bedevilled by high rates of client drop out – or attrition, as it is usually called – and by the risk of various kinds of bias (Cuijpers, 2017).[8] Nevertheless, Cuijpers managed to extract hopeful conclusions about the power of psychotherapy for those afflicted with malignant sadness.

In the talking therapy research literature, 'success' is usually defined by a drop in the scores below a given threshold on a mental health questionnaire. But this often amounts to a modest reduction, rather than erasure of the client's problems – even for those who are experiencing less intense 'symptoms'. For the more representative client of public health services – in terms of their overall levels of distress – things may be worse (Atkinson, 2014;

---

6. See also William Epstein's incisive and critical discussion of this research project, in his book *The Illusion of Psychotherapy* (1995). For a more general critique of the systematic tendency for researchers and reviewers in the field of the treatment of depression to over-rate the power of psychological therapies, see Cuijpers et al. (2010b).

7. Shedler (2015) offers an informative account of the spurious authority that the MHCRP study continues to enjoy within the CBT therapist training literature and beyond.

8. This pattern, demonstrated by Cuijpers, of cautious scientific fault-finding followed by endorsement, tepid or warm, is a recurrent one within the current psychotherapy research literature, and even within the official clinical treatment guidelines for the UK. For a discussion of these general trends within the field, see Epstein (2019). For a trenchant analysis of the construction of UK NICE guidelines for psychological treatment as an all-too arbitrary and essentially bureaucratic process, see Mollon (2007).

Dalal, 2015; Scott, 2018; Timimi, 2020). In their painstaking review of clinical trials of the most widely used evidence-based talking therapies, the American psychologist Drew Westen and colleagues found that, at the end of the course of therapy, the 'typical' client was experiencing a panic attack on a near-weekly basis, and for those suffering from eating distress, a bulimic binge 1.7 times per week and a purge 2.3 times each week. Moreover, the benefits of most treatments seemed to drop quickly: more than half of those who received an evidence-based therapy sought to restart their therapy six to 12 months later. This did not necessarily mean that the remainder were well, of course; many of them may have simply given up (Westen et al., 2004). Two fairly recent follow-up studies appear to give more encouraging long-term results for some evidence-based treatments for severe anxiety, but these findings must be interpreted with caution: they are small-scale, observational investigations, rather than randomised clinical trials, and they suffer from many of the key methodological issues discussed in this chapter – including client attrition (Bilet et al., 2020; Hoffart, et al., 2016).

Indeed, a similar story can be told for some of the most vulnerable groups, such as children and young people. In the 1990s, the largest ever controlled trial of community-based mental health services for children and their families, the Fort Bragg program, was unable to show that the recipients of 'integrated services', featuring heavy doses of psychotherapy, did better than their peers who got paediatric outpatient treatment as usual (see the discussion in Dineen, 1998).

Poor performance in RCTs and real-life settings is not the only issue. There are longstanding (and long-ignored) questions about the way that data from clinical trials are harvested and analysed. The vast majority of studies use statistical tests that aggregate the outcome scores for a group of recipients. They then seek to establish either the odds that any observed improvement might be due to chance or the magnitude of the difference in scores between the comparison groups – that is, the effect size.

However, there is an unacknowledged problem with both approaches. Small groups of participants can have disproportionate effects on the outcome. This can happen via the small minority who are scored as having done particularly well under the given therapy. By the same token, a result that has a high significance level or strong effect size might say little about whether *any* of the participants have returned to normal functioning or have achieved worthwhile change, however defined.[9] As we touched on in Chapter 3, the alternative is clinical significance testing, which usually gives a more modest

---

9. See Michael Billig's critical discussions of the shortfalls of psychological and clinical experiments reliant on averaged group data (Billig, 2015). For a detailed conceptual exploration of this issue (and critique of standard psychological experimental statistical analyses) see Gigerenzer (2004).

picture of the strength of psychological treatments. Perhaps unsurprisingly, then, this approach is yet to make headway in outcome research, although it has long been advocated (Jensen & Corralejo, 2017).

A growing number of researchers also argue that trial results should include fine-grained analyses of the progress of each participant, which can be added together to create a more meaningful portrait of what has transpired. This strategy would address the problem of 'depopulation' in psychological research (also referred to in the previous chapter). In doing so, it would supply a more detailed and clinically useful picture than the inferential statistical methods routinely used.

If the statistical issues are far from minor, defining and measuring the effects of a therapeutic conversation is considerably harder than might be supposed. For instance, it is often unclear what is meant by success. There is no consensus about which outcome measures are the most important and why. Research has focused more on the measurement of distress than on improvements in the sufferer's ability to cope with or enjoy daily life (Epstein, 2006; Morgan, 2008; Smail, 1978). Among more vulnerable groups (children, older people, adults with learning disabilities), there is often a gap between what they want from therapy and the priorities of their relatives and carers (see, for example, Rapley, 2004; Strenfert Kroese & Holmes, 2000).

There is also the more general issue of simplistic tick-box assessment. If the client indicates that they are happier, this does not always imply that they have recovered from their problems (and vice versa). Also, the disappearance of one problem can mean that it has simply been displaced by another. Reports of clinical practice contain many instances of this 'symptom substitution', but the reader will look in vain for mentions of it in the clinical trial literature.[10] Finally, it is hard to distinguish difficulties that were brought to therapy from those that might have emerged legitimately within it – from growing insight on the part of the client, for example, or due to mistreatment or neglect by the practitioner.[11]

If all this is beginning to sound complicated and difficult, then it should. This is positivistic research, which – as the previous chapter explained – always struggles to capture the complexities and subtleties of human social life.[12] Unlike molecules and mainsprings, clinicians and clients have interests

---

10. Epstein's *Psychotherapy and the social clinic in the United States: Soothing fictions* (2019) offers a comprehensive summary of these and many other longstanding methodological deficiencies within the research field.

11. An insightful discussion of these issues can be found in Zilbegeld's (1982) *The Shrinking of America: Myths of psychological change*.

12. See, for example, the critical discussion in Epstein (2006) of widely used therapy outcome checklists like the Beck Depression Inventory. For a more general discussion of these measurement issues, see Smail (1978).

and aims. Their responses to research questions can be subtle, sometimes untruthful, and often unpredictable, especially when they know they are being judged. The very act of asking someone to relate the usefulness or otherwise of treatment can distort what gets reported.

One way to understand the effects of psychotherapy is by comparison with placebo effects in medicine. Just as there is a lot of ritual in the practice of psychotherapy, so there is a longstanding debate about the clinical power of ceremonies that bring feelings of comfort, hope and control. For a third of patients, placebos have both subjective and objective therapeutic properties, especially for stable but chronic conditions such as musculoskeletal pain, asthma and high blood pressure (Jopling, 2008). Where they convince, fake remedies can ease the symptoms of anxiety, pain and perhaps inflammation. They seem to do this via a threefold process in which patients may deceive both themselves and others, find new zeal for health-giving actions, and experience a temporary quickening of their immunological and parasympathetic nervous systems (Jopling, 2008; Fisher & Greenberg, 1989).

In one sense, all this is good news for psychological treatment practitioners: persuasive conversations sometimes heal. In another, more fundamental sense, however, it is bad news. If placebos act through generalised healing rituals, then we are maybe approaching the essence of professionalised talking treatment itself – an encounter saturated with enough hopes, dreams and needs to induce everyone involved to exaggerate the benefits and overlook the problems.

Consider, for instance, that intimacy and trust, the hallmarks of good psychotherapy from the client's viewpoint, are themselves palliatives for the loneliness and confusion that drive many to seek help in the first place (Sands, 2000; Stivers, 2004). Few of us, in such circumstances, would be inclined to criticise the one who gave succour. Moreover, clients often expend considerable time, energy and sometimes money on therapy. Not many might countenance their efforts having been fruitless, even if this were true. A further consideration is that most therapists in research trials are trained to project confidence and optimism about the intervention. Fervour is contagious but can also browbeat, making it harder for clients to admit poor progress, above all to themselves.

This problem is compounded by the way in which most psychotherapeutic theories and practices celebrate, even fetishise, what they take to be our boundless personal autonomy.[13] In this early 21st century neoliberal era, we are expected (and expect ourselves) to be confident, bold and striving.

---

13. For example, some widely regarded writers and practitioners in the field go so far as to describe the 'heroic client' as the key agent of change, catalysed, of course, by whatever encouragement and techniques the therapist can muster (Bohart & Tallman, 2010).

Consequently, we may be too willing to equate loss of nerve and inability to benefit from therapy with moral and personal failure (Illouz, 2008; Rose, 2007).

This is a heady mix of inducements and beliefs that could ultimately shape clients' own judgements about their treatment. More than 30 years ago, the American clinical psychologist Bernie Zilbegeld noticed that many clients would routinely enthuse about their progress, only to admit, when pressed, that their original problems were unresolved or worse (Zilbegeld, 1982).[14] And this reluctance is not just on the client's side, since:

> ... there is little space in the therapist community to discuss failure [of therapy]. Academic and practitioner conferences are like fashion shows: therapy models are presented by emphasising the benefits without mentioning their limitations. (Rousmaniere & Wolpert, 2017, p.43)

But not everyone has ducked this issue. The American social scientist William Epstein begins his analysis by discussing 'demand characteristics': the covert and usually unconscious prompts transmitted by researchers in psychology experiments. In response, research participants can shape their opinions and actions in the direction that they believe the researchers desire, thus systematically distorting the results (Epstein, 2006, 2019; and see, Orne, 1962a, 1962b for early and still seminal discussions of these issues).

Demand characteristics are very likely a contributory factor to the replication crisis discussed in the previous chapter (Staddon, 2017). Stage magicians and fraudsters have known about and exploited them for centuries, since they work best when the persuader projects confidence and prestige. In clinical medicine, for instance, remedies and procedures that are sheathed in impressively technical-sounding names and esteemed institutions are usually experienced as more effective, while a physician's tone of voice can predict their credibility when it comes to the acceptance of treatment, and conversely their proneness to being sued (Cialdini, 2008).

Effects like these, when investigated and measured on scales analogous to those used to assess psychological therapy, routinely surpass the degree of change ascribed to talking treatments. If clinical trials are not to be hobbled by such issues, they must be planned and executed to a very high standard. Double-blind assessment is one requirement: both investigators and clients must remain ignorant of who has had what kind of remedy, and why. But this is tricky to accomplish. Experimental blinds can slip when there are tangible

---

14. For a similar account from closer to our own time, see the psychologist Anne Kelly on what she calls the 'self-presentational view of therapy'. She argues that, as their therapy progresses, the first priority for many clients is not to recover from their ills but to please their therapist (Kelly, 2000).

differences in how treatments are delivered, in the side effects to which they give rise and when non-blinded participants inadvertently signal their allocated treatment to supposedly blinded outcome assessors.

In recent years, psychiatric drug research has been strongly criticised for such failings (Kirsch, 2010). Yet very similar issues apply to psychotherapy research, where it is often simply assumed that blinding was successful. However, the vast majority of published RCTs in the field are woolly on the details of how blinding was managed. A survey of nearly 300 psychotherapy trials found widespread problems, including an over-reliance on small samples; high drop-out rates; failure to name the primary outcome measures, and a puzzling vagueness about procedures for randomly assigning clients to different groups (Hróbjartsson et al., 2014). Current guidelines for reporting RCTs are not being properly followed, more than a decade after their inception.

These problems are longstanding. In the early 1990s, Epstein examined some of the most reputable research in this field, and found it to be badly wanting (Epstein 1995). He reprised this work 10 years later (Epstein, 2006), and again in 2018 (Epstein, 2019). Each time, the best studies in the top international journals were scrutinised for their ability to scientifically assess leading therapies (including CBT) in the treatment of common clinical problems. Throughout a span of almost 30 years, none of this literature was able to sustain its own claims, and, indeed, the standards of the research had scarcely improved.

In addition to the various concerns described in this chapter, Epstein also identified other pervasive flaws. First, the questionnaires used to assess outcomes were often of dubious validity, or vulnerable to second-guessing. Second, research was frequently conducted at centres of high clinical repute, with practitioners who were intensively coached, supervised and monitored – very different circumstances from ordinary clinical practice in the overstretched public health services where the majority of psychotherapy is delivered. Third, there was typically total reliance upon what the clients said about the helpfulness or otherwise of treatment. Attempts to observe how interventions might have shaped wellbeing, social affiliations, economic status, and other real-life mental health-related indicators were vanishingly rare.[15]

The overall effectiveness of the leading brands of psychological therapy is therefore questionable. This is especially so for the many people whose lives have been blighted by impoverishment or chronic social and economic

---

15. Two therapeutic approaches that are less prone to make this error include positive behavioural support (or PBS), as discussed in Chapter 8, and nidotherapy, which seeks to adapt the environment to the needs of the sufferer, rather than vice versa. For some critics, the scientific coherence and clinical utility of nidotherapy are hampered by its reliance on dubious constructs like 'personality disorder'. For an accessible summary of the approach by its creator, see Tyrer & Tyrer (2018).

insecurity. Such people are often the majority of the clientele of the publicly funded health services that – in countries including the UK – have steadily increased their provision of psychological therapy in recent years (Davies, 1997; Jackson & Rizq, 2019; Moloney, 2013).

Conclusion

Many policy makers, researchers, practitioners and consumers claim the triumph of psychotherapy – its arrival as a 'reliable technology of personal change'. There is no good evidence that specific clinical techniques are crucial, that qualified practitioners do better than amateurs, or even that therapists improve because of their training, and for some recipients, talking therapy does more harm than good. At the same time, a quiet groundswell of emerging work questions how therapy outcomes in the research literature are reported, and how confident we can be about the effectiveness of many current interventions.[16] After almost a century of research, there is no good evidence that any approach can outperform another, or even a convincing placebo. Considered by its own lights, research suggests that the power of therapy is modest: typically, between 15–20% more than a placebo, as acknowledged even by therapeutic optimists like Martin Seligman (Sykes, 2003).

This does not mean that these established therapies never produce any successful outcomes. It does mean that successes are very far from guaranteed and that, overall, therapeutic efficacy is hard to demonstrate. As we suggested at the beginning of this chapter, if therapy cannot be justified on the grounds that it simply works, then there must be other, more ideological reasons for its continuing pre-eminence. We will revisit this issue at the end of Chapter 5, which critically assesses some of the newer brands that have appeared in the psychotherapeutic marketplace.

---

16. Similar arguments are increasingly being made about the presence of pervasive bias and distortion in the clinical research literature for many current medical interventions, including any widespread pharmacological treatments in general and psychiatric medicine, such as statins and antidepressants, respectively. Thought-provoking and incisive analyses can be found in Stegenga (2018) and Broadbent (2019). And for a very similar argument made from the perspective of a practicing clinician, see O'Mahony (2019).

Chapter 5

The latest technologies of the self

The title of this chapter is a knowing nod to Foucault. For him, technologies of the self are bodies of knowledge and practice that encourage individuals 'to transform themselves in order to attain a certain state of happiness, purity, wisdom, perfection or immortality' (Foucault, 1988) – a definition that includes psychotherapy. As ever in Foucault's work, issues of power and its relation to knowledge are never far away, and so the chapter title also hints at its eventual conclusion: that the current cultural and psychological prominence of therapy might owe as much to ideology as to scientifically demonstrable efficacy.

The previous chapter reviewed the evidence base for well-established psychological therapies, such as CBT, and concluded that overall therapeutic efficacy is difficult to demonstrate. In this chapter, we first critically assess the evidence in support of four of the more recent psychological interventions: mindfulness, dialectical behaviour therapy (DBT), eye movement desensitisation and reprocessing (EMDR), and cognitive behaviour therapy for psychosis (CBTp). Our analysis will sometimes engage with the methodologies of the studies we discuss. Among other methodological issues, we will frequently highlight:

- problems in defining or isolating the interventions (in the language of clinical research, the independent variable)
- problems in defining or isolating the outcomes achieved (the dependent variable)
- uncertainties regarding the populations these interventions are purported to benefit.

As suggested above, we will then conclude this chapter with a discussion of the ideological functions of therapy.

Mindfulness – the bottled holy water of the therapy industry

One technology for self-improvement that has been particularly successfully marketed is mindfulness. It is increasingly seen as an intervention for social problems, and is encouraged and practised in homes, schools, prisons, health services and workplaces across the UK.

The set of treatments and techniques known as mindfulness can be traced to the spiritual traditions of ancient India, especially to the Mahayana and Theravada schools of Buddhism, where the aim was to free the seeker from all desire, fear and confusion. Mindfulness had several meanings in the Pali language spoken by the historical Gautama Buddha (Bodhi, 2011). But for present purposes, and especially in its therapeutic guise, it is perhaps best described as the practice of being aware of and paying attention to whatever is happening in the present moment (Stanley, 2012). Since the 19th century, Western imperialists, academics, mystics and adventurers have sought to bring Buddhist teachings back to their homelands. In the 1950s, with the advent of global air travel and tourism, Monastic Buddhism – and above all its meditational aspects – gained still wider attention in Europe and the US, as a potential refuge for those suffering the strains of an accelerating commercial and technological world (Crook, 2009; Mishra, 2004).

It was then but a short step to clinical application, and the 1970s saw the creation of mindfulness-based stress reduction (MBSR) by the American microbiologist, Jon Kabat-Zinn. MBSR was (and is) a classroom-friendly educational package, designed to ease a range of health conditions – initially, mainly chronic tension and pain, and the demoralising effects of long-term physical illness.[1] MBSR has since been exported throughout the world, accompanied by new varieties, woven by psychologists and psychiatrists into the many shapes of 'mindfulness-based cognitive therapy' (MBCT) (Lehrhaupt & Meibert, 2017). Most are intended to treat traditionally intractable mental health problems, including those described as psychosis, 'complex PTSD', obsessive-compulsive disorder, anxiety disorder and, of course, depression – 'the common cold of psychiatry' (Segal et al., 2002).

Mindfulness has indeed won official and popular approval. In the UK, the Bangor Centre for Mindfulness Research and Practice, a partly NHS-funded training institute, has produced more than 2,500 teachers, in hopes that they will disseminate the technique to upward of 200,000 people each year. There are now more than 1,000 fee-paying courses for mindfulness in the UK. Mindfulness is also a publishing bonanza. The works of Kabat-Zinn help to swell bookshelves packed with works by New Age therapists, life coaches, Zen therapists and celebrities. For those too unsettled or bemused

---

1. See, for instance, the account in Kabat-Zinn (1994).

to read, there are crayoning books for grown-ups, with titles like *Colour Your Way to Calm*. Simultaneously, there are mindfulness websites and smartphone apps that enable paying subscribers to practise mindfulness anywhere they want.

Little surprise, then, that in the UK in 2014 an All-Party Parliamentary Group (APPG) was established to investigate how public policy might incorporate mindfulness-based practices. The group's report, *Mindful Nation UK* (MAPPG, 2015), outlined key policy recommendations for funding, implementation and research. Taking as one of its key metaphors the fluoridation of the water supplies in the last century as a preventative public health measure, *Mindful Nation UK* urges the national adoption of a mindfulness hybrid consisting of Vipassana meditation and CBT. One aim is that, within the NHS, half a million adults a year might be using these techniques by the third decade of this century. The report advocates establishing national institutes to develop the teaching of meditation to schoolchildren, combined with a million pound 'challenge fund', for which schools might compete for staff to become mindfulness experts. Public sector workers from police officers to nurses might also become practised in the art, together with the many criminal offenders who struggle with poor impulse control.

Economist Richard Layard, one of the co-authors of *Mindful Nation UK*, has spent most of his academic career at the London School of Economics – well known as one of the main engines of 'new management' and of the neoliberal initiatives that have so drastically reshaped our healthcare and public services. *Mindful Nation UK* follows on from *The Depression Report* (CEP Mental Health Policy Group, 2006), in which Layard had a leading role, and which successfully prompted the creation of the massive, publicly funded primary care talking therapy service in England and Wales, the Improving Access to Psychological Therapies (IAPT) programme.

Mindful Nation UK builds its authority in a very similar way to *The Depression Report*. It does so first on the apparently solid scientific credentials of CBT and mindfulness. Second, it makes a fiscal argument for the widespread application of the new therapy as an effective and compassionate way to reduce mental healthcare bills, cut sickness rates, get more people back to work sooner, and alleviate misery. In doing so, *Mindful Nation UK* evades the many unanswered questions about the state of the evidence base for CBT, the dubious performance of the IAPT scheme, and the political controversy surrounding its covert role in forcing people with long-term health conditions into debilitating work and deeper impoverishment (Friedli & Stearn, 2015). Above all, *Mindful Nation UK* ignores the problematic evidence base for mindfulness itself.

Recent reviews confirm that, when enthusiasts and researchers mention mindfulness, they are in fact referring to a very large array of teachings and interventions.[2] Just as with many other psychological therapies, so large and various is this assemblage that it is hard to isolate the precise therapeutic ingredients for study. In addition, mindfulness training entails a set of powerful, interlocking demand-and-expectancy effects: a strong belief that the practice works, commitment to a time-consuming and rigorous regimen, and the fusion of specialness, conviviality and peer pressure. To this set of persuasive influences might be added the knowledge that one is embarking on a new and promising treatment, seemingly backed by the latest neuroscience. All of this might go some way to explaining anecdotal reports of mindfulness not being helpful to some people using mental health services: perhaps hearing the rumble of an approaching bandwagon, they feel the need to flee in the opposite direction.

The sheer weight of these placebo influences should set a very high standard for the quality of the studies – a standard that is scarcely ever met. Reviewers almost invariably begin with a statement of optimism about the promise of mindfulness. They then reluctantly admit that variance in outcomes is wide, and that there is pervasive ignorance about the nature of the active ingredients, the duration of the benefits, and how far they might be down to other competing variables. However, important cautions like these rarely if ever find their way into the declarations of public policy thinktanks and interest groups, such as the one that produced *Mindful Nation UK*.[3]

Indeed, *Mindful Nation UK* highlights a large meta-analysis that included 209 studies and more than 12,000 participants. It showed that mindfulness had 'large and clinically significant effects in treating anxiety and depression' (MAPPG, 2015). But this meta-analysis is much weaker than its authors admit. The apparent clinical value of the meditation training varied considerably across the different studies. Most importantly, the benefits declined as experimental control increased. They dropped to clinical marginality, or insignificance, when careful blinding and active placebo regimes were introduced.[4] And although the reported benefits of mindfulness training in these analyses are usually bigger for psychological than for physical or medical conditions, this is not particularly reassuring. Experiences described

---

2. In the words of the venerable Buddhist monk and teacher Bhikkhu Bodhi, mindfulness as a concept has 'become so vague and elastic that it serves almost as a cipher into which one can read virtually anything we want' (Purser et al., 2016).

3. For a sobering discussion of the difficulties of demonstrating that mindfulness leads to predictable outcomes, and that indeed it might be unhelpful for some people, see Farias & Wikholm (2015). For an extended analysis of the many unresolved but widespread methodological issues that have hampered the research in this area, see Moloney (2016). On the rather too comfy relationship between mindfulness, neoliberalism and extravagant claims of personal transformation, see Purser (2019).

4. This pattern is typical for the leading meta-analyses in this field, suggesting that experimental control is routinely lax (see Moloney, 2016).

as symptoms of depression and anxiety (for example) are among the most elusive, variable and prone to distortion. As is so often the case, the authors of this meta-analysis concluded that more and stronger research is needed.

In fact, there are significant methodological problems with the evidence base for mindfulness more generally. These include (but are not limited to): problems defining the independent variable, as there is not one universally accepted definition of mindfulness (is it a practice, a state or a trait?); problems measuring the independent variable, since mindfulness itself is intrinsically difficult to observe and therefore to measure; problems measuring and comparing dependent variables, or outcomes achieved (because there is no single widely used outcome measure), and lack of clarity regarding the populations for whom mindfulness is purported to be beneficial.

Clinical outcomes research is sometimes categorised into stages, according to the extent to which it assesses actual clinical practice. Estimates suggest that only 30% of research into mindfulness-based interventions (MBIs) has moved beyond stage 1, which refers to the early stages of research when an intervention is being developed. A further 20% is at stage 2a, looking at efficacy in a research clinic, with control groups. Only 1% of research into MBIs is from real-world clinical settings, outside of research contexts. This has led some to argue that the research base does not warrant mindfulness being used in routine clinical practice, at least not until there is a more robust and compelling evidence base (Van Dam et al., 2018).

The gold standard as an independent variable is the eight-week MBSR course, with a clear structure involving 20–26 hours of formal meditation training. However, a variety of course formats and activities have evolved and been adapted from this. In addition, outcome studies include CBT, Acceptance and Commitment Therapy (ACT) and DBT courses that also incorporate mindfulness practices. This diversity makes it hard to meaningfully compare clinical trials with each other.

Cognitive neuroscientist Peter Malinowski directs the Meditation Research Lab at Liverpool John Moores University. He also has more than 25 years of his own meditation practice, including many years as a meditation teacher. He might therefore be seen as a fan of mindfulness. Yet even he points out that, while NICE includes mindfulness in its guidelines for people described as having depression, the recommendation is in fact very specific. NICE only recommends MBCT, and only for the particular situation of people who are judged to be at significant risk of relapse and have been given a depression diagnosis on three or more previous occasions (National Collaborating Centre for Mental Health, 2010, p.299). Moreover, this recommendation is based on just four studies, with 411 participants. Compared with so-called antidepressants, MBCT showed a small to medium effect of lowering scores of experiences associated with a depression diagnosis at one month and 15 months follow-up.

In other words, NICE guidelines cannot be used to justify the use of mindfulness for anything other than relapse prevention for a subset of people labelled with depression. In addition, there is a further concern regarding the populations for whom mindfulness is purported to be beneficial. Both the University of Massachusetts Center for Mindfulness and the Oxford Mindfulness Centre recommend that people expressing current suicidality and/or experiencing any current psychiatric disorder should not be included in standard MBSR and MBCT courses. Nevertheless, the internet is awash with articles, blogs and claims about mindfulness, and this has had a powerful influence on practice in mental healthcare settings. Consequently, the ad hoc promotion of mindfulness has become ubiquitous, even though the scientific evidence for its effectiveness is limited. Many schools in the UK are also keen to sign children up to mindfulness practice, supported by organisations such as the Mindfulness in Schools Project, a charity dedicated to improving the lives of children by teaching mindfulness as a 'life skill'.[5]

Wise up with dialectical behaviour therapy

Mindfulness plays a significant part in DBT. DBT was originally developed to treat chronically suicidal individuals given a diagnosis of borderline personality disorder. Its creators, Behavioral Tech, claim it is 'the gold standard psychological treatment for this population' and that 'research has shown that it is effective in treating a wide range of other disorders such as substance dependence, depression, post-traumatic stress disorder (PTSD), and eating disorders' (Behavioral Tech, n.d.). Developed as a variant of CBT by psychologist Marsha Linehan, DBT:

> ... emphasizes individual psychotherapy and group skills training classes to help people learn and use new skills and strategies to develop a life that they experience as worth living. DBT skills include skills for mindfulness, emotion regulation, distress tolerance, and interpersonal effectiveness. (Behavioral Tech, n.d.)

However, research suggests that empirical reality differs from the claims about DBT's efficacy, which appear to have been somewhat exaggerated. Methodological issues with DBT research are numerous. First, with regard to the independent variable, DBT is supposed to be a 'psychological therapy program', not an individual psychological intervention. Specifically, it

---

5. See https://mindfulnessinschools.org/

is organised into four stages of treatment, involving weekly individual psychotherapy and psychoeducational and skills training. It is therefore even more multifactorial than an individual intervention. So, as well as it being difficult to find trials investigating effects of a precise programme being carried out in the same way, there are also problems isolating the independent variable if DBT is a programme. This then causes problems evaluating the outcomes achieved – the dependent variable. It is difficult to show that particular outcomes are associated with specific treatments, when the treatments involve a range of different activities.

If these issues were not enough, there is also concern regarding the population for whom DBT is said to be beneficial. As NICE explains:

> Borderline personality disorder is one of the most contentious of all the personality disorder subtypes. The reliability and validity of the diagnostic criteria have been criticised, and the utility of the construct itself has been called into question. Moreover, it is unclear how satisfactorily clinical or research diagnoses actually capture the experiences of people identified as personality disordered. (National Collaborating Centre for Mental Health, 2009, p.17)

Indeed, NICE is very clear about the methodological issues with clinical trials of treatments for people given this diagnosis:

> There is no agreement on what constitutes the 'core' problem in borderline personality disorder. As the diagnosis merely requires five out of nine operational criteria to be present there are many different ways to qualify for the diagnosis, resulting in considerable heterogeneity among trial populations. This heterogeneity and variation in severity is compounded by frequent co-occurrence of other personality and axis 1 disorders, the detail of which is often not reported. A related difficulty is in choice of outcome measures, as different treatments target specific problems and use measures designed to capture a specific outcome… A challenge in conducting trials, and an important issue in developing clinically effective treatment models, is to engage and retain a representative sample of people with borderline personality disorder, since disengagement with services is common and high attrition rates from trials are usual. (National Collaborating Centre for Mental Health, 2009, p.102)

Returning to DBT specifically, the type of DBT assessed by NICE (in the guidelines for borderline personality disorder) is a 'psychological therapy programme' that involves 'weekly individual therapy and a weekly psychoeducational and skills training group... offered concurrently for a contracted period (usually 1 year)'. NICE draws the following conclusions from just five RCTs involving 280 patients:

> The RCT evidence for psychological therapy programmes showed some benefit in reducing symptoms such as anxiety and depression. They also have some benefit on rates of self-harm. Most of the evidence is of moderate quality. (National Collaborating Centre for Mental Health, 2009, p.170)

While DBT is being rolled out across the UK, services do not always introduce the comprehensive programme from which NICE describes its evidence. Instead, they offer watered-down versions, such as a 20-week course covering the four modules, but without the individual therapy sessions. In the service where one of us works, the psychoeducational material, provided to patients in locally produced workbooks, includes powerful statements presented as fact, for which there is no evidence: 'People with personality disorders have a more active amygdala, so feel stronger emotions (good news is they feel more positive emotions too). Their frontal lobes are smaller, so don't have chance to act, meaning that the individual is more impulsive. Distress tolerance strengthens the frontal lobes.'

Not only is there no compelling evidence for running these courses, there are also implications for patients who do not want, or are unable, to access them. Increasingly, patients referred to secondary mental health services will be allocated to a group of this nature. Then, if they do not want to attend the course, or would have significant difficulties doing so, they are discharged on the basis of their unwillingness to commit to treatment.

People referred to these courses are often those who struggle the most with daily living and are therefore precisely those who, for various reasons, would struggle to attend a course like this. In a service known to one of us, a person was required to commit to a course that was only available in a town 30 miles away, which necessitated a train and bus journey of approximately an hour and a half each way, once a week. This person was eventually discharged from the service. While this was due to a general lack of engagement, it is evident that organising psychological services in this way does not fit with claims of patient choice and does not help to engage people who are already disenfranchised.

So NICE does not specifically recommend DBT for borderline personality disorder, but rather 'an explicit and integrated theoretical approach used by both the treatment team and the therapist, which is shared with the service user'. A 'comprehensive dialectical therapy programme' is only recommended by NICE for 'women with borderline personality disorder for whom reducing recurrent self-harm is a priority' (National Collaborating Centre for Mental Health, 2009, p.208). Yet the developers of DBT have been so successful at marketing their product that many UK mental health workers erroneously assume that DBT is recommended wholesale by NICE for people given a borderline personality disorder diagnosis.

There are other reviews in addition to that by NICE, which similarly conclude that there is as yet no robust evidence for the use of DBT to treat people labelled with borderline personality disorder (Reddy & Starlin Vijay, 2017). For example, a Cochrane review[6] reports that there are 'indications of beneficial effects' of psychological therapies for borderline personality disorder, but also concludes, in line with NICE, that 'none of the treatments has a very robust evidence base, and there are some concerns regarding the quality of individual studies' (Stoffers-Winterling et al., 2012).

Anecdotal accounts suggest further problems with DBT. An aspect of experience strongly associated with the diagnosis of borderline personality disorder is difficulty controlling emotions, often called emotion regulation. Part of DBT is about using 'wise mind': getting a balance between two other minds, rational and emotional. While many of us might acknowledge that it is easy to get caught up in emotions, to some it doesn't make sense that getting stuck in 'rational mind' could also be a problem. On the one hand, feeling numb and cut off from all emotion can be deeply disturbing. On the other, emotions can sometimes be seen, and experienced, as entirely rational. There is also an issue here regarding what in fact it means to be wise. Many would see wisdom as involving ethics, morality and sound knowledge, along with both good judgement and the power and resources with which to exercise that capacity. DBT massively oversimplifies the concept of wisdom by implying that being wise is about nothing more than balancing emotions with reasoning.

Another concern is the potential contradiction experienced by people who may feel they are being encouraged to cultivate awareness of the present moment, at the same time as distracting themselves in order to tolerate distress. For people who are already hypervigilant as a result of trauma, practising awareness of the present moment can lead to feeling overwhelmed with emotion. The contradictory direction to use distraction techniques can

---

6. Cochrane reviews are systematic reviews of primary research in human health care and health policy, and are internationally recognised as the highest standard in evidence-based health care.

then be confusing and unhelpful for those who feel this is colluding with their already unhelpful coping strategy of dissociation.

Supporters of DBT may well argue that this is not the intention of treatment, but this is how those on the receiving end can experience it.

Where there are reports of people finding DBT helpful, it is worth considering that, just as with the clinical trials for mindfulness, there are other methodological issues. First are the expectancy effects, where the expectations of the therapist influence the outcome of the therapy – it is likely that the person delivering DBT is invested in it and believes it to be an effective treatment, which in itself makes it more likely to be successful. Second, DBT programmes require quite intense participation, therefore the populations it serves are likely to include self-selected, highly motivated people, which also makes success more likely. Third, in group sessions people get emotional support simply from being in the group, which itself can be healing. In short, if you take some highly motivated therapists and some highly motivated participants, and have them work intensively on a focused project for a year, there may be some positive outcomes at the end.

May the force of EMDR be with you

One legendary day in 1987, somewhere in America, psychology student Francine Shapiro made a seemingly chance observation:

> While walking through the park one day, I noticed that some disturbing thoughts I was having suddenly disappeared. I also noticed that when I brought these thoughts back to mind, they were not as upsetting or as valid as before. Previous experience had taught me that disturbing thoughts generally have a certain 'loop' to them; that is, they tend to play themselves over and over until you consciously do something to stop or change them. What caught my attention that day was that my disturbing thoughts were disappearing and changing without any conscious effort. Fascinated, I started paying very close attention to what was going on. I noticed that when disturbing thoughts came into my mind, my eyes spontaneously started moving very rapidly back and forth in an upward diagonal. Again the thoughts disappeared, and when I brought them back to mind, their negative charge was greatly reduced. At that point I started making the eye movements deliberately while concentrating on a variety of disturbing thoughts and memories, and I found that these thoughts also disappeared and lost their charge. My excitement grew as I began to see the potential benefits of this effect. (Luber, n.d.)

Over the next six months, Shapiro worked to develop her experience into a protocol for treating people experiencing anxiety, and by 1995 had published her first book about what she called eye movement desensitization and reprocessing (EMDR). The book explained how, following the evaluation of hundreds of cases, 'when the procedure was done correctly, there was a simultaneous desensitization and cognitive restructuring of memories and personal attributions, all of which appeared to be by-products of the adaptive processing of the disturbing memories' (Shapiro, 1995, p.2).

EMDR is described as:

> ... an eight-phase treatment. Eye movements (or other bilateral stimulation) are used during one part of the session. After the clinician has determined which memory to target first, he asks the client to hold different aspects of that event or thought in mind and to use his eyes to track the therapist's hand as it moves back and forth across the client's field of vision. As this happens, for reasons believed by a Harvard researcher to be connected with the biological mechanisms involved in Rapid Eye Movement (REM) sleep, internal associations arise and the clients begin to process the memory and disturbing feelings.[7]

An array of shiny gadgets and machines that go 'ping' are now available to supply suitable external stimuli. Anyone looking for a new technology of the self that is a little more exciting than boring old conversation can head to one of the EMDR kit internet shops. There they will find a range of toys to augment the delivery of this therapy, beyond resorting to the standard finger movements needed to achieve bilateral stimulation. The light tube, a little reminiscent of a light sabre, may be particularly appealing, although savvy consumers can watch a moving light for free courtesy of YouTube.

EMDR is most closely associated with treatments for people described as having post-traumatic stress disorder (PTSD). Advocates claim it to be an extremely effective and efficient treatment for people given PTSD or anxiety disorder diagnoses. NICE guidance on EMDR, found in the guidelines for PTSD, is based on just 11 studies, totalling 188 participants, comparing EMDR with waiting list or other psychological interventions (NICE, 2005). Again, we see problems with regards to precisely defining the independent variable – the presumed key element(s) of treatment. It is recognised by many that eye movements, or bilateral stimulation, are not the most important aspect of treatment (Landin-Romero et al., 2018), and NICE points out that

---

7. Taken from the EMDR Institute Inc website www.emdr.com/what-is-emdr/

several empirical studies have suggested that eye movements might not even be necessary to produce the therapeutic effects observed with EMDR. This has led some critics to suggest that, although EMDR appears to be a complicated technique that requires specific training, its key elements are not necessarily different from well-established psychological interventions and that gradual exposure to threats may be the most important element of this treatment (NICE, 2005, p.55).

NICE suggests that EMDR might be better than nothing, standard care or being on a waiting list; however, the evidence is 'limited' (NICE, 2005, pp.58–62). One study showed little effectiveness for EMDR over a waiting list control group (Jensen, 1994). Further limited evidence favours EMDR over waiting list on reducing the likelihood of having a PTSD diagnosis after treatment; on reducing the severity of experiences described as PTSD symptoms (self-report measures), and on reducing the number of experiences categorised as anxiety symptoms (NICE, 2005, p.58). There is also some evidence favouring EMDR over waiting list on reducing the severity of experiences described as PTSD symptoms (clinician-rated measures), and of those described as symptoms of depression (p.58). However, in one of these studies (Rothbaum, 1997), the author herself was the therapist for all participants in the EMDR condition, and was trained by Francine Shapiro. This methodological weakness casts doubt on its findings in favour of EMDR.

NICE also concludes that EMDR is no better than trauma-focused CBT (TFCBT) and that the 'effectiveness of EMDR was also generally supported by the meta-analysis, but the evidence base was not as strong as that for trauma-focused CBT, both in terms of the number of RCTs available and the certainty with which clinical benefit was established' (NICE, 2005, p.58). Alongside this, a Cochrane review concluded that evidence in support of TFCBT and EMDR is very low quality (Bisson et al., 2013). However, as is often the case with NICE, after it has established that there is a poor evidence base for a particular therapy, EMDR is recommended, along with TFCBT. It is also common for EMDR to be the 'go-to' therapy suggestion for combat veterans referred to secondary mental health services, yet in a recent update to the NICE guidelines, EMDR is no longer recommended for combat trauma (NICE, 2018).

The research base has, naturally, grown in the 13 years between the first guidelines and the 2018 update. The updated version is more complicated as it now considers prevention, early treatment (less than three months) and delayed treatment (greater than three months), with the majority of studies in the latter category. However, NICE maintains that the updated evidence remains largely of low or very low quality.

Aside from its problematic evidence base, there is a lack of a clear theoretical rationale for EMDR. In the words of one sceptic:

A recent attempt by Shapiro to elaborate on EMDR's mechanism of action may mystify even those familiar with the technique: 'The system may become unbalanced due to a trauma or through stress engendered during a developmental window, but once appropriately catalyzed and maintained in a dynamic state by EMDR, it transmutes information to a state of therapeutically appropriate resolution.' (Lilienfeld, 1996)

> *One of us works in adult mental healthcare, where it is typical to receive referrals of people who have completed a course of EMDR, followed by discharge from services, only to be re-referred at a later date, due to ongoing problems related to the experience of trauma, which have not been resolved by EMDR. In such cases, there are requests for more EMDR because 'it has helped in the past'. When EMDR is then offered, it is common to see decisions documented in patient notes explaining how the person was 'not in a position to use EMDR', that the person had 'difficulty engaging with EMDR' or that further sessions are needed 'preparing for EMDR'.*

In addition, and as we have seen previously in relation to other therapies, there are numerous methodological problems in evaluating the effectiveness of EMDR. First, the studies are not comparing like with like, such as the number of sessions, type of trauma, duration of sessions, and so on. Second, there are vast differences between different experiences of trauma and how they play out within differing social and material circumstances. The experience of a car crash for a wealthy adult is very different to that of physical abuse for a child living in deprived circumstances. Third, many studies are based on completer analyses, not intent-to-treat analyses. That is, they only include people who completed treatment, not those who dropped out. They may therefore overestimate treatment effectiveness, as we may expect that people who withdraw from treatment, on average, respond less well than those who complete it.

Fourth, participants in research trials are not necessarily representative of people using mental health services. Studies often exclude people if they have characteristics that might interfere with the intervention, but this frequently means that those with the most complex difficulties are not included in these trials. For example, one study excluded people who exhibited 'concurrent severe depressive illness; past or present psychotic illness; history of alcoholism or drug abuse within the last 6 months as defined by *DSM-IV*; suicidal ideation or intent as assessed at clinical interview; physical illness of clinical significance' (Power et al., 2002). For all these reasons, in our judgement, EMDR offers significantly less than meets the eye.

Putting the p into CBT: Cognitive therapy for psychosis

In the 60 years since their chance discovery, so-called antipsychotic drugs have become central to the practice of psychiatry and the management of severe distress, but they have proven less effective than hoped. Rather than targeting specific experiences described as psychiatric symptoms, these powerful neurotoxic agents achieve their results mainly through blunting capacities for feeling and thought. They also have other effects, which can be fearsome, ranging from diabetes and chronic drowsiness to disfiguring facial tics and irreversible cognitive impairment (Moncrieff, 2017). In the shadow of these treatments, talking therapists have sought to find their own ways to treat people labelled as psychotic. In 1952, the year in which chlorpromazine was heralded as the first medication for schizophrenia, Aaron Beck published a case study in which he claimed to have successfully treated an individual suffering from delusions (Beck, 1952). Despite this, most therapists continued to assume that those experiences categorised as positive symptoms of psychosis – delusions and hallucinations – were beyond the reach of mere talk.

In the UK, the therapeutic community movement in the large psychiatric hospitals took a different direction in the attempt to help severely disturbed people tackle their problems by psychological means. At its best, this involved the creation of more benign and democratically run psychiatric wards, where inpatients and staff collaborated to find meaning in distressing experience. However, this movement had all but vanished by the end of the 1980s, owing to its limited clinical success, the resistance of many in the psychiatric profession, and the rise of community care. In contrast, cognitive therapy for severe psychological disturbance continued to fascinate a small group of clinical psychologists and researchers. They were encouraged by the apparent success of CBT as a general-purpose mental health treatment, and by its conceptual framework, which holds a common genesis for all forms of distress. They were also heartened by epidemiological surveys and cognitive laboratory research, which implied that unusual or disturbing mental states, the bases of so-called psychotic symptoms, were more widespread than previously supposed and did not necessarily imply mental illness.

In the 1990s, clinical psychologists began to adapt CBT designed for the control of anxiety and low mood to the treatment and management of people with a diagnosis of schizophrenia. Cognitive behaviour therapy for psychosis (CBTp) was born. In contrast to the biomedical, psychiatric approach, the individual's personal understandings and ways of coping with distressing experiences became the focus of treatment. Thought-challenging techniques were used to combat stigma, create hope and recalibrate the flaws in attention and ascription believed to foment persecutory beliefs and delusions. Emotions, feelings, sleep patterns and self-protective behaviours were explored and therapy sessions were shortened and simplified to make them more palatable. Most of this early work was published in the form of case studies (Boyle, 2002).

These developments, which continued into the 21st century, are laudable and humane by comparison with the mainstream psychiatric alternative of simply numbing people with stupefying and toxic drugs. Unfortunately, they are not backed up by the research literature. The NICE *Psychosis and Schizophrenia in Adults* guidelines (National Collaborating Centre for Mental Health, 2014) recommend 16 sessions of CBT using a treatment manual, but this is at odds with its reported evidence. NICE considers nine different psychological interventions within these guidelines. Aside from CBT, these include adherence therapy ('no robust evidence'); arts therapies ('currently the only interventions (both psychological and pharmacological) to demonstrate consistent efficacy in the reduction of negative symptoms'); cognitive remediation ('no consistent evidence'); counselling and supportive therapy ('do not improve outcomes'); family interventions ('robust and consistent evidence'); psychodynamic and psychoanalytical psychotherapies ('no clear evidence'); psychoeducation ('no robust evidence') and social skills training ('no evidence').

As is so often the case in psychological therapies, CBT is the most widely researched therapy on offer for this population. NICE highlights a range of methodological problems with the existing research. Of particular concern is training. The inconsistency in reporting what training the therapists in trials had received meant it was impossible to determine the impact of level of training on the outcomes of the trial. Therapists could have entered the study with different levels of competence, making it impossible to assess the impact of the specified training programme. One study indicated that training in general CBT did not necessarily produce proficient CBTp therapists. Although the therapists had undergone CBTp training, when their practice was assessed on a fidelity measure, they did not appear to be using specific psychosis-focused interventions (Durham et al., 2003). A number of other studies included in the CBTp meta-analyses used CBT fidelity measures to determine the quality of the therapy delivered, and again there were inconsistencies between them (National Collaborating Centre for Mental Health, 2014).

NICE derives its conclusions from 31 RCTs (N = 3052), with sessions ranging from four to 156. Again, such variability between interventions makes it hard to trust that any conclusions are reliable. In general, NICE concludes that CBT (but not necessarily CBTp) reduced hospitalisation rates at 18-month follow-up, and reduced the severity of experiences categorised as symptoms up to 12 months afterwards. It declares 'some evidence' for reduced misery and for improvements in social functioning up to 12 months follow-up. Evidence was limited for the reduction of experiences described as positive symptoms: there was some effect on hallucinations, but inconsistent evidence for effect on delusions. Finally, it was concluded that individual therapy was more effective than group therapy (National Collaborating Centre for Mental Health, 2014, pp.232–233). NICE also acknowledges that previous recommendations are no longer valid, due to insufficient evidence:

> ... effectiveness of CBT has been corroborated by the evidence for symptom severity, which included reductions in hallucination-specific measures and depression in addition to total symptom scores. However, it must be noted that despite general confirmation of the 2002 recommendations...there is insufficient evidence to support the 2002 recommendation about the use of CBT to assist in the development of insight or in the management of poor treatment adherence. (National Collaborating Centre for Mental Health, 2014, p.239)

While advocates of CBT might view these conclusions as broadly positive, because CBT appears to have some effect in reducing symptom severity, the issue of the independent variable again rears its head. This is not least because these findings fail to differentiate between the type of CBT being practised. Add to this the usual problems with comparing outcomes, the potentials for experimenter bias, population definitions and so on, and it is understandable that some critics argue that claims regarding the effectiveness of CBTp are unfounded.

Proponents of CBTp maintain that the efforts to create an effective CBTp should not be abandoned, because it is a uniquely collaborative and benign treatment. However, drop-out rates seem to be high and estimates suggest that more than half of those given a schizophrenia diagnosis who are offered CBTp decline it (Royal College of Psychiatrists, 2014). The offer of a journey through the gates of one's personal hell or heaven, even if it is a collaborative journey, may indeed be a step too far for many. This raises the issue of potential client harm, which, as we saw in the previous chapter, needs to be considered in relation to the talking therapies.

Therapy as ideology?

We live in an era where psychological techniques and therapies can flourish. Climate change is accelerating and threatens us all. At the same time, under neoliberalism, feelings of anxiety and fear proliferate, driven by cuts to welfare and disability benefits, an unstable and precarious employment market, corroded communities, and work regimes ever-more subject to intensification, regulation and surveillance. These feelings both generate misery and render people vulnerable to the idea that it is themselves they need to work on if they are to have any hope of thriving, or indeed surviving. So demand for psychological therapies continues to grow, even though scientific evidence for their overall efficacy remains poor. Moreover, this disappointing conclusion about the lack of overall efficacy applies to the newer therapies reviewed in this chapter as well as to the established approaches reviewed previously. Given this, it seems reasonable to ask whether the basis for the high profile given to therapy is at least as much ideological as therapeutic.

While this might at first seem a strange question to pose, it is self-evident that people are the bearers of moral, ethical and political dispositions. It follows that therapeutic practices intended to change those people will also have moral, ethical and political aspects. Consequently, some scholars suggest that therapy – and psychological practices more generally – have always had ideological dimensions (Wain, 1998). Therapy was first popularised in Europe under the banner of psychoanalysis toward the end of the 1800s. This was a time of considerable upheaval. The explosion of new technologies, industrialisation and urbanisation that we call the Industrial Revolution was still profoundly changing the character and tempo of everyday life. Religion was in decline (in 1882, Nietzsche declared that 'God is dead'), other established forms of authority were being challenged, and what would become the first mass democracies were beginning to emerge. These social and political changes required a notion of the person that was able to accommodate them: a secular, non-religious one that emphasised struggles to achieve rationality, to defer gratification and constrain the many impulses and appetites that could readily be sated in the newly anonymous cities.

Psychoanalysis not only provided such an image of the person; it supplied a practice to perfect individuals who fell short of its precepts. Seen from this perspective, psychoanalytic therapy is a way of regulating behaviour that was entirely suited to the emerging modern era (Wain, 1998). In positing basic drives that recognised the legacies of our animal origins, psychoanalysis provided a way of working on and crafting identities in a culture still trying to accommodate Darwin's ideas about evolution (published in 1859). At the same time, its emphasis on continuous striving for rational control over animalistic impulses ('where Id was, there Ego shall be' (Freud, 1973, p.112)) resonated both with the nascent liberal democratic regimes and with the managerial ethos of the mass-producing Fordist capitalism that very soon came to dominate. So, in accommodating the cultural shock of evolutionary theory and simultaneously promoting beliefs and practices of rational self-management, psychoanalysis was aligned with the needs of both the state and capitalism.

Indeed, sociologist Nikolas Rose has argued strongly that the legitimation and transmission of power has always been a dominant function of all the 'psy' disciplines (Rose, 1985). Psychology and its practices produce supposedly scientific knowledge about individuals at specialist sites, including the school, the clinic and the prison. In these ways, Rose argues, it helps police the bounds of normality while simultaneously generating templates for subjectivities aligned with the status quo. These subjectivities, sometimes imposed through the operation of power, are widely held up as seductive enticements that we should strive towards in order to better ourselves. As we observed in Chapter 2, under neoliberalism these subjectivities are often characterised by such qualities as responsibility, flexibility, adaptiveness and resilience.

So our argument is not that neoliberalism distorted a previously unsullied practice of therapy by bending it to ideological goals. Therapy, and psychology more generally, has always had ideological dimensions – inescapably so, since both concern humans for whom values and beliefs of all kinds are of enduring significance. Neoliberalism transformed, renewed or updated the ideological aspects of therapy – it did not simply invent them. Consequently, therapy today helps smooth the exercise of power by encouraging subjectivities aligned with the demands of neoliberalism. We can understand this with respect to three overlapping groups of people: those who are distressed, those who would heal them, and the general population.

First, therapy functions to manage, console and sometimes repair the subjectivities of those who seek its help. While there are undoubted compassionate aspects to this work, the goal of transforming these people from being a burden on the state into fitting productively into society is also frequently important. As we have seen, with regard to both IAPT and mindfulness this imperative is stated explicitly, and in IAPT it is mandated. In this respect, it seems possible that the prominence of CBT in the many clinical trials that we reviewed says less about its efficacy and more about the especially close fit not only between CBT and the precepts of outcome research methods, but also between its core practices and the ideological utility of a technology of the self that can function in a strongly disciplinary fashion (see, for example, Dahlstedt et al., 2011; Ferguson, 2007; Rizq, 2012). Homework, monitoring negative automatic thoughts, challenging irrational beliefs, completing questionnaires, practising new ways of thinking: what these practices all have in common is the extent to which they make the individual responsible for resolving their own distress. The very practice of CBT reflects and supports neoliberal ideals such as notions of ill health being an individual responsibility rather than the outcome of the complex interplay between environmental factors such as poverty and social inequality (Ferguson, 2007).

Second, therapy shapes the subjectivities of therapists themselves. It fosters the development of sensibilities thoroughly attuned to the identification of psychological phenomena such as behaviours, conflicts, information processing errors and so on. However, these are all to be understood as 'inner' phenomena that seemingly arise and persist with only optional reference to social, material, political and economic forces. While these forces can then be considered in therapy as largely abstract and contextual (to the extent that they get considered at all), they in fact create the life events and circumstances that in turn influence the 'inner' difficulties upon which therapists work. At its worst, then, training and expertise in therapy can encourage therapists to unsee the connections between what has happened to people and how they are able to act and to be; to unfeel the impulses of ordinary empathy, and instead act on the basis of what appear to be simply technical imperatives ('watch the moving light'), and so to naïvely understand themselves as nothing more than specialist technicians wielding the latest value-neutral, marketable, branded, scientifically proven technologies of the self.[8]

Third, and most widespread and pervasive of all, therapy functions ideologically by promulgating the cultural ideal that subjectivities *can actually be worked on effectively* with sufficient deliberate effort. The high-profile promotion of therapy, coupled with the widespread belief in its efficacy, together seem to 'prove' that subjectivities are ours for the making. These beliefs are now largely taken for granted by a therapy culture (Furedi, 2003) that presumes both vulnerability and the efficacy of techniques to rectify it. These cultural presumptions have several ideological consequences. Like Western orthodox psychology, they infuse everyday understandings of self with individualist and subjectivist tendencies, encouraging people to locate the sources of their suffering inside their own (supposedly deviant or irrational) thinking processes. In so doing, they also reproduce the heroic myth that social and material circumstances affect us only to the extent that we let them do so. Both self-help and therapy imply that within all of us there are hidden reserves of willpower, strength and moral fibre that, if only we but tried, we could draw on to improve our lot.[9] In these ways, the widespread belief that therapy is efficacious functions in everyday life to encourage people to take individual

---

8. 'Technologies of the self', defined by Michel Foucault in a seminar of the same name, 'permit individuals to effect by their own means or with the help of others a certain number of operations on their own bodies and souls, thoughts, conduct, and way of being, so as to transform themselves in order to attain a certain state of happiness, purity, wisdom, perfection, or immortality' (Martin et al., 1988).

9. 'Between 1971 and 1984, 700,000 people underwent the three-day long training of est (Erhard seminars training), where they learnt to put themselves first, to recognize that they were fully responsible for their own fates, to understand that there were no victims in the world, and to realize that they created their own reality.' (Cederstrom & Spicer, 2017)

responsibility, to believe that it is always worth working on themselves in quasi-therapeutic ways. Yet this ignores the extensive epidemiological evidence showing that greater levels of distress, in all its forms, are consistently associated with adverse life events and circumstances (see Chapter 2 of this book). In short, the idea of therapy as efficacious helps console, soothe and pacify the population. It paints a mask of fake compassion over the snarling teeth of neoliberalism, warrants its individualism, and presents its unrealistic demand for continuous self-improvement as something positive and good.

There is a damaging contradiction here that the ideological aspects of therapy help to conceal. Neoliberalism encourages people to live their life as if it were an enterprise, emphasising ambition, responsibility, autonomy and self-belief. It privileges insight into what is supposedly wrong with individuals, at the expense of helping them develop outsight and an understanding of what is wrong with their worlds. In truth, though, the ability to live life as an enterprise depends very much on the powers and resources people have available in the first place. It is difficult to be enterprising if everything you need to initiate new projects is unavailable to you. Consequently, neoliberal subjectivities are simply more accessible, and have a better fit with the lives of – and make more immediate and intuitive sense to – the entrepreneurial members of the already wealthier and privileged classes. Conversely, telling a distressed, precariously employed and overworked single parent struggling to make ends meet that they simply need to be more flexible and creative seems unlikely to be helpful.

In much the same way, the ability to make use of psychological techniques to manage overwhelming feelings, to break unhelpful habits, or to come to terms with traumatic memories also depends, to a large extent, on the various powers and resources – economic, material, personal, relational and so forth – to which people have access. To be able to gain enduring benefit from therapy, individuals need to have it within their grasp to actually make meaningful changes.

This, in a nutshell, is why therapy sometimes works, but also why – overall – therapeutic efficacy is difficult to demonstrate. Even the determined, well-intentioned efforts of the most dedicated and compassionate therapist can do little more than provide temporary comfort if, at the end of treatment, the person can do nothing other than simply return to toxic circumstances quite similar to those in which their distress was initially forged. This is often not clear to those on the receiving end of interventions, and can lead people to feel a sense of failure and hopelessness when their difficulties are not resolved. In these ways, therapeutic practices can even have the opposite effects to those they seek to achieve – of increasing feelings of isolation, anxiety, shame, insecurity, misery and hopelessness.

Chapter 6

Psychology and the construction of consent

It's useful at this point to briefly summarise what we have discussed in this book so far. We have described how neoliberalism, an invigorated form of capitalism, was imposed in this country. We have explained how its imposition was accompanied by attempts to implement a cultural shift, and that it has negative impacts on mental health. Then we discussed mainstream psychology and showed how two pervasive features of the discipline – its claims to be a positivist science and its individualism – align it with neoliberal ideology. This involved looking at specific examples (resilience, stress, optimism) where this ideological influence could be traced. After this, we presented a detailed analysis of the evidence for psychotherapeutic efficacy, where we concluded that – overall, rather than in specific, selected cases – efficacy is hard to demonstrate. On this basis, we argued that psychotherapy itself serves a pervasive ideological function. The belief that psychotherapy works individualises the effects of inequality and exploitation. It supports the myth that, if only people try hard enough, subjectivities can be remade through deliberate effort, regardless of the abuses and injustices that have forged them, and despite the persistence of adverse social and material circumstances.

If our arguments so far have been persuasive, you may by now be wondering why mainstream psychology and psychotherapy not only continue to exist but appear to be flourishing. In this chapter, we address this question by focusing on the ideological alliance between psychology and neoliberalism as it has unfolded in recent years.[1] We contend that mainstream psychology not only reflects but significantly contributes to the functioning and legitimation

---

1. We base our conception of ideology on the work of the literary theorist Terry Eagleton (1991), who defines ideology as 'false or deceptive beliefs... arising not from the interests of a dominant class but from the material structure of society as a whole' (p.30).

of neoliberal policy and practice. David Harvey proposed that, 'For any way of thought to become dominant, a conceptual apparatus has to be advanced that appeals to our intuitions and instincts, to our values and our desires, as well as to the possibilities inherent in the social world we inhabit' (Harvey, 2005, p.5).[2]

In what follows, we propose that psychology functions with regard to neoliberalism in precisely the manner that Harvey suggests.

We place our discussion of psychology at this point in the book firmly within its very recent societal context, with the aim of discussing in the final three chapters how an alternative social materialist psychology might offer more progressive alternatives. Specifically, then, in this chapter we consider the role of mainstream psychology in either supporting or challenging recent and contemporary neoliberal practices. Along the way, we consider several things. We reflect on so-called austerity and the responses to it. We reflect on the nature of work and the seductions of consumerism, on wellbeing, and on squids. But to set the scene, we begin by reflecting on today's neoliberal culture. In a society pervaded by and organised in accord with neoliberal values and precepts, what kind of culture dominates?

Capitalist realism

The late British cultural studies scholar, Mark Fisher, began his acerbic book, *Capitalist Realism*, with the provocative statement that 'it is easier to imagine the end of the world than it is to imagine the end of capitalism' (Fisher, 2009, p.1).[3] Fisher's book reflects on how the rich and powerful seem to have managed to persuade the majority that capitalism is the only viable social, political and economic system, and that this will be true forever.

This has been possible because we live in the historical shadow of momentous changes that include the fall of the Soviet Union,[4] the transformation of China into a totalitarian market economy, and the introduction of market initiatives into Cuba. These geopolitical and economic changes have not only reshaped the political and commercial practices of governments and big business. They have also reconfigured and, in Fisher's terms, *deflated* the collective imagination. Vitally, this has happened *here* – not just in the countries where those changes occurred. The demise of what were widely understood as alternatives to capitalism – however flawed or corrupt

---

2. For example, the ideology of individualism arises within a capitalist society that is materially structured around the idea of the sovereign individual consumer. In our view, this operates to deceive people into believing that, for example, inequality is 'natural'.

3. The author attributes this phrase to Frederic Jameson and Slavoj Zizek.

4. It could be argued that the resurgence of Russia as a global threat, as evidenced in its invasion of Ukraine in the spring of 2022, relates at least partly to economic power gained through its control of oil and gas prices in the global marketplace.

they actually were – has restricted or deflated our own consciousness of other ways of living.

In the wake of these historic changes, capitalism now so dominates the globe that it appears synonymous with reality itself. Our feelings and memories, our habits of reasoning and speaking, have been shaped and colonised by the interests of those who gain from capitalism the most. Illustrating this, Fisher discusses the work of historian Francis Fukayama. Influenced by the fall of the Berlin Wall in 1989, Fukayama proclaimed 'the end of history' (Fukayama, 1989) – the idea that politics will now consist of only minor changes within and between capitalist regimes. He proposed that capitalism – rather than some version of communism, as Marx once predicted – was actually the final phase, the endpoint, of human societal development.[5] For Fisher, Fukayama's analysis accurately identifies certain aspects of how contemporary culture feels. Unlike Fukayama, though, Fisher takes a wholly critical stance towards this state of affairs and does not see it as simply inevitable.

Capitalist realism describes a culture within which our capacity to imagine that there could ever be any alternatives to capitalism has been deflated. More profoundly, it describes a culture within which any awareness that this deflation has occurred has itself been largely obliterated. We simply don't realise, argues Fisher, that our collective imagination has already been so thoroughly deflated. We only dimly perceive how previous visions of a better way of living are neutralised, incorporated, commodified and sold back to us: the recycling of punk, of Che Guevara's face, of Banksy's street art. Capitalist realist culture is like a museum, with the passive 'consumer-spectator, trudging through the ruins and the relics' (Fisher, 2009, p.4) of old belief systems.

Fisher's book highlights a major challenge: how to understand and resist what, on the surface, appears to be 'common sense', 'taken for granted' and 'just the way things are'. Neoliberalism has survived and thrived, to the huge benefit of a few, due to its ability to insinuate itself into our feelings, arguments and actions. It has produced a world characterised by appalling economic inequality, a trampling on human rights, the destruction of social services, a severe lack of secure employment, falling average incomes and rising rates of homelessness, crime and community degradation. And yet, overall, there has been relatively little public outrage.

A regular day in a regular community mental health service. As is usual, the weekly multidisciplinary team meeting (MDT) is taking

---

[5]. Somewhat ironically, perhaps, the liberal democratic capitalism Fukayama had in mind has now itself been more or less extinguished, supplanted by neoliberalism.

> place. A group of mental health workers discuss the people they are working with – talking together about the difficulties that people are experiencing and if and how they can offer help. During the course of the meeting, one team member comments on the malign social and material circumstances many people are living in and the significant effects these have on mental health. This receives a comment from another team member to the effect of suggesting that their colleague seems angry. This elicits the rejoinder: 'Of course I'm angry; have you not looked out of the window?!!'

The neoliberal squid

It seems to us that the movements and tactics of neoliberalism somewhat resemble those of the predatory Humboldt squid. Like the squid, neoliberalism conceals how it consumes everything that comes its way. The squid uses rapidly shifting colour patterns that distract and disguise, allowing it to engage in sudden attacks (including on members of its own species). Similarly, neoliberalism hides its predatory, cannibalistic tendencies behind the seductive, shiny surface of consumerism. Unsuspecting victims are attracted by the bright flashing lights, dazzled into immobility, then devoured by the razor-sharp teeth of debt and insecurity. But how does this combination of seduction and coercion explain why so many appear to be entirely satisfied as passive consumer-spectators? We need to better understand how the squid manages to hold us so effectively in its dangerous tentacles, so that we might begin to wriggle free.

Without the squid comparison, these kinds of concerns were central to the early work of Karl Marx. In his analysis, capitalism is structured by a conflict between the interests of the rich and powerful, on the one hand, and those of the workers on the other. The primary interest of the rich and powerful is to generate increased profit for themselves, but this necessarily means attacking workers by reducing their pay, introducing harsher working conditions and so on.

The psychological effect of this, for workers,[6] is to create a pervasive sense of *alienation* – a 'dislocation from the inherent life-affirming possibilities of existence' (Roberts, 2015, p.36). Under capitalism, we become alienated from other *people*, who are reduced to competitors, rivals or resources. We become alienated from our *work*, which is organised by the need to enhance profit rather than the desire to do a good job. Finally, we become alienated from the

---

6. Marx also argued that capitalists themselves are alienated, in analogous ways.

products of our work. The things we make, or the services we provide, become commodities for sale – rather than accomplishments of which we can feel personally proud.

In this state of alienation, people often act in compliant, unquestioning and uncritical ways. The feelings of connection they would otherwise share with others are stunted by social relations structured by competition, and by interactions that are purely instrumental. People at work often live reduced, inhibited, false versions of themselves, with the particular form of their work regulating which aspects of their selves they should accentuate, and which they should diminish (Lordon, 2014). Fordism, for example, often required docile compliance from the majority of its workers. But in today's precarious, service-dominated economy, workers must frequently be more proactive. Increasingly, even the lowly paid must now masquerade as persons animated only by corporate values, who behave in purely 'professional' ways. This affective or emotional labour can take the form of 'deep acting', within which the distinction between person and pretence is all-but dissolved (Hochschild, 1983). Some even take satisfaction from their own ability to unfeelingly comply with procedures and inflexibly impose rules ('Computer says no'[7]). When you are merely a cog in the machine, becoming the best cog possible is one way of retaining some dignity.[8]

The unquestioning compliance that alienated work can inculcate helps explain its valorisation under neoliberalism. Anthropologist David Graeber (2018) argued that the disciplinary effect of employment is one reason why 37% of workers occupy what he called 'bullshit jobs' that seemingly serve no meaningful productive purpose. At the same time, historically high levels of consumption – largely made possible by increased consumer debt (facilitated by the ready availability of credit) and soaring house prices – also seem to have helped generate assent to a society structured by neoliberal principles.

These three factors – alienated work, employment-based compliance and credit-fuelled consumption – help explain how, despite the continuing unpopularity of its policies, the spread of neoliberalism has mostly been achieved through democratic means.[9] Nevertheless, psychologically we must also consider the inescapable symbolism of the growing numbers of emaciated people reduced to working as beggars and *Big Issue* sellers. Their spectacular immiseration functions as a highly visible warning to those who can't or won't join the productive economy. We must consider, too, the continuous work

---

7. www.youtube.com/watch?v=0n_Ty_72Qds

8. For some, the secret knowledge that simply being the best cog possible can actually undermine corporate goals is presumably a further source of satisfaction.

9. Neoliberalism was violently imposed in Chile in the 1970s, with the support of the USA. See Klein (2008).

of right-wing politicians and their allies who own media and advertising companies. This work constantly regulates how we feel about ourselves and the values we hold (Chomsky & Herman, 1995; Monbiot, 2017), telling us to forget the intrinsic values associated with relationships and embrace extrinsic values associated with status, self-advancement and celebrity culture (Monbiot, 2017), and all the while presenting scapegoats to blame when self-advancement falters. Also, as we have seen, neoliberalism was designed to appeal to a generation dissatisfied with the conformity expected by Fordism's hierarchical institutions, and hungry for greater personal freedoms (Harvey, 2005).

By these means, then, the gaudy squid of neoliberalism pervasively influences what people feel, recall, attend to and ignore. Using both seduction and coercion, it organises much of the social, economic and material basis on which our subjectivity emerges and develops. But while politicians and the media (and the rich and powerful whose interests they promote) are continuously instrumental in all this, it is our contention that orthodox psychology also contributes.

Psychology and ideological power

Building on the critiques of a small number of others (some of these are discussed in Chapter 3), clinical psychologist David Smail identified ideological power as central to the exploitation of capitalism, writing that:

> Our capacity as human beings for imagination and storytelling makes us exquisitely vulnerable to exploitation by those who understand the properties of ideological power. (Smail, 2005, p.54)

It is our very abilities to speak, to feel and to imagine that enable us to be manipulated by the rich and powerful. Smail even nominated Margaret Thatcher as his choice for 'best applied psychologist' (Smail, 2006). She seemingly understood that, while people can be coerced into behaving differently, it is better to persuade them that doing so is in their own interest – or, at least, that there is no alternative.

Many of Smail's later writings were dedicated to exposing how mainstream psychology and its applied arm of psychotherapy aid and abet this ceaseless work of persuasion. Moreover, Smail is not the only critic to have made such observations. As long ago as 1974, psychologist David Ingleby argued that, rather than adapt the political structure to the needs of people, the primary role of psychology is to adapt people to the dominant political structure of the day. This, he suggested, is why so many of the ideas and theories that dominate psychology coincide with the interests of the rich and powerful (Ingleby, 1974).

We have described how mainstream psychology is profoundly individualist, predominantly treating human beings as separate from the circumstances that shape them. This false belief reflects the material structure of a contemporary neoliberal society dominated by competition and markets. In this society, a psychology characterised by the primacy of the supposedly sovereign individual entrepreneur and consumer can flourish. Hence, psychology frequently reproduces an image of humans as asocial consumers, mostly driven by self-interest, and largely immune to the suffering of others (Nafstad, 2002). This image reflects and reinforces the ways that advertisers market products by appealing to individuals to look after themselves, even at the expense of loved ones, so presenting self-interest as a desirable psychological attribute. And why not? After all, you're worth it.

As we have seen, consumerism is central to the economics of neoliberalism that we are exhorted to celebrate. Neoliberalism positions us all as buyers and sellers, rather than as citizens with rights and responsibilities, and this generates profit. Getting suckered by the brightly coloured, mobile and initially attractive neoliberal squid is exhausting and oftentimes hellish. At every turn, you are lured into believing that [item of choice] will immediately and wholly resolve all your worries, and life as you know it will immeasurably improve – at least until the new, improved version of [item of choice] arrives.

Today, the ideological work of mainstream psychology also has a moral dimension. Neoliberal culture places high moral value on the idea of a particular version of the self, one closely associated with ideals such as autonomy, individuality, liberty, choice and fulfilment (Rose, 1996). Mainstream psychology echoes this by defining a 'good' person as one who makes the right choices towards self-fulfilment or self-improvement projects. This can be illustrated with regard to the current national obsession with health and wellbeing – an agenda strongly pushed by government and by myriad business interests, including gyms, personal trainers and nutraceutical manufacturers. Psychology has been quick to support to this agenda, not only through the established subdiscipline of health psychology but also by spawning a new specialism – coaching psychology.[10]

Critics have described how the wellbeing agenda, with its dominant narrative that links health with individual responsibility, leads to the shaming of poorer people when they get ill or die – presumably for their lack of commitment to achieving immortality (Ehrenreich, 2018). Trying to get by[11]

---

10. www.uel.ac.uk/postgraduate/courses/msc-applied-positive-psychology-and-coaching-psychology-by-distance-learning

11. Getting by is, of course, far more challenging for those most negatively impacted by neoliberal policies. See McKenzie (2015).

in chronically constrained, stressful conditions can mean that engaging in unhealthy habits, such as smoking cigarettes, might be the only thing that helps someone to feel momentarily better before the almost intolerable material stresses reassert their grip (Torado, 2014). These stresses are compounded by the reduced availability of healthy environments for the poor, due to closures of public swimming pools, playing fields and parks. Simultaneously, the rising cost of high-quality, wholesome food has moved it out of the reach of many. Instead, every high street is now saturated with inexpensive, readily available 'fast food', particularly in areas of high social deprivation. For growing numbers, too, there is increasing reliance on the food banks that now seem to have become a permanent fixture in our country.

But rather than acknowledge the many associations between increasingly toxic environments and ill health, mainstream psychology is in practice largely complicit in a powerful process of victim-blaming (see Sontag, 1978). Getting by is aided by a psychology industry that offers 'comfort and advice to those who identified themselves as falling short of the norm in "coping skills", the "management of stress", etc.' (Smail, 1993, p. 115). Downplaying the material determinants of illness, psychology locates its causes within 'unfit' individuals who do not measure up to the healthy productive norm and so must be coached to conform.

This psychological work of individualising and internalising is deeply ideological because it enables a double concealment. First, it conceals the relevance of social and material drivers of ill health, including unemployment, gender violence and poverty. Second, it conceals the underlying norm of good health that is promoted – a superficial individualistic hedonic norm primarily about 'looking and feeling good' (Fisher, 2009, p.73). This in turn serves the interests of corporations, whose profits depend on the continued consumption of the latest superfood, exercise fad or fitness gadget.[12]

The oppressive effect of moralising about illnesses as individualised problems signals the tentacular presence of the neoliberal squid. The most pernicious aspect of this moralising is the way it influences how we view and feel about ourselves. It seems churlish to argue against something so self-evidently beneficial as physical fitness, but this is not our intent. Our intent is to challenge its packaging as a consumer product, and to reject its repeated association with individual responsibility and moral superiority.[13] This association positions those who do not pursue wellbeing as, at the very least, deservedly guilty of ill health, if not as downright failures as human beings (Cedarstrom & Spicer, 2015).

---

12. Emily Martin traces how social discourse around the body, such as the idea of the 'fit' individual as flexible and adaptable, is deeply intertwined with modern capitalism's focus on flexible accumulation (Martin, 1995).

13. On neoliberal responsibilisation, see Brown (2015).

The flipside of neoliberal consumerism is work and production. In this regard, psychologist Ron Roberts (2015) argues at some length that the whole edifice of orthodox psychology is built on an internalisation of the effects of capitalist exploitation. Core psychological concepts such as 'intelligence' and 'personality' are used to distinguish the performance of workers, thereby deflecting attention from a critical analysis of their working conditions and the demands made upon them. In the neoliberal workplace, a fit employee is a productive employee. By implication, those who are unfit or unwell have committed the greatest sins – laziness, irresponsibility, a lack of resilience. It is no coincidence that, as trade union membership has reached an all-time low, work environments have become increasingly degraded and harsh. Collective resistance is neither welcomed nor tolerated, even from teachers, lecturers and doctors, as the disputes of recent years have shown.

Of course, pointing out the systemic flaws in the neoliberal squid's invitation into employer-employee nirvana (shareholder and executive pay-outs, zero-hours contracts, the absence of living wage rates) requires considerable bravery. Such bravery is nigh-on impossible to sustain among members of the increasingly numerous precariat (see Chapter 2). Insecure, intimidated and poorly paid employees are easier to control or (in the popular parlance) 'performance manage'. Those who comply are more likely to climb the corporate ladder. Falling off, or not being aided up the rungs, is solely attributable to slack individual performance.

So, from a psychological perspective, if you fail at work it is because you have an 'inadequate personality' or are not 'resilient', rather than because you are exposed to an exploitative culture. Psychology helps relationships of dominance and submission, intrinsic to capitalism, to be hidden from public awareness by locating them within the individual psyche. In promoting these individualised concepts as if they are facts, psychology colludes in a process of mystification 'where what is actually being done or what is taking place or being experienced is obscured behind a set of constructions which suggest something else entirely' (Roberts, 2015, p.43). Today, we are all exhorted to 'become the best me I can be' by engaging in constant self-optimisation projects. However, this hides how, through such efforts, the power structure of neoliberalism is interiorised, such that individuals engage 'willingly' in a form of auto-exploitation where their very selves or psyches have become a productive economic force (Han, 2017).

> *Mary – a middle-aged woman living in a working class area of a big city – had spent most of her adult life at home raising her three children, while her husband worked in a nearby factory. At the age of 43, Mary*

> got a part-time job on a checkout in a big supermarket. She was initially happy to be earning some extra income and was enjoying meeting some new people. However, after two years in the job, she began to experience significant anxiety about going to work and her physical health was suffering. Her GP signed her off for four weeks and referred her to a local primary care psychology service. Here she talked about how everything she did at work was constantly monitored and measured. In her case, this mostly referred to the data collected on how quickly she could scan items through the till. She was not allowed to 'waste time' in talking to customers, and this was strictly enforced by the presence of CCTV cameras. She said that the most difficult part of the job for her was how, in the staff changing room, an employee of the month award was put up on the wall, leading to a constant feeling of not measuring up and being in competition with colleagues. After a number of psychology sessions talking about this, Mary concluded that the best course of action for her was to leave her job. She reported a significant reduction in anxiety and a huge sense of relief on reaching this decision.

Given its scientific credentials, it may appear counter-intuitive to argue that psychology operates ideologically, helping to conceal the brutal realities of a deeply unjust world and facilitating the work of the neoliberal squid. Yet we have already described how psychology's claims to be scientific often rest on an outdated philosophy of science: positivism. Some have gone even further and argued that psychology is actually a 'fake science' because, while it has all the trappings of science (laboratories, experiments, statistical analyses), these are not grounded in any valid understanding of the human beings that it studies (Parker, 2007). In any case, even the psychological subdiscipline that today arguably appears to be the most scientific – cognitive psychology – can be shown to be deeply ideological (Prilleltensky, 1990).

Histories of the discipline typically describe how cognitive psychology emerged during the 1960s as a reaction against the perceived shortcomings of behaviourism. The Chomsky-Skinner debate about language learning is often cited as a turning point that, alongside insights from cybernetics and systems theory, produced a renewed psychological focus on inner cognitive processes. However, while this is accurate so far as it goes, this account ignores a vital economic and material driver of cognitive psychology's rapid rise.

Early in the 1960s, the US military began developing missiles that could guide themselves to hit pre-programmed targets, navigating around obstacles where necessary. Since humans carry out such navigation tasks fairly effortlessly, it was supposed that identifying the cognitive processes involved might enable them to be copied. Consequently, the military directed large amounts of (mostly covert) funding to cognitive psychology, and this significantly accelerated its development. So, far from simply reflecting the inevitable superiority of a scientific approach, cognitive psychology's rapid rise was in considerable part due to its alignment with US cold-war military strategy – specifically, the invention of the cruise nuclear missile (Bowers, 1990).

From its inception, then, cognitive psychology was shaped by ideological interests.[14] Taking a broader perspective, the American psychologist Edward Sampson (1981) describes how cognitive psychology, as a whole, combines both individualism and subjectivism. As we have seen, individualism refers to psychology's all-but ubiquitous tendency to imagine that individuals can be sensibly understood separate from their circumstances. Subjectivism (touched on in Chapter 3) is a related tendency that refers to the way that psychology distinguishes fairly sharply between the world and our individual cognitions of it, and then strongly emphasises those cognitions.[15]

So, for cognitive psychology, the world is constituted by individual thinking and reasoning processes, and 'objects of reality are seen as products of individual cognitive operations rather than as products of social and historical constitution' (Sampson, 1981, p.731). This contrasts with the materialist understanding that individual understanding and experience reflect our embodied situation in the physical world.

By combining individualism and subjectivism, cognitive psychology fosters the illusion that psychological processes are not inextricably entwined with and constituted in and through the social, historical, economic political circumstances in which individuals exist:

> The cognitivist emphasis that marks much of contemporary psychology participates in presenting a portrait of humanity in which mental events, mental activities, mental operations, mental organization, and mental transformations are of greater importance than events, activities, operations, organization, or transformation of the external world. (Sampson, 1981, p.733)

Under neoliberalism, this emphasis on supposedly wholly internal processes has considerable destructive potential. At best, cognitive psychology can deflect attention from analysing and acting on the world we live in in

---

14. Again, there were some countertrends: for example, the European Association for Experimental Social Psychology created links with Eastern European networks in ways not entirely aligned with the US Project. Relatedly, Tajfel's cognitive approach to intergroup relations was also guided by the post-Holocaust necessity of feeling part of a broader social order.
15. See also our discussion of social psychology in Chapter 3.

favour of transforming our interpretations of it. At worst, its combination of individualism and subjectivism, which de-emphasises collectivity and makes everything a matter of interpretation, means that cognitive psychology can be instrumental in supporting and maintaining neoliberal practices of exploitation.

Far from being scientific and ideologically neutral, in this way cognitive psychology is in fact ideological to the core. Its very character facilitates both individualism and the denial of material influences. With respect to mental health, for example, cognitive psychology promotes the view that 'Men are disturbed not by things, but by the views which they take of them' (Robertson, 2010, p.5) – a view that conveniently ignores the robust evidence linking psychological distress with material factors such as poverty and unemployment (Fryer & Stambe, 2014).

In contrast, we recognise that the intrapsychic is continuously intimately connected to, and formed by, social relations, cultural resources and material conditions. This implies that the subject matter of psychology – human beings – can only be understood when fully situated within their actual circumstances. All of our understandings, feelings and actions are constituted in and through the social and material structures into which we are born and live out our lives. While Thatcher seemed to understand this, orthodox psychology seemingly does not – and this failure of understanding continues to have far-reaching ideological effects. We will now further illustrate this with reference to psychology's response to the sweeping cuts to welfare, social services, health and social care spending imposed in the UK and elsewhere since 2008.

So-called austerity[16]

From the early 1980s onwards, the interests of the rich and powerful were already being powerfully served by neoliberal policies. These policies facilitated a steady transfer of wealth upwards, from the majority to the already very wealthy (James, 2008). However, following the global economic crash of 2008, the governments of many developed nations (backed up by international organisations such as the European Union, the International Monetary Fund (IMF) and the World Bank) significantly ramped up their implementation (Farlow, 2013). This was justified by arguing that it was necessary for economic recovery (see Allen, 2009; Elliott & Wintour, 2010), and (as noted earlier) that former 'profligate' spending on welfare could no longer be afforded.

Indeed, in the UK, politicians even falsely claimed that it was this welfare spending – rather than the hundreds of billions paid to bail out the banks – that was responsible for the national debt. These arguments, perhaps

---

16. In fact, a programme of ideologically driven, economically damaging spending cuts.

somewhat surprisingly, were not immediately rejected by the mass of people.[17] This provided those wedded to neoliberal ideology with a golden opportunity to argue that welfare was too expensive, stifled individual freedom, was against the spirit of entrepreneurship, and was therefore bad for national competitiveness (Dardot & Laval, 2013). In 2010, George Osborne, UK Chancellor of the Exchequer, announced a package of measures estimated at saving £40 billion, which included cuts of up to £11 billion to welfare spending (Elliott & Wintour, 2010). The cuts imposed on the EU countries most severely impacted by the crash (Portugal, Ireland, Greece and Spain – the so-called 'PIGS') were even more extreme, due to their reliance on financial bailouts from the troika of the European Commission, the European Central Bank and the IMF (Allen & O'Boyle, 2013).

This wave of savage cuts and public sector privatisations is widely described as 'austerity'. Naming these deliberate policy choices as a 'thing' facilitates their presentation as something like a naturally occurring event, something inevitable and beyond human control ('We'd rather not make cuts, but it's austerity you see'). At the same time, this harking back to the language of wartime invokes images of mutual aid and collective effort, of equal rationing of both rich and poor. It knowingly recalls a time when we really were all in it together, fighting for survival against an external enemy. Austerity sounds so much more acceptable than 'programme of ideologically driven, economically damaging spending cuts'.

So-called austerity was also used as a cover for malign policies, including the creation in the UK of an environment that was expressly 'hostile to immigrants'. Alongside legislation making it more difficult for them to access rented accommodation, hospitals and bank accounts, the 'hostile environment' policy included vans touring areas with high multicultural populations, emblazoned with the phrase 'In the UK illegally? Go home or face arrest'.[18] Inevitably this escalated tensions within and between ethnic communities. A crackdown on documentation led to some who had lived, worked and paid tax in the UK for many years, most notably first-generation immigrants from the Caribbean, described as the 'Windrush generation', being wrongfully deported to countries they had not lived in for decades. Following widespread criticism, in 2018 the policy was suddenly rebranded as the 'compliant environment'.

---

17. There are various possible explanations for this acceptance. For an overview, see Clarke & Newman (2012). Chapter 2 described how benefit claimants were demonised and a false picture of widespread fraud was disseminated. In addition, Maurizio Lazzarato suggests that being used to living enmeshed in debt itself could have rendered many people susceptible to accepting so-called austerity as the 'price' of previous 'good times' (Lazzarato, 2012).

18. Policies initially implemented by Theresa May, who at that time was Home Secretary, with the full support of the then prime minister, David Cameron. See Savage (2018).

However, like many rebranding exercises, nothing fundamental changed. Hostile, compliant; austerity, ideologically driven cuts: a squid is still a squid, whatever colours it's flashing.

Even before so-called austerity, neoliberalism was already damaging mental health. Mark Fisher described how many of the students he taught in further education colleges were afflicted by what he called 'depressive hedonia' – a state 'constituted not by an inability to get pleasure so much as by an inability to do anything else except pursue pleasure' (2009, p.22). When you are enmeshed within a culture that insists that nothing fundamental can ever change, a culture where imagination is impeded and desire harnessed to the merely trivial, it makes considerable sense to:

> ... seek indulgent comfort from the ubiquitous meaninglessness of exploitation, to anaesthetise, divert and moderate the senses: as Jarvis Cocker and Pulp eloquently put it, to 'dance, and sing, and screw, because there's nothing else to do'. (Cromby, 2018, p.21)

So depressive hedonia is what psychologists call a coping strategy. That it did not always work was clear even before 2008 from the evidence that misery, worry, self-harm and other forms of distress were increasingly prevalent, particularly among young people and the unemployed (James, 2008).[19] While some of these were 'people psychologically damaged by the capitalist realist insistence that industries such as mining are no longer viable', others 'have simply buckled under the terrifyingly unstable conditions of post-Fordism' (Fisher, 2009, p.37). But, said Fisher, we are encouraged to understand these reactions as individual 'chemico-biological' problems because this furthers individualism, depoliticises distress and generates massive profits for the pharmaceutical industry:

> It goes without saying that all mental illnesses are neurologically instantiated, but this says nothing about their causation. If it is true, for instance, that depression is constituted by low serotonin levels, what still needs to be explained is why particular individuals have low levels of serotonin. This requires a social and political explanation; and the task of repoliticising mental illness is an urgent one if the left wants to challenge capitalist realism. (Fisher, 2009, p.37)

It is difficult to fully assess the negative impact of so-called austerity on mental health. The ways in which social and economic policies operate are

---

19. On the relationship between unemployment and suicide, see Nordt et al. (2015).

complex, vary between countries, and are assessed using different indicators. In general terms, though, these policies adversely affect mental health in two ways: first, through a reduction in the provision of mental health services (Duffy, 2013), and second, through the increase in poverty and economic inequality resulting directly from their imposition (Stuckler & Basu, 2013). Allied with these effects, the damning language increasingly used in recent years to describe benefit claimants and people in poverty (see Chapter 2) has sought to make individuals feel personally responsible for their problems and predicaments.

The UK government's so-called austerity policies were designed to cut public spending by £63.4 billion by 2015. They disproportionately targeted the most vulnerable: people living in poverty and people with disabilities and their families (Duffy, 2013; Ryan, 2019). And, whether by accident or design, these policies disproportionately affected women – in the UK, they are estimated to have borne 86% of the impact (Stewart, 2017). Despite high-profile promises to protect NHS spending ('I'll cut the deficit, not the NHS' (Open Democracy, 2013)), so-called austerity meant significant cuts to real-terms health budgets at the same time as demand increased (Kings Fund, 2017). Simultaneously, massive reductions in local government funding led to cuts in social care services, including those for people with mental health problems (BBC News, 2019). Voluntary sector support was also cut disproportionately in areas of higher need (Jones et al., 2016).

In combination with cuts to welfare payments and intense pressure to return to work, all this significantly exacerbated the distress of many already very vulnerable individuals. Consider 44-year-old Mark Wood, who was found dead in his home in August 2013 following a cut to his benefits due to his having been declared fit for work. This was despite a GP's letter stating that Mark was 'absolutely unfit for any work whatsoever'. At the inquest into Mark's death, the GP expressed the view that the cut to Mark's benefits was an 'accelerating factor' in his decline and eventual death (O'Hara, 2015).

In one of the most thorough analyses of the negative health impact of so-called austerity, policy analyst David Stuckler and epidemiologist Sanjay Basu reviewed a decade of research evidencing the devastating effects of such measures (2013). Greece, which implemented these policies despite massive public resistance, experienced 'a 52 percent rise in HIV, a doubling in suicide, rising homicides, and a return of malaria – all as critical health programs were cut' (p.xiv). Likewise, here in the UK there is evidence that so-called austerity is linked to marked increases in distress, particularly amongst the workless and those with less education (Barr et al., 2015). Stuckler and Basu argue that these adverse health consequences were not the inevitable effects of recession so much as the result of (neoliberal) policy decisions. They observe that the government of Iceland, for example, chose to protect its social welfare programmes during the recession following the 2008 crisis, and consequently saw no significant rise in health problems.

Psychology's response

Superficially, we might expect psychology to have been vocal in strongly condemning so-called austerity. Its self-image is largely one of benevolent moderation. Its practitioners, for the most part, are liberal-minded, well-meaning people. And health and illness are frequent topics within the discipline, and focal to the specialisms of clinical and health psychology. Nevertheless, for the most part, psychology's response to these toxic policies has been quiet acceptance.

That said, a handful of psychologists in the UK have spoken out about the damaging effects of so-called austerity on our psychological and physical wellbeing. Most notable is the excellent work of the small group Psychologists Against Austerity, which we discuss further in Chapter 8. Similarly, clinical psychologist Carl Harris provided a powerful analysis of how damaging these policies have been on an already deprived housing estate in Birmingham (Harris, 2014). Harris observed that the imposition of the so called 'bedroom tax' resulted in significant cuts to welfare payments for families who were already struggling to survive, with particularly damaging effects on children.[20] Additionally, the closure of facilities such as day centres for older people and people with mental health care needs removed some of the few safe social spaces for some very isolated and vulnerable individuals. Similarly, other psychologists have discussed the growth in unemployment caused by neoliberal policies, with reference to the extensive research linking joblessness with 'mental health problems including anxiety, depression, negative self-esteem, dissatisfaction with life, social dislocation, community dysfunction and population morbidity' (Fryer & Stambe, 2014).

For the most part, though, psychologists have remained politically mute about the effects of so-called austerity. Their individualist, positivist and subjectivist allegiances seem to have left them unable to offer psychologically informed criticism. Worse, there are even claims that psychologists have colluded with its implementation. This makes sense once we identify, as we do here, the affinity between elements of orthodox psychology and neoliberal ideology. This affinity facilitates what has been described as 'psycho-compulsion':

---

20. Under this policy, people living in council or housing association homes suffered a cut in their housing benefits if they were considered to have a 'spare' bedroom. The initial expressed aim was to encourage older people to give up their family-sized social housing when their children had grown up and left home.

> ... the imposition of psychological explanations for unemployment, together with mandatory activities intended to modify beliefs, attitude, disposition or personality. (Friedli & Stearn, 2015)

Psycho-compulsion involves the use of psychological technologies, including psychometric tests, and techniques such as those from positive psychology to coerce unemployed people back into the workplace, regardless of how unsuitable the job might be. Under this approach, unemployment is presented to the unemployed person as a personal failure and a psychological deficit, not the outcome of policy decisions. In their exposure of this approach, Friedli and Stearn (2015) pointed out that psychologists were effectively being recruited into 'monitoring, modifying and punishing people who claim social security benefits'. This raises wider questions about the role of psychology in the support and maintenance of a damaging status quo. Psychologists who have not worked in these 'workfare' settings may challenge the implication that they are supporting a toxic culture. However, it is important to remember that the economic justification for the mass implementation of the IAPT NHS psychological therapies programme was always that the service would pay for itself by getting people off benefits and back to work (see, for example, Pilgrim, 2018).

The increasingly coercive nature of the system that administers social security benefits in the UK was starkly portrayed in Ken Loach's 2016 film *I Daniel Blake.* Loach's film graphically showed the horrors inflicted on a 59-year-old carpenter who tried to claim sickness benefits following a heart attack.[21] Its real-life nature was highlighted by the case of Mohammed Ameripour, a man diagnosed with severe cerebellar disorder affecting his speech and vision. Mohammed was declared fit to work and deemed to have no problem with mobility, despite having a full-time carer and using a wheelchair. This led to his benefits being cut and his having to appeal this decision with help from a law centre (Younge, 2017).

Yet, relatively speaking, Mohammed was lucky in one sense, at least: he got legal support. Increasingly, the ability to challenge such decisions is out of reach of many, due to restrictions on legal aid funding. The great majority of legal challenges that have proceeded have reversed the initial decisions, resulting in more money for claimants with disabilities and illnesses (Independent Living, n.d.). The financial costs of this undermine any supposed economic savings claimed by the government, so highlighting the ideological agenda driving the way that severely ill and disabled people are currently being treated (Ryan, 2019).

---

21. Journalist Frances Ryan documents many more examples of the callous treatment of people with disabilities under so-called austerity (Ryan, 2019).

Gone too far?

When the UK coalition government of David Cameron took office in 2010, it embarked on a programme of cuts and privatisations that were, in the words of then Environment Minister Greg Barker, 'on a scale that Margaret Thatcher in the 1980s could only have dreamt of' (Peev, 2011). Now, more than a decade later, there is some concern that this programme was excessive. Even the IMF, an organisation entrenched in the ideology of neoliberalism, has admitted that so-called austerity has resulted in increased inequality and negative effects on economic growth (Elliott, 2016). At the 2019 World Economic Forum (an annual meeting of politicians, billionaires and other influential people), Dutch economist Rutger Bregman made headlines with his talk suggesting that the best way to quell growing social unrest was for the rich to pay more tax, in order that public services could be adequately funded (his suggestion was met with incredulity from the billionaires in the audience (Elliott, 2019)). And in the UK, former health secretary Jeremy Hunt openly admitted in a 2019 speech that, under his leadership, cuts to social care funding went too far (Courea, 2019).

Headlines and speeches apart, though, in practice little has changed. The rich and powerful remain rich, powerful, and – mostly – unconcerned (to invoke Jarvis Cocker again, they are indeed still running the world[22]). Some among their number – perhaps dimly sensing the public mood, perhaps concerned that growing social unrest could be bad for investment – have begun talking about 'philanthrocapitalism'. Among those with unimaginable wealth, some now appear keen to give away significant amounts to help others. This, surely, is a good thing?

It seems to us that this is primarily a form of image management. It is an attempt to reduce the tension between an economic system steeped in the idea of 'everyone for themselves', and the public face of that system, which proclaims that increased wealth and resources trickle down to benefit us all. In other words, philanthrocapitalism is precisely the latest slick manoeuvre of the neoliberal squid. The insertion of its tentacles into the domain of charity shows how apparently benign appearances can be misleading. While corporations and billionaires proclaim their social responsibility, they continue to operate in their own self-interest (Cloud, 2007). Cultivating the appearance of decency and behaving decently are not the same thing.

In his book, Mark Fisher (2009) concluded that, if history really has ended, nothing truly new or original can ever be produced. Culture must endlessly recycle what already exists, because what already exists is what will always be. Art loses its ability to inspire and can only shock – think pickled

---

22. www.youtube.com/watch?v=xRGGbyZzuTg

sharks, unmade beds and pottery decorated with pretty scenes of child abuse. Indeed, as feelings of fear and cynicism predominate, inspiration itself becomes suspect. There is fear – well-founded, in the face of climate change – that things will only get worse. And there is cynicism about alternatives that, seemingly, have already failed. In such circumstances, it is easy to imagine that the best we can hope for is some version of the neoliberal capitalism we already have. But, says Fisher, this seemingly permanent alignment of art and imagination with the beliefs and values of neoliberalism inevitably produces a sterile, immiserated culture of shock, parody and repetition.[23]

We agree with Fisher that, today, believing in alternatives to neoliberalism seems absurd. But not believing in alternatives is equally absurd, because it condemns us to simply being passive consumer-spectators of our own extinction. Support for the workless or disabled is ever more restricted and deliberately humiliating. Work is increasingly precarious and poorly paid, dominated by vacuous mission statements and stupefying training courses. Policies that leach money and resources upwards to the already rich and powerful continue to be implemented, and cuts and privatisations of health, welfare, social care and education continue. Yet we are simply told that we must go on this way, forever, confining our hopes and dreams to the small – a new TV, the latest iPhone, more social media followers. But the damage this continually inflicts upon our bodies, upon our minds, upon the very planet, tells us we cannot.

This is why neoliberalism continuously generates resistance and opposition; again, it is so exploitative and damaging it could do nothing else. The years since the financial crash of 2008 have seen a powerful resurgence of political activity. Not all of this activity has been either helpful or welcome – Brexit for example, and the antics of Donald Trump. But we also (briefly) saw the re-emergence of the UK Labour Party as an avowedly socialist force – a change driven by grassroots campaigning that particularly involved younger people.

With particular regard to younger people, political economist Keir Milburn presents evidence showing that, internationally, the current generation is the most left wing so far (Milburn, 2019). Importantly, these people were not born with progressive political ideals, and nor did they blindly follow their parents or older siblings. They have been radicalised, Milburn argues, in two ways. First is, their material constitution as a generational cohort facing

---

23. While Fisher's argument is primarily a cultural one, there are relevant historical and economic aspects. Historically, as previously noted, the collapse of 'actually existing communism' and the decline of trade union power left many exploited people both weakened and somewhat directionless. Economically, this cultural stagnation could be linked to the generational aspects of financialisation in which resources disproportionately flow to those who already own assets.

a historically unique set of challenges and setbacks, all of which are linked to neoliberal policy decisions. Climate change, precarious employment, low pay, unaffordable housing, high rent, massive student fees and cuts to education, social care and health have all hit younger people harder, will affect more of them, will affect them for longer, or all three. Second, young people were radicalised by both the financial crisis of 2008 and the contrasting responses to it: from neoliberal governments, so-called austerity; from the mass of people, Occupy, UK Uncut, Momentum, Extinction Rebellion, the school strikes and so on. In short, a generation of young people enduring broadly similar adverse economic circumstances experienced a historical event that magnified these adversities, but also highlighted their cause: the result, says Milburn, is what he calls 'generation left'.

The emergence of this new, progressive generation suggests that maybe history has not ended after all. Perhaps we can develop the outsight needed in order to imagine a better world. Perhaps we can begin to feel, act and argue in ways informed by a critical consciousness, and in doing so challenge the interests and abuses of power inflicted by the neoliberal predator. And along the way, perhaps we can respond in more caring, humane and effective ways to the psychological damage neoliberalism has inflicted. In the remaining chapters of this book, we describe some psychological resources, initiatives and practices that might support efforts of this kind.

Chapter 7

A social materialist psychology

This chapter marks the beginning of a change in tone. Until now we have been largely critical – of current social and economic arrangements, of growing inequality and injustice, and of mainstream psychology. In this, and in the chapters that follow, we will present and evaluate alternative ideas and initiatives that, in our view, have some potential to get us out of the mess we are in.

In presenting our critiques, we frequently asserted that individuals cannot be understood separately from their circumstances, as mainstream psychology erroneously supposes. We were critical of the individualism and subjectivism of mainstream psychology, and of its self-serving endorsement of positivism. Instead, we suggested, psychological processes do not merely take place against a backdrop of social and material influences and resources. Rather, these influences and resources function to actually constitute and produce individual subjectivities. We call this approach to psychology *social materialist*, and in this chapter we begin to describe some of its elements.

Simply put, in place of individualism and subjectivism, we propose a psychology continuously intertwined with social influences and material circumstances. From this perspective, mental processes are always dependent on cultural resources, and always shaped by social influences, relationships and material circumstances. At the same time, mental processes are never separate from the bodies that enable them – bodies that are always part of a social and material world.

Here, we present a small set of concepts that are important in social materialist psychology – feeling, language, memory, habit, interest and power. We have already been using these concepts throughout this book; we now want to discuss them explicitly. Some – feeling, language, habit and memory – are already familiar topics in psychology, although not always as we develop them here. Others – interest and power – will be less familiar to many psychologists. Each concept has two things in common: first, that they are both individual and social *at the same time*; second, that they necessarily operate within a material world of actual objects and physical bodies.

Each concept recognises that our experience is personal and, to a considerable extent, private. And each recognises that our experience is unique: that no one else will ever occupy precisely the same circumstances as us, or do so in exactly the same bodies. At the same time, each concept recognises that our individual, unique experiences are mostly forged from shared elements of our historical and cultural milieu. Each recognises that the unique lives we live are made possible by human bodies that are broadly equivalent,[1] that have roughly similar dimensions, potentials, limits and lifespans. The concepts recognise that our lives are given sense and meaning by shared cultural knowledge and discourses, and shaped by the social practices, cultural norms, collective memories and hierarchies of power that we jointly reproduce. We are unique individuals, for certain: but both our uniqueness and individuality are in large part social accomplishments (Cromby, 2015).

Each concept also inextricably connects psychology to the material world and the bodies that locate us within it. Rather than presume an inner world where disembodied cognitions predominate, these concepts identify ways in which circumstances, in the present and to which we have been exposed in the past, continuously shape experience. They show how environments, situations, objects, artefacts and resources both enable and constrain activity – not only regulating what we can do, but also shaping what we *imagine* we can do.[2]

Our social-materialist psychology is (the mere beginning of) a theory, emerging in dialogue with other developments in psychology, social science, neuroscience, philosophy and social theory.[3] It draws extensively on, and was

---

[1]. This does not mean that each concept applies uniformly to every person. If we consider people with profound and multiple learning disabilities, some have little or no language (receptive or expressive), and it is difficult to know what they remember. At the same time, it is impossible to doubt that they feel. Many also display habits and have at least some language ability, and of course all are subject to power relations. In these senses, at least, they are – in a phrase sometimes attributed to clinician John O'Brien – 'just like the rest of us, only more so'.

[2]. The concept of subjective possibility spaces from German critical psychology captures how imagination is structured by materiality and social relations – see Tolman (1994).

[3]. Three developments are especially relevant. First, among psychologists and social scientists there has recently been increased interest in process philosophy – the ideas of Deleuze, Langer, Whitehead and others, and the emphases upon affect, emotion and feeling they suggest – see for example Brown & Stenner (2009). Second, our ideas are influenced by an emergent tendency in the social sciences called 'the new materialism'. This awkward term refers to a disparate body of research that treats material things as vectors, mediators and products of social influence: that shows how soil, for example, is modified by human activities (agriculture, irrigation, enrichment) at the very same time as it enables them (by making it possible to plant, grow and harvest crops) – see Papadopoulos (2018). And third, our thinking reflects the influence of critical realism: an attempt to sketch a philosophy that is consistent with both the natural sciences and the social sciences, and that reconciles the experience of agency with the influence of social structure. Alongside these three, social scientific concepts of assemblage and hybridity, and the bodies of work known as actor-network theory and sociotechnics, lurk in the background.

made possible by, a large body of scholarship conducted by critical researchers both within and outside of psychology. The nature and purpose of a theory is that it is a guide to understanding. As such, it is there to be supported or challenged. This means that the set of concepts we present is neither exhaustive nor definitive. As our ideas develop, we may add more, revise these, and so on. Nor are most concepts overtly aligned by their originators with our social materialist approach, although in our judgement each is at least broadly compatible.[4] We begin with the concept that identifies what is most continuous, most intimate and yet in some ways most mysterious within our experience – feeling.

Feeling

In recent years there has been a sharp increase in interest across the humanities and social sciences in the phenomena variously described as affect, emotion and feeling. This work is far from homogeneous, with variable emphases on each of these three different terms, and different conceptualisations of each. Arguably, the only thing that this work shares is some kind of focus on the bodily aspects of experience. Mainstream psychology has a problematic history with the body, tending either to ignore its influence (cognitive and social psychologies), or to treat it as reductively determinist (biological and neuropsychologies). This recent wave of scholarship, this 'affective turn' (see, for example, Athanasiou et al., 2008; Clough & Halley, 2007; Cromby, 2012b; Gregg & Seigworth, 2010; Massumi, 1995; Wetherell, 2012; Willis & Cromby, 2020), offers a potential way of sidestepping this unhelpful forced choice.

As we conceive of it here, feeling is social, material and psychological, all at the same time. It is social because it reflects the influence of culture, history and upbringing. Parenting styles, for example, have been shown to predict levels of pain sensitivity in children (Evans et al., 2008). Likewise, cross-cultural and historical variation in emotion, and in the social standards by which it is felt, expressed and acted on, are well documented (Dixon, 2003; Shweder, 2004). Feeling is also material, because it reflects the location, position and orientation of our bodies in the world. Where we are and what we are doing continuously influence our bodily feelings (of temperature, fatigue, pain, hunger, thirst and so on), as well as shaping our emotions. Simultaneously, feeling is psychological: it is always experienced in and through the body, and known directly only by the experiencing individual.

There is evidence that feeling can be considered the most basic element of experience. Some research in neuroscience suggests that feeling is the raw, primordial stuff of consciousness itself (Damasio, 1999). Indeed, all moments

---

4. And so we apologise to any who feel that their work has been traduced by its inclusion in this book.

of experience include a feeling aspect. There is not a (waking) moment when we are not feeling something – some emotion, some sensation, some mood – even though feeling is only rarely the focus of our attention. This is reflected in the languages we use to describe our experience, where feeling is known as a 'linguistic prime' (Shweder, 2004). This means that a word that translates as 'feeling' appears in every language that has been studied.

Feeling is so fundamental to experience that philosopher Suzanne Langer proposed, 'The entire psychological field... is a vast and branching development of feeling' (1967, p.22). In other words, both (what we call) thought and (what we call) emotion share a common root of feeling. Misled by the computer metaphor of cognitive psychology, and rendered professionally alexithymic by their training in a version of the scientific method, psychologists have struggled to recognise the extent to which thought is both guided and motivated by feeling. Feeling is integral to processes of reasoning, deciding and judging, although many of the feelings involved are fleeting, subtle and not emotional in conventional terms. These feelings – for example, connection, association, tension, disjunction, obstruction and flow – can be called *feelings of knowing*, because they continuously shape what we attend to, how we evaluate it, and how we connect it to everything else (Johnson, 2007). Similarly, the silent self-talk in which reasoning is sometimes conducted occurs:

> ... in the unspoken equivalent of tones of voice that are emphatic, querulous, excited, despondent, impatient, measured, despairing, confident, bored, hopeful and so on. (Cromby, 2015 p.77–78)

It is fair to say that the growth of so-called trauma-informed approaches demonstrates that mainstream psychology has recently started to pay more attention to feeling. Psychologists, along with the people referred to them, are beginning to talk more about feelings, bodily sensations and emotions, and to explore ways of better managing these. Unfortunately, though, such work still often disconnects feelings from the social and material world in which they occur.

Language

Language is the most prominent, pervasive and valuable carrier of history and culture. It is also the dominant medium of human social interaction. In recent decades, critical perspectives in psychology and social science have often strongly emphasised the functions and workings of language. The movements known as social constructionism and discursive psychology, for example, provided theoretical models, novel research methods and empirical evidence that foreground the constitutive power of language – that is, the extent to which psychological phenomena are not simply represented or talked about in language but are also shaped and made possible by it.[5]

The great majority of our everyday communications and interactions rely on language. Simultaneously, language permeates our individual psychological experience. Its categories and terms provide much of the content of thinking, which to a considerable extent involves the self-talk that the Russian psychologist Vygotsky called 'inner speech' (1962).

Vygotsky described how conversations, particularly in educational or instructional settings, provide templates for our own subsequent reasoning. When learning a new skill, we often talk out loud to ourselves, and when we do this we typically use words and phrases with which we have been coached. Some readers will recall the debate between Piaget and Vygotsky about this kind of talking out loud. Piaget called it egocentric speech and largely dismissed it, seeing it primarily as a function of egocentricity, of a failure to see the world from the viewpoint of others. But Vygotsky described it as a highly significant transitional form. For Vygotsky, this kind of speech is actually a halfway stage between the conversation from which it was derived and the inner speech it will later become.

While feeling can be considered the most basic element of experience, language is massively important too. As inner speech, it becomes part of the very fabric of our being, weaving overt elements of culture and social relations into our subjectivities. Language makes explicit many of the rules, norms and codes of conduct that we acquire as we become ourselves. Simultaneously, it provides the narrative forms, the stories that we tell ourselves and others, which do so much to make our feelings intelligible, accountable and publicly shareable. As David Smail put it:

> Without there being public forms which (nearly always) pre-exist our bodily experience of the world, resonate with it and give meaning to it, we should live in a completely unintelligible, unarticulated and nondiscussable fog of confusion. (Smail, 1993, p.87)

So language is inextricably linked with feeling. We have already suggested that human thinking, by contrast with computer information processing, is always in some measure the product of feelings. These feelings embody within us the values, principles and commitments of our time and place, providing a kind of baseline for judgements and decisions (Shotter, 1993a). This, in turn, means

---

5. On social constructionism, see, for example, Berger & Luckmann (1966); Burr (2003); Gergen (1985); McNamee & Gergen (1992); Nightingale & Cromby (1999); Parker et al., 1995). On discursive psychology, see, for example, Edwards & Potter (1992); Potter & Wetherell (1987).

that thinking is very often a matter of ethics, relationality and morality, as much as it is of identifying and evaluating information (Shotter, 1993a). As a result, the words and phrases we use to express ourselves are overwhelmingly those that *feel* right in that moment.

> *For the last three years, Natalia has been employed as a carer in an old people's home at the edge of a small seaside town. When she first arrived from Poland in search of steady work, many of the locals were quite friendly. Since the time of the Brexit referendum, however, some of those she once saw as friends no longer speak to her. In others, she can't help noticing a new curtness and distance when she tries to greet them. A few people have remained as warm as ever, and sometimes Natalia worries that she is simply making too much of the more unsettling encounters and the hurtful newspaper stories (the worst of which imply that immigrants and guest workers are parasites).*
>
> *What is not in doubt is that she struggles more and more to concentrate on the stories and poems she once loved to read. Her movements have started to feel awkward and slow. She sleeps poorly and in the daytime her body is inhabited by a feeling that is somehow both jittery and leaden, but which is hard to pinpoint – perhaps it is mainly in and around her head, which doesn't exactly ache. Her inability to describe what she feels has itself become a hallmark of her troubles. She cannot decide if she is confused by what is happening to her, or if her confusion is the core of the problem. When speaking on the phone to her family and friends back home, Natalia sometimes tries to explain by telling them that she is tired, or that her back hurts. She half hopes for a tangible suffering that would at least be simpler to deal with. Her understanding of pain is growing to encompass this new namelessness.*

In the process of thinking, then, language interprets the meaning of what we feel. It allows us to comment on our feelings, to represent and reflect upon them. In doing so, it also creates possibilities for confusion. Deception, of oneself as of others, is often conducted in language. Similarly, the error of reification (treating concepts or processes as though they are things) depends on words. Language is also how the magical thinking that characterises many therapeutic encounters gets transmitted. So language can mystify, misdirect and obscure, just as much as it can clarify and stabilise. This means that painstaking attention to its movements, patterns and forms, as it gets used in everyday settings, can yield psychological insights (see also Tavris and Aronson, 2007).[6]

Memory

Most cognitive psychology treats memory as a particular kind of accomplishment (procedural, semantic, episodic, autobiographical) made possible by a series of distinct cognitive processes (rehearsal, encoding, storage, retrieval). In most cognitive psychological research, the activity of remembering is conducted by individuals, takes place within the confines of their skulls, and is only minimally dependent on social and material circumstances.

While this cognitive approach to memory persists, alternatives have started to emerge. Notions of embodied, situated and extended cognition have begun to supplement the disembodied, decontextualised and individualised notions that previously reigned supreme (Anderson, 2003). Likewise, approaches developed to address trauma are increasingly drawing on the embodied elements of remembering. For example, psychotherapist Babette Rothschild (2000) discusses the impact of trauma on the body in terms of what she calls somatic memory. She argues that it is increasingly recognised that people who have been traumatised may hold implicit memories of traumatic events that are known through and re-experienced by their bodies, rather than simply occurring in their brains.

In relation to memory, an early challenge to individual cognitive approaches came in 1990. Psychologists Dave Middleton and Derek Edwards' account of collective remembering (1990) used empirical qualitative analyses to show how memories get worked up in conversation. Their analyses demonstrated how it was in the conversations themselves that remembering took place, rather than conversations merely reflecting prior cognitive processing. Subsequent work by other psychologists, notably Steve Brown, has further developed this perspective by drawing out not just the social but also the *material* aspects of remembering.

There is of course a banal sense in which memory is material: the sense in which its very possibility requires an adequately functioning brain. But remembering is also material in the more interesting sense that 'People, places and objects intertwine together to mark memorial processes in specific ways' (Brown & Reavey, 2015, p.xiii). Remembering gets enacted by individuals using collective resources, most obviously language. It is also context bound and activity dependent: as they go about their business, people reproduce

---

6. Once its unhelpful excesses of relativism (its denial of embodiment and materiality, its downgrading of power, its myopic conception of sociality) are accounted for, discursive psychology can be a valuable resource for such investigations.

and reformulate memories of the past to serve differing functions in the present. At the same time, memory is intrinsically linked to material objects and places. Physical settings and the artefacts they contain serve to 'emplace' memory (Middleton & Brown, 2005), to concretise and anchor it in relation to particular sets of circumstances and relations. This happens whenever parents keep their children's milk teeth, lovers exchange rings, and any of us store treasured photographs. Importantly, however:

> The objects are not 'cues' to memories that are beneath the skull. They are constituent parts of the material-communicative-neural process that, as a whole, enables the past to be mobilised in the present, and that is irreducible to any of its individual elements. (Brown & Reavey, 2015, p.43)

Photographs, for example, are not mere external objects that trigger memories. They are material elements within hybrid circuits of remembering that people create and re-create as circumstances require. These circuits may include objects, places, practices, rituals, symbols, words and images, as well as brain functions and activities. The activity of remembering is then revealed as embodied, material and social: it is dependent just as much on objects, places and communicative activity as it is on neural systems.

Applying this perspective to mental health, Steve Brown and Paula Reavey analyse medium-secure psychiatric wards (Brown & Reavey, 2015). Their analyses identify how the material environment of the ward reflects two sometimes conflicting social imperatives: to contain and to manage risk, and to care and be therapeutic. These imperatives are reflected in the ways that spaces and material objects are configured and designed. Together, they encourage an environment where 'institutional forgetting' of the detail and intricacy of patients' pasts takes place.

Habit

Psychology has long recognised that many aspects of experience and activity are habitual. The behaviourist psychological paradigms – classical and operant conditioning, and social learning – dominated psychology for the middle part of the last century, and strongly emphasised the importance of habit. As a result, the idea that we have habitual or 'conditioned responses' that shape what we do is widely accepted in mainstream psychology.

Like feelings, language and memory, habits are intimately individual. But they are also, inescapably, the product of environments and biographies – biographies that are both moulded by social interactions and aligned with (sub-) cultural norms. This means that habits can be seen as 'mind-body-environmental assemblages' (Bennett et al., 2013) – organic connections between the material, the social, and the realm of experience. Habits operate by structuring psychological and bodily potentials. How we *could* react is limited only by the material bounds of our bodies and our circumstances, but how we are *likely* to react will be shaped by the habits we have acquired.

> *Jane was a 34-year-old woman who was referred to a primary care psychology service by her GP. She reported long-standing feelings of low mood, negative thoughts and feelings about herself, and a habit of 'bingeing' that had resulted in her gaining a lot of weight. When asked about her childhood, she said that her mother had been diagnosed with depression and was often angry and upset at home. She remembered many experiences of feeling scared, unsafe and worried about her mother's health. The only times she remembered feeling better were when she retreated to her bedroom, where she developed a routine of hiding 'treats', which she ate secretly.*
>
> *Jane had been given diagnoses of depression and bulimia by her GP but, despite years of taking medication, her mood had not improved significantly, and she continued to retreat to her bedroom to binge on high-calorie foods when feeling stressed. During therapy, Jane seemed to find it helpful to link her current issues with past events, and began to remember many experiences that she previously appeared to have forgotten. During sessions when her mood appeared relatively positive, Jane recalled more happy memories of her relationship with her mother; equally, when her mood was low, she mainly remembered more difficult times. It became clear over many conversations that her memories were not simply stored details of the past. They were active accounts, influenced by combinations of past events and current feelings, which in turn were reciprocally influenced by the social and material circumstances of her ongoing day-to-day life.*
>
> *While therapy helped Jane to develop a richer account of her experiences, it did not facilitate radical change in her habitual feelings and behaviours. At best, it assisted her to understand herself better, to blame herself less for her struggles, and to try to develop new habits, such as meeting friends more often.*

In social science, habitual tendencies of gesture, posture, movement, feeling, preference, taste and style are associated with repetitive social practices that communicate values and norms. Some scholars propose that they form recognisable clusters that reflect distinctions such as class and gender.

Sociologist Pierre Bourdieu argued that social class is transmitted between generations as sets of embodied dispositions – habitual tendencies to use and relate to our bodies in particular ways (Shusterman, 1999). Accents are a good example. They are typically acquired at an early age and without conscious effort or intention. Once acquired, they become part of us in ways that make them difficult to change. At the same time, accents indelibly mark their bearers as coming from a certain location and social strata, including their class origin.

Similarly, political theorist Iris Marion Young proposed that some girls get socialised into a restrictive style of habitual body movement that hinders their actual ability (Young, 1990). This 'feminine' style is transmitted through gendered practices of parenting and education that typically attach greater fragility and danger to female bodies. It is contrasted against a more expansive and freer 'masculine' style, more typically adopted by boys. However, since both styles are the product of socialisation, they are not forced to be associated with their respective genders, and so we have both 'feminine' boys and 'masculine' girls.

These claims have been challenged, both empirically and conceptually. Empirically, some studies find that these classed and gendered body styles are both less prominent and more diverse and nuanced than Bourdieu and Young seem to suggest (Mutch, 2003). Conceptually, it is argued that accepting analyses such as Bourdieu's locks us into a pessimistic world where actions are forcefully determined by social influences that largely elude reflection and rationality (Evaldsson, 2003).

These are complicated debates with implications for such profound notions as free will and consciousness. It is important to emphasise, then, that habits have contradictory potentials. On the one hand, they are the source of unthinking compliance with social conventions. They can embed the effects of power deep within subjectivity, by aligning what we do, feel and say with regimes of discipline and authority ('Keep your head down, don't ask awkward questions, don't make a fuss'). On the other hand, and at the same time, habits are potentially liberatory. In freeing us from the need to continuously monitor our activity, they generate capacities for reflection, deliberation and choice. Once labour becomes so unthinking and habitual that no conscious oversight is needed, this creates conditions in which we have time and energy to think about something else instead ('Why am I working all these hours for so little pay?').

Matt, a young man in a residential rehabilitation setting, had withdrawn from most aspects of life. Mute for more than a year, socially isolated, eating minimally, he had virtually given up. Therapeutic interventions,

> of which there had been many, had made little difference. The prolonged neglect and abuse suffered throughout childhood had made Matt immune to others, causing frustration for the psychiatrists who oversaw his inpatient stays. Nevertheless, Matt had established routines of cleaning and caring for where he was living; while he had given up speaking, he still communicated in other ways.
>
> 'What's the point in talking?' Matt would occasionally scribble on a piece of paper, 'They never listen.' I later learned that 'they' referred to psychiatrists. Through many more notes, Matt explained that he wanted psychiatrists to be more human, to listen properly and to take people seriously. We tentatively agreed to work on a plan to address this. I was involved in training and teaching, and could see a prospect of involving Matt.
>
> Eventually Matt took risks and started to talk minimally. I gained a sense of the abject abuse Matt had suffered but he never wanted to talk about it, preferring to focus on what he wanted to say about his current circumstances. I was aware that we were trying to break several historically imposed damaging habits. After some time, Matt joined me in teaching and training psychiatrists. He went on to work as a health care assistant on a psychiatric ward, and has undertaken a number of care services jobs. He is now happily settled, with his own family, and has not taken psychiatric medication for 15 or more years.

Interest

Attempts by David Smail to introduce the concept of interest into psychology were, he said, often met with either incomprehension or indignation:

> This idea seems to be seen often not just as uncomfortable but as, literally, unthinkable. 'Yes, but what do you *mean* by interest?' people say, puzzlement written all over their faces; 'Could you *define* it?' (Smail, 2005, p.5.)

Some psychologists would seem to simply not understand his claim that the material demands of existence continuously influence what we feel, say and do. Others would react emotionally, as though pointing this out was somehow outrageous. Even though notions of interest are established in sociology (in relation to so-called 'interest work' (Bartley, 1990)), mainstream and clinical psychologists often reacted as though the concept was utterly impenetrable. Perhaps, though, these reactions were only to be expected. The American novelist Upton Sinclair, writing in the 1930s, neatly summarised how interest frequently operates when he said, 'It is difficult to get a man to understand something, when his salary depends upon his not understanding it' (Sinclair, 1935, p.109).

The concept of interest was introduced in Smail's writing by discussing the contrast between Sigmund Freud's published theoretical writings and his private letters to Fliess, a longstanding friend and collaborator. Particularly noteworthy, Smail suggests, is a letter from 21 September 1897. In this letter, Freud described the beginning of a significant shift in his thinking: from the view that many of his patients had been sexually abused as children to the view that they had merely fantasised about or imagined this abusive sexual contact (Masson, 1984).

Smail observed that in this letter (as elsewhere in Freud's correspondence) 'there is a continuous theme of financial insecurity running alongside his reasons for abandoning some of his previously held key contentions (e.g. that fathers could so often be involved in 'widespread perversions')'. Smail then suggested:

> Could it be that Freud's gradual shifting of the blame for his patients' 'neuroses' from the fathers and uncles of his 'hysterical' female patients to, eventually, themselves... might have been something to do with who was paying his bills? (2005, p.2–3)

This suggestion illustrates a more general issue:

> What it reveals is not a shameful flaw in Freud's character, but the extent to which we all manage to avoid reference to the way that our actions are governed by our interests. (p.3)

However, some people saw Smail's observations as 'a kind of below-the-belt slur on Freud's character – rather as if I'd uttered an obscenity so out of context that people couldn't be quite sure they'd heard it right' (2005, p.5). Ironically, Smail said, it is Freud's own concept of repression which best explains the way that his own theories downplayed how struggles for material security shape our conduct. In a further ironic twist, the outrage and indignation Smail encountered when he proposed this are precisely the kinds of responses that, for Freud, indicated that repression might be occurring.

So the concept of interest involves two psychological phenomena that frequently co-occur: getting our needs met, at the same time as not appearing to be purely self-serving. Interest is a feature of the continuous influence of our needs on what we feel, say and do. These needs include 'biological necessities such as food, sex, security, pain avoidance and pleasure, and shade into the rather more obviously social requirements for attachment, association, money and status (Smail, 2005, p.35). Interest is also a feature of how, in polite society, we frequently disavow its influence – even though there seems to be no necessary reason why we practise such disavowals (in fact, the disavowal of interest seemingly functions primarily to mask the operation *of* interest).[7]

Interests are similar to the more familiar mainstream psychological concepts of need and drive. But interests are not *additional* to needs and drives; instead, they offer a fuller explanation of what influences human behaviour – one that takes proper account of cultural and social forces. In psychology, needs and drives are seen as biological urges that push activity in certain directions: to seek food, sex, shelter, affiliation and so on. By contrast, interest is a more sophisticated concept, already both biological and social. It refers to bodily or biological necessities, and simultaneously to the ways in which they get taken up or acted on by social forces. This explains why money, for example, can be a target of interest. Although money itself is not biological, it recruits interest because it can marshal resources that meet biological needs.

So, by adding interest to the equation, what is actually proposed is a more sophisticated understanding of motivation. Psychological theories of motivation typically imply a biological core with its own largely independent dynamics that drive our conduct. By contrast, interest implies a continuous meshing of the biological and the social, where social influences (e.g. status, money) are made attractive by biological necessities (e.g. food, warmth, survival). This hooking together of the biological and the social means that, rather than being pushed from within by needs and drives, we are '*pulled from without* by the social manipulation of, in the last analysis, inescapable biological features of being human' (Smail, 2005, p.35).

The ability to satisfy interests depends on power to do so. Likewise, the operation of power often involves the exploitation of interest. While brute force and coercion always remain possible, in practice they are rarely used. Most often, in contemporary neoliberal societies, power works by exploiting interest. Indeed, under neoliberalism, interest all too readily becomes narrow self-interest[8] – a perversion that may help explain the disquiet Smail encountered when introducing the concept to psychologists. But the distortions of neoliberalism do not negate the central observation

---

7. The research on cognitive dissonance perhaps offers one way of illustrating this. These studies focus on conflicting attitudes, beliefs or behaviours. This produces a feeling of discomfort, leading to an alteration in one of the attitudes, beliefs or behaviours to reduce the discomfort and restore balance. If a person is prioritising their own needs over those of other people, in a cultural context where this might be seen as selfish, then they need to have a way of justifying their behaviour in order to continue prioritising their own needs – just as Freud did.

8. As discussed in Chapter 1.

that individuals can get recruited to the goals of powerful others when their interests become aligned with those goals. This smooths the operation of power, helping to conceal its dynamics and effects (Smail, 2005, p.34).

Power

Power is fundamental to the operation of all social systems, and has been extensively discussed and theorised by critical psychologists and social scientists (see, for example, Bourdieu, 1991; Foucault, 1977; Hagan & Donnison, 1999; Hook, 2007). In relation to clinical psychology, David Smail defined it as the means of gaining security and advantage (2005, p.28). We will use this definition as our starting point as it usefully emphasises how power is about influencing people and situations in order to satisfy one's own interests. At the same time, because power is varied and complex, it is useful to identify some of its different forms:[9]

- Biological power – physical strength, fertility, conventional attractiveness, skin colour, embodied talents e.g. sport, musicianship. All these are significant because of the cultural meaning and potentials associated with them.
- Interpersonal power – the capacity to give or withhold care, love, protection.
- Coercive power – war, terrorism, combat, military or police force.
- Legal power – the use of arrest, imprisonment or enforced hospitalisation, together with all of the other enforceable rules and sanctions of our complex societies.
- Economic and material power – access to things such as money, housing, employment transport, education, medical treatment and leisure facilities.
- Ideological power – the control of meaning by setting agendas, prioritising what gets discussed (what is relevant or newsworthy), and deciding what terms and concepts are legitimate.

While biological power is the most readily available to many, it is also the most restricted in reach and flexibility. Its operation tends to be relatively obvious, and its influence mostly confined to immediate personal encounters and relationships where, for those with the least power overall, it is often their main or only recourse: the man or woman with a learning disability, for example, who has no other way to express their frustration than through the 'challenging behaviour' of absconding or hitting out with their fists; the

---

9. These categories are adapted from Johnstone & Boyle (2018).

impoverished and poorly educated youth whose world has presented few options other than to become an expert at intimidation and violence. Overall, the ability to wield biological power is disproportionately concentrated among those who are younger and physically fitter, which means that its possession is often temporary.

By comparison, the other forms of power can affect more people and be applied over greater distances and in a wider range of situations. Legal power, for example, gets used very flexibly and its parameters can easily be revised; similarly, money can influence a dazzling myriad of outcomes.

Ideological power is probably the most influential of all, while tending to be the least visible. Indeed, its very invisibility helps make it so profoundly influential. Those who control agendas control what gets talked about. Likewise, if the terms of discussion are those ordained by the powerful, critical reflection will be more difficult. Debates about social causes of distress, for example, tend to be framed in terms of psychiatric categories such as schizophrenia. But these categories already presume an illness model with an underlying biological cause, and this inflects debates about them with unhelpful suppositions. It also means that debates that reject them instantly appear more controversial, however strong the evidence, or reasonable the claims. So ideological power functions largely by setting the bounds of what we accept as simply true, reasonable and appropriate. It does this increasingly through journalism and the media, which in turn rely on material resources, or money, to make their activities possible.

Ideological power can work psychologically: it can cause us to distrust our feelings, doubt our memories and blame ourselves for unhelpful habits. Crucially, it can lead us to imagine that our interests are other than they actually are. Anti-apartheid activist Steve Biko put this well when he said, 'The most potent weapon in the hands of the oppressor is the mind of the oppressed' (Wilderson, 2008 p.107). Other than this, ideological power primarily works by regulating other powers. Similarly, changing our own thoughts and behaviours is only influential depending on the material resources we have available. For example, governments telling people they are lazy and need to work will only be effective if they have the means of compelling them to do so (for example, by changing the law or the benefits system).

A particularly noxious example of the operation of power is the scandal exposed in 2019 at Cygnet Healthcare, a US-owned company that describes itself as 'one of the UK's largest independent providers of inpatient mental health care, giving individuals the time and care they deserve'.[10] Cygnet's sites include Whorlton Hall in County Durham, an NHS-funded, privately-run

---

10. https://wearewaterloo.co.uk/business/cygnet-health-care-limited

hospital for people with learning difficulties. Undercover filming there by the BBC revealed shocking abuse of the residents (Plomin, 2019). It showed many different forms of power being used to the detriment of these most vulnerable people. This abuse was in effect sanctioned by the government, via the Care Quality Commission, which failed to act on concerns raised at the hospital. At the same time as this case revealed abuses of power within a hospital, it also highlighted the workings of ideological power. Astonishingly, perhaps, Cygnet's website continues to assert that 'We have integrity; We Trust; We Empower; We Respect; We Care'.[11]

Proximal and distal powers

It is useful to distinguish between proximal and distal powers. Proximal powers are those we tend to most readily notice in everyday life. They are the powers most often discussed in therapeutic conversations – the powers that flow through relationships between parents and children, between siblings, or between lovers, friends and peers.

Because proximal powers loom so large in everyday life, it is easy to proceed as though they are the most important influences upon us. However, this leads us to ignore the vastly more influential distal powers wielded by governments, multinationals, religions, the military, the police and other institutions. In truth, the great majority of parents and their children are enmeshed within intersecting networks of distal powers over which they have almost no control. Their proximal interpersonal relationships are constantly shaped and buffeted by this wider field of distal power relations.

The mistake we can make, then, is to simply attribute the dynamics of family and other close relationships to the malice, obstinacy, generosity or empathy of others. In so doing, we blind ourselves to the operation of distal powers that continuously supply the potentials and constraints which ultimately regulate these interpersonal dynamics. For example:

> ... while the father's work situation affects him massively, and by extension his family, his ability to influence it is (unless he is well up the hierarchy) likely to be slight. From the family's perspective, the father mediates a view of power that extends not much further than his workplace, but what seems to them a matter of the good will or otherwise of his managers, the cooperativeness or recalcitrance of his fellow workers, and so on, may in fact be much more a product of economic policies determined beyond even national borders. (Smail, 2005, pp.30–31)

---

[11]. https://www.cygnethealth.co.uk/about/our-values/

In this example, gendered power relations transmitted through cultural norms (fathers as 'breadwinners') intersect with economic power relations transmitted through hierarchies of employment. Neither of these forms of power arise within the individuals – the father, the family members – affected by them. Yet both play themselves out intimately within the family where, because their distal origins are unlikely to be recognised, their effects will often be understood as the mere capriciousness of members: 'Dad shouted at me, he's in a bad mood today.'

The power horizon

The distinction between proximal and distal powers is the basis for David Smail's concept of the power horizon. This concept describes our frequent tendency to see the world as though we are simply at its centre. It is an effect of the way we typically ignore or downplay distal powers, focusing instead on what we feel, and on the feelings and actions of those close to us. Broadly speaking, there are three reasons why we adopt this focus.

First, we are encouraged to do so. Media, culture, art, news and entertainment promote trivial debates and ignore profound ones, selectively emphasise certain issues, and identify and berate scapegoats. It is not that debate and dissent are outlawed; they are actively encouraged, but only within certain bounds and about particular topics. So, debate about migration is encouraged, while debate about its *causes* – war, totalitarian governments, famines, environmental disasters, neoliberal capitalism – is not. Hence the influence of distal power is frequently downplayed, circumscribed or ignored.

Second, while education that enables critical thought is vital, too often education does the opposite. Education frequently enforces conventions, discourages 'awkward' questions and reproduces disciplinary knowledge that is ostensibly neutral but is, in fact, value laden. We have seen, for example, how psychology emphasises the isolated individual, and how this reinforces neoliberalism. Notably, in this country, education is stratified by social class: working-class children get less of it, and what they receive is focused less on critical thinking and more on immediately practical skills such as reading, writing and mathematics (Ferguson, 2017). And, of course, education transmits cultural values and norms. In an individualist culture, then, education will often foreground the proximal and obscure the distal.

Third, we are misled by the sheer prominence of our own experience. In particular, says Smail, we are misled by the immediacy of the realm of feeling that gives such continuous, intimate and seemingly profound insights into our being and activity. Feeling can seem like the absolute guarantor that we are sovereign individuals, in sole charge of the bodies that constitute our physical being. In reality, how we feel is continuously impelled by circumstances, activities and relationships. Nevertheless, because we actually *feel* our actions as we perform them:

> We cannot but conclude – so powerful is the impression – that the embodied sensation of action is actually its cause. However constrained – even determined – our own conduct may be, it is extremely difficult to feel it as anything other than of our own creation. (Smail, 2005, p.32)

So ideological forces combine with culture norms and educational practices, and with elements of our very species nature. Their joint effect is to create 'a horizon of power beyond which all sorts of things might be happening, but it's too dark for us to see' (Smail, 2005, p.32)

The social unconscious

For Smail, this means that the unconscious is a very real phenomenon. But the unconscious, here, is thoroughly dynamic and social. Rather than being dominated by psychosexual dramas, repressed desires and familial conflicts, it is continuously constituted and maintained by largely unrecognised distal powers. This means that, far from being an individual phenomenon, the unconscious is in many respects shared.

For example, clinicians may encounter clients who seem unable to perceive what, from the clinician's perspective, are obvious links between their prior experiences and their current distress. While for any one individual this may be the result of many different factors, a shared contributory element is often the psychiatric diagnoses that clients have been given. These diagnoses crystallise the influence of the psychiatry-dominated services with which many clients are engaged. In misrepresenting distress as symptoms of medical disorders, backing up this position with the authority of medicine and science, psychiatric diagnosis obscures the connections between experience and distress, so pushing them deep into the social unconscious.

Another example was touched on in Chapter 1: the way neoliberal culture teaches us to feel empathy only selectively in relation to certain groups such as the homeless (see Olson, 2013). Empathic feelings that would run counter to neoliberalism then go quite literally unfelt, although they may be replaced by flashes of irritation when the abject presence of the destitute disrupts or intrudes on our routines. A third example is provided by journalist Ian Cobain. He conducted important investigative work revealing the systematic but hidden use of torture by the British state, concluding that torture 'is as British as suet pudding and red pillar boxes' (Cobain, 2013, p.309). For present purposes, what is most relevant about this conclusion is Cobain's surprise at his own initial felt reluctance to accept what he eventually discovered:

> ... even as I was helping to unearth the evidence, there was a self-imposed handicap. I hadn't wanted to accept that figures of authority in British public life would arrange for their fellow citizens to be tortured. Back then, I hadn't realised how strongly rooted my assumptions about my country and its values had been. (p.307)

All three of these examples suggest that the social unconscious, rather like the Freudian one, harbours understandings that can be difficult, dangerous and threatening – understandings that can potentially transform our sense of world and self. But in contrast to Freud, the dynamics that maintain the social unconscious, and indeed its contents, originate *out there* in the world to which we are jointly subject. Consequently, we are continuously vulnerable to having our interests manipulated, without necessarily being aware of it, by those who wield power. And it is precisely because the hidden dynamics that shape individual experience are much more external than internal that we need outsight rather than insight.

Implications

We have presented six initial concepts that are important elements of a social materialist psychology: feeling, language, memory, habit, interest and power. We began with feeling because it is the most basic, continuous and intimate stuff of experience. It is also through feeling that many mental health problems are primarily known – feelings of profound misery, persistent fear, numbness, shock and so on. But the dynamics of feeling are not simply internal to individuals: feeling is continuously responsive to where we are, who we are with, and what we are doing. Likewise, the language that we use, including the unspoken inner speech that prominently shapes subjectivity, gets derived from, and is continuously responsive to, shifting social relations and changing cultural forms.

Memories, similarly, are not solely the result of cognitive processes 'in the head': they are accomplished within dynamic networks of material objects, communicative practices and psychological activity. Habits, meanwhile, are an important but often subtle way that elements of biography, of prior experience of social relations, get embedded within our very selves. And interest describes how fundamental biological needs get continuously recruited within social relations to pull our activity in particular directions.

But all these capacities are constantly shaped by power. Power relations organise feelings, get communicated through language, structure memory, get embedded within individuals as habits associated with social positions, and have their operation smoothed by the recruitment of interest. So, while in our experience feeling often looms largest, power relations are the biggest influence. Yet we rarely recognise this, instead tending to attribute our actions and choices to our own capacities and decisions. The ideology of individualism blinds us to the profound influence of distal power, just as it leads us to understand ourselves separately from our circumstances. As a result, those who benefit from the operation of power often congratulate themselves, whereas those damaged by it very frequently blame themselves.

Combinations of these six capacities give rise to other phenomena that – in mainstream psychology – are often erroneously treated as though they were both individual and fundamental. Beliefs, for example, can be understood as organisations of feeling that have come to be habitually associated with certain linguistic positions and claims (Cromby, 2012a). This is why deliberate attempts to inculcate belief so often depend on ritual, repetition and the invocation of feeling (Smith, 2007): their goal is to forge habits that consistently link certain feelings with particular symbols and ideas, often stated in language. Likewise, imagination might be understood as bringing to mind circumstances and events that have not (yet) occurred – as opposed to memory's function of bringing to mind circumstances and events from the past. Like remembering, then, imagining is infused with feeling, and dependent for its character on hybrid networks of social relations, physical objects and material circumstances. Self-esteem, similarly, describes how we have come to habitually feel about our own subjectivities (Scheff & Fearon, 2004). More precisely, it refers to how particular aspects of our subjectivities are reflected back to us, all too often with negative judgements attached, through social relations enmeshed within networks of power and interest.

Similar reconceptualisations are possible for clinical phenomena described as aspects of mental ill health. For example, the extremes of misery and worry associated with diagnoses of depression or anxiety can be understood as complex mixtures of feelings induced by toxic combinations of adverse circumstances caused by the negative operation of power (Cromby, 2004). Experiences of voice-hearing appear as instances of inner speech that, through force of circumstance, individuals have come to attribute to non-present others (Ferneyhough, 2016). And so-called eating disorders may represent efforts to re-assert control by individuals who lack power, just as so-called personality disorders imperfectly describe the kinds of subjectivity often forged by sustained experiences of early adverse or abusive circumstances. And running through these experiences, we see the force of memory as source or reminder of trauma, and the force of habit that easily embeds responses to adverse power relations as involuntary reactions that, when transferred to other situations, are then misunderstood as quasi-medical symptoms of fictional psychiatric disorders.

Overall, what we propose is a reconfiguration of psychology's understanding of subjectivity to necessarily include the social and material influences and resources through which it is actually produced. We want to emphasise, again, that this does not mean any denial or negation of individuality or uniqueness. Instead, it means recognising and exploring how individuality and uniqueness already emerge from particular intricate, dynamic and highly variable combinations of feeling, language, memory and habit. These combinations are forged in social relations hierarchically organised by powers both proximal and distal – relations within which we may be enmeshed largely to the extent that their potentials align with our interests.

The image of subjectivity we have in mind somewhat resembles that once proposed by psychologist John Shotter, who characterised subjectivity as a 'boundary phenomenon' (Shotter, 1993a). In other words, subjectivity is not simply 'inside' the person, but nor is it 'outside'. It is on the boundary between, where, instead of being separate from external events, it is in continuous transaction with them. Our subjectivities are continuously being remade as new elements of feeling and language impinge, new memories are made and new habits of feeling and speaking are forged.

Ultimately, this means that subjectivities are somewhat vulnerable accomplishments. They are vulnerable to manipulation, to be sure, but they are also vulnerable in themselves. Some, of course, are more vulnerable than others: notably, those whose early experience was characterised by abuse, neglect and adversity are, on average, significantly more likely than others to experience distress (see Johnstone & Boyle, 2018, pp.102–105). In truth, though, we are all ultimately dependent for our wellbeing on the ways that our acquired habits (of feeling, of inner speech, of remembering) resonate or 'fit' with prevailing social and material circumstances. So, when power causes these circumstances to change, and especially when those changes are sudden or unpredictable, the sensitive interdependence between subjectivities and the conditions that sustain them is revealed.

When this occurs, the distressed and distressing states that psychiatry calls mental illness can get produced. This is what happened when what Mark Fisher (2009, p.37) called the 'terrifyingly unstable conditions' of neoliberalism were first imposed and then, in the wake of 2008, intensified in the name of so-called austerity. It is why we now have an epidemic or crisis of mental health. It is also why this crisis is concentrated particularly among young people, who on average are affected most adversely by neoliberal policies (Evans et al., 2018; Gunnell et al., 2018). Yet we cannot simply wait for neoliberalism to collapse under the weight of the misery it produces. Accordingly, the next two chapters will describe some initiatives and developments that, in our opinion, represent more useful or hopeful ways of responding to distress. Chapter 8 will consider institutional or organisational initiatives, and Chapter 9 will describe individual and activist developments.

Chapter 8

Doing psychology differently

The previous chapter described a small set of psychological concepts that are part of a social materialist psychology. In this chapter, we discuss some organisational or institutional initiatives that, broadly speaking, are compatible with a social materialist approach. By this we mean that these initiatives locate the origins of psychological difficulties not simply inside people's heads but in the shared world they occupy. They propose that social and material circumstances, not inner dynamics that supposedly proceed largely of their own accord, are the primary source of people's problems. This, in turn, means that all these initiatives take account of the most important of our social materialist concepts: power, and the ways that it structures experience. Sometimes this also means recognising how abuses of power can have damaging psychological consequences, most obviously in the form of trauma.

Our examples come from three areas of applied psychological practice: criminal justice, adult learning disabilities and mental health. None of the practitioners whose work we describe are partisans of a single movement, and there are important disagreements between some of them (Brewer & Lait, 1980; Epstein, 2018). Also, as we will describe, each initiative has some shortcomings that sit alongside its positive implications. Nevertheless, their existence points toward a common terrain upon which a more helpful form of applied psychology might take root.

'Don't fence me in': psychology in prison settings

More than half a century ago, Otto Fenichel, one of Freud's foremost successors, noted that the 'neuroses' are social diseases: products of the disordered world we have created (Fenichel, 1994). Forensic psychologists based in prisons, secure hospitals and offender rehabilitation services work with some of the most emotionally wounded individuals. Yet many only just seem to have woken up to Fenichel's insight. Perhaps this is proof of forensic psychologist Eli Godsi's 'second law of personal distress': the more troubling or frightening someone's expression of misery, the more it will be seen as a medical problem lurking inside them (Godsi, 2004).

Indeed, the prison population in England and Wales has nearly doubled since 1990. The UK holds the doubtful distinction of having the highest incarceration rate of any Western European jurisdiction (Sturge, 2019). Far from reflecting scientific progress, criminal justice policy and psychological practice in the English-speaking world has always been a curious cocktail of ill-assorted ingredients: public opinion, as expressed through vindictive infotainment and crime reporting; the punitive and cost-cutting ambitions of reactionary leaders, and – more laudably – the influence of human rights activists and progressive journalists. A small but important contribution comes from the work of forensic psychologists. As consultants, researchers and therapists, they have helped steer offender management towards the handling and re-adjustment of those deemed to be wayward, or deviant (Garland, 2002).

Within this culture of control, one simple question has been paramount: what works best in deterring convicted offenders from a career of crime? From the early 1990s the main answer, at least so far as mainstream psychologists are concerned, has been CBT. This treatment has been touted for every kind of impulsive offending, from violent and sexual misconduct to petty theft and bad driving. Proponents claim that CBT bestows improved thinking skills on 'high risk individuals' (Burnett & Roberts, 2004). There have always been sceptics of these claims, mainly from outside the carceral system. They have drawn attention to the quality of the research (Mair, 2004; Smith, 2004; Moloney, 2013)[1] – abysmally poor, even by the usual standards of the field – and organised in a climate of near 'evangelical fervour, in which managers discouraged the open expression of doubt as "unprofessional"' (Moloney, 2013, p.125). For the most serious kinds of offending however, where the conduct of ex-prisoners is more closely monitored, it becomes much harder to fudge the outcome data.

In the last 10 years, some forensic psychologists have reluctantly acknowledged the low quality and inconclusiveness of the outcome literature for CBT in their field, versus the stark reality of increased violence, self-harm and suicide in prisons today (Adair-Stantiall & Needs, 2018; HM Inspectorate of Prisons, 2015; Smith, 2004). Their doubts have been vindicated in recent reports that acknowledge that long-standing cognitive therapy-based thinking

---

1. The egregious and numerous failings of this research literature include just about all of the issues discussed in Chapter 4 of this book. However, the problems of recruitment bias, high attrition rates, lack of long-term follow-up and questionable outcome measurement loom especially large. For more details, see Forde (2018) and Moloney (2013).

skills programmes for sex offenders do not work (Mews et al., 2017),[2] and that British prisons do not rehabilitate (see, for example, Taylor, 2019; Grierson, 2019).

So instead, psychologists like Alethea Adair-Stantiall and Adrian Needs argue that the correctional system should, as far as practicable, strive to mentor and even nurture its charges. They suggest that a key step would be to recognise that trauma has distorted the lives of most inmates. Further, they propose acknowledging that more subtle forms of maltreatment, such as indifference and disdain, continue to have baleful effects (Adair-Stantiall & Needs, 2018). The exercise of power in the present inevitably evokes echoes of its abuse in the past. A lifetime of having to get by, within harsh families and impoverished, hostile neighbourhoods, can manifest as aggression toward self and (especially) others. Those who have suffered relentless cruelty can become experts in re-enacting what befell them – especially in prison, where violent, callous conduct can bring its own rewards. One hallmark of spiritual mutilation is the urge to avoid or escape any reminder of the original harm through actions that shock or disturb: stealing away, hurting oneself, blowing up into anger, or threatening suicide (Jones, 2018a).

While such damage cannot be altogether unravelled, durable emotional bonds with others can offer a strong bulwark against the worst reactions. Some prison-based psychologists therefore concentrate on working as much with the social milieu as with individuals burdened with it. This means concentrating on how the institution and its rules, roles and rituals shape the way in which people act and feel toward each other. Staff and convicts are encouraged to confront the long tradition of mutual silence about personal suffering, vulnerability and self-harm, and to question myths about the resilience-building value of mockery, chiding or wilful ignorance. Instead, they are helped to find ways to respond with thoughtfulness and compassion to the signs of emotional injury (Jones, 2015, 2018b).

Looking even further into the outside world in their efforts to alleviate individual distress, some forensic psychologists argue for a radical change

---

2. For a damning analysis of why it took 25 years for the very obvious failings of this CBT-based Sex Offender Treatment Programme (SOTP) to reach public attention, see the *Lancet* article by forensic psychiatrists Penelope Brown and Callum Ross (2020). One of their main concerns is that the results of earlier investigations of the SOTP programme (sponsored and overseen by the UK's Ministry of Justice) were not published and seem to have been suppressed. They note that research in the UK Criminal Justice system has long been fraught with ethical tensions, yet nowhere is there any attempt to address the key ethical and governance requirements that would have made its predecessors into sound clinical trials, and might well have led to a much earlier exposure of the weaknesses of the whole programme: 'Any health institution or industry trial on the scale of the SOTP study would require a steering committee, data monitoring committee, independent statistical oversight, robust ethical and peer review, and comprehensive conflict of interest statements for all involved.'

of institutional climate. These climates are comprised of people and their dispositions, their social rituals and the institutions and buildings that enclose them (Lewis, 2018). Climates are felt more than seen, just as we might sigh upon entering a cold, gloomy room. They can change across time and place, and their influence can linger like a chill in the bones. Even where the architecture is similar, one wing of a prison may have a more sinister character depending on how prisoners are categorised, the purposes the wing serves, and the norms of conduct that have grown there (Nylander et al., 2011).

A well-designed prison can improve how people get along, while poor design can stifle and isolate. Spaces that foster calm, dignity and imagination are key. An experimental prison on the island of Bastoy in Norway offers a beach and a green space for family visits without scrutiny by guards. As we have seen in our discussion about memory in Chapter 7, physical settings, including built environments, can function as elements within material-neural circuits that embed remembering and forgetting within institutions. This suggests that more amenable environments will promote recall of positive experiences, as well as beneficent feelings. Indeed, this design appears to have encouraged amity between prisoners and their families, and may have reduced reconviction rates (Lewis, 2018).

The psychologists within this loosely defined movement share an optimistic belief that, during a time of authoritarianism and poor funding, 'pockets of humanistic growth' can be seeded within prisons and forensic services. Clearly, this will be a struggle when attitudes toward offenders seem to be hardening, in a time when the current UK Home Secretary (responsible for criminal justice policy) is able freely to proclaim her desire for criminals 'to literally feel terror' (Gayle, 2019).

A cure for the institution? Positive behavioural support

Behaviour described as 'challenging' is common in adults with learning disabilities. It can take many forms – shouting, hitting, hair-pulling, self-harm, or breaking furniture or valuables. At any one time, 10 to 15% of people with learning disabilities may bear this label of quintessential awkwardness. When it is witnessed in public places, challenging behaviour contributes to the stigma that already imbues this most disempowered segment of society. It can have terrible consequences, including long-term hospital admission and the over-enthusiastic use of physical restraint. In over-stretched care homes and hard-pressed families, possession of this label can sanction avoidance and neglect. Challenging behaviour is also associated with the abuse of psychiatric medication as a 'chemical straitjacket', the extent of which has been described as a scandal of national proportions (Rapley, 2004; Lovett, 1996).

> *Jenny was described as having profound and multiple learning disabilities. She was unable to speak, and it was hard to know what she understood. Jenny was also physically impaired. Her spine was twisted; one of her arms and both her legs were paralysed; and she was blind in one eye. Jenny developed a habit of constantly rubbing the lid of her sighted eye with her fingers. It quickly became sore and inflamed as the skin got rubbed away. A psychological assessment was requested to find a behavioural solution, but there was a long wait, due to staff shortages.*
>
> *Meanwhile, care staff started to worry that Jenny might lose her sight. They agreed that, whenever possible, they would sit with Jenny, hold her hand away from her eye, and talk soothingly to her. But there were only two staff on each shift, caring for 26 doubly incontinent adults. So when nobody could sit with Jenny – inevitably, most of the time – they tied her arm to her wheelchair. This prevented Jenny's fingers reaching her eye, allowed the eyelid to heal, and prevented her blinding herself. Jenny was greatly distressed by having her arm tied down, and the staff hated doing it. However, they faced a dilemma. They could allow Jenny's eyelid-rubbing to continue, risking blindness, or they could use physical restraint to immobilise her arm. Weighing permanent sight loss against temporary distress, they chose the latter.*
>
> *We might expect poorly paid care workers not to have to face such distressing decisions. But this expectation was flouted both by managers and, ultimately, politicians wielding powers that intimately affected the entire care team and Jenny herself.*

In the UK and elsewhere, people with learning disabilities who challenge those who care for them are increasingly subject to an approach called 'positive behavioural support', or PBS. What is interesting to us is that PBS constitutes a 'whole-environment' perspective. It strives to prevent and manage challenging behaviour by modifying the circumstances within which it arises. Its literature looks almost entirely to the once-mainstream psychological principles of conditioning, derived originally from experiments, mainly with animals, by B.F. Skinner and others. In its modern guise, PBS is in large part about the use of rewards and the arrangement of environments to 'shape' behaviour in directions that reduce risk and are deemed more desirable for the key individual and others with whom they share their life. More fundamentally, this framework can also be described as a way of enabling the most marginalised to finally get their ordinary human needs met.

If the more technocratic facets of PBS sound Orwellian, they can be. Behavioural approaches of this kind always bear considerable potential for misuse (Rapley, 2004; Lovett, 1996). Used with insight, sound ethics and compassion, however, and with attention to the wider systems in which behavioural methods are deployed, PBS could potentially improve the quality of life of many people who, in dull and unresponsive residential homes, have grown used to a languishing existence punctuated with bouts of angry protest.

PBS is based on careful assessment of where and when problematic behaviours occur. It attempts to create socially valid interventions that improve quality of life: for the person themselves, and for their relatives, carers and other service users. PBS is founded, humanely enough, on an understanding that actions that challenge represent efforts to manage an environment that is challenging. People may, for instance, be seeking escape from noisy or crowded situations. They may want relief from boredom, to distract themselves from fear or anxiety, or to convey anger or frustration at not getting the recreation or social stimulation they need. If we had an aversion to spinach but found that it featured in every other meal, regardless of our expressions of disgust, then would we not become annoyed, and perhaps annoying'? In addressing such concerns, PBS is said to combine the technology of behavioural intervention with a respect for the human rights and autonomy of all involved (NICE, 2015; Care Quality Commission, 2018).

In the NHS, training seminars on PBS use the marketised language of managed care. There is a recognised system of accreditation and courses are provided by specialists. To attend one of these courses can be to enter a world of supreme confidence in the power of behavioural interventions. And for all that these courses proclaim shared ethical values, the practical emphasis is on Skinnerian behaviourist psychology.

From a clinical perspective, this is not altogether a bad thing. A full account of the environment and how it can generate and maintain distress and distressing behaviours is what so much of mainstream therapeutic psychology lacks. However, the difficulty lies in how 'the environment' is conceived: in essence, as a series of micro-interventions aimed at rewarding the constructive or benign conduct of the targeted individual. Yet this myopic, proximal focus downplays the very problems that led to the widespread endorsement of PBS in the first place. The institutional abuse and neglect of people with learning disabilities is a recurrent national scandal that, inflamed by a blame-seeking media, often leads to new policies intended to ensure the policing and support of vulnerable people (Shakespeare, 2018). Indeed, a longstanding critique of learning disability policy is that it is too often driven by knee-jerk political responses to scandals – such as Cygnet Healthcare and Winterbourne View

– rather than being based on comprehensive, evidence-based assessments of strategic priorities (Whittock, 2016).

This is why no amount of behavioural work by itself is likely to produce lasting improvements in the lives of people with learning disabilities. For one thing, behavioural methods appear far less effective for any client group when the evidence is weighed critically.[3] For another, many paid carers are unable to follow the PBS recommendations because they lack the necessary support from their employing organisation.

This missing support is not necessarily in terms of understanding how to use behavioural techniques, although this may contribute. It is also not just about understaffing due to cost-cutting, although again this can be a factor. More fundamentally, it is about workers not being valued and treated respectfully and decently. It is about employers who pay minimal wages for extremely demanding work, and who take little interest in workers' professional development. This lack of interest doubtless owes much to the fact that most care workers are working-class women or immigrants, with few avenues for communicating their own unhappiness to managers (Epstein, 2006; Timms, 2015). If there is to be meaningful progress, power must be genuinely in the gift of those seeking to do the empowering. This is seldom the case for employees in the caring professions – and especially those who provide personal assistance to people with learning disabilities, who are frequently among the least valued and worst paid of workers (Epstein, 2010).

As for the people these workers support, their plight reflects a culture that sometimes sentimentalises but more often ignores or despises them (Shakespeare, 2018; Whittock, 2016). The things most likely to ease their malaise are those that would benefit almost anybody: an environment rich enough in resources and relationships and free enough from threats to allow people to flourish and care for each other. Unfortunately, many people with learning disabilities (and often their families and carers) have, in the last decade, suffered reductions in income and access to housing and all varieties

---

3. See for example, Chapter 6, 'The Owl and the Pussycat: Behavioural treatments', in Epstein (2006). For a recent example of a 'pragmatic' RCT, specifically investigating the use of the PBS approach in the care of adults with learning disabilities in the UK, see Hassiotis et al. (2018). This study found that an educational programme designed to equip the staff in a community adult learning disabilities team to confidently train and advise the carers of people with learning disabilities in the use of the PBS approach led neither to meaningful reductions in challenging behaviour, nor to any tangible improvements in client wellbeing. However, this study had a number of shortcomings, which included the poor quality of the behavioural plans themselves. It may be telling that the carer teams suffered very high rates of employee turnover, while the team managers were unable or unwilling to reduce the caseload of the participating health professionals, even though this was seen as an essential pre-requisite for the demanding and time-consuming work of creating a useful PBS plan.

of public participation. This has happened overtly, as funding for health and social care services has been cut under so-called austerity. It has also occurred more insidiously – by sleight of hand – in the form of redesigned benefits and services that present diminished opportunities as greater 'freedom' and 'choice'.[4] It is therefore unsurprising that too many people with learning disabilities and their families and friends have suffered a heavy burden of distress under the social distancing and isolation measures imposed in response to the recent Covid-19 pandemic (Willner et al., 2020).

Mental health

> *Lisa shares a flat with her father who 'doesn't talk much' but drinks heavily. She is lonely, anxious and has little trust in her neighbours, some of whom cannot allow her to forget that she is a graduate of a much-stigmatised 'special school'. She sorely misses her late grandfather, the only person she feels really understood her.*
>
> *On bad days, Lisa believes that she can hear her grandfather muttering prayers of comfort from the 'other side'. She has reluctantly accepted treatment with psychiatric drugs for these 'auditory hallucinations' – which nevertheless persist. Her twin preoccupations with the afterlife and the paranormal have found expression in her new-found hobby of ghost hunting. Pursued in derelict buildings and deserted parks, Lisa's nocturnal sojourns have made her the target of malicious social media gossip, and mockery and personal threats on the street. The police have provided the family with CCTV equipment as protection. But since the closure of the local police station, there is no strong law enforcement presence in the area. The blurred digital images of perpetrators are never enough to warrant meaningful deterrent action. Meanwhile, the police have cautioned Lisa for her attempted acts of violent retaliation at her tormentors. So, besides the risk of seriously hurting someone, Lisa is herself in danger of falling into the criminal justice system.*
>
> *Several years ago, Lisa visited a day centre for people with disabilities, and enjoyed some support from a local authority personal assistant. Both these services were deemed unaffordable during successive rounds*

---

4. Assessments of the social and economic marginalisation of people with learning disabilities in the UK in recent years can found at Redley (2008) and Malli et al. (2019). For an incisive look at the neoliberal thinking that tacitly underlies so many recent policies that purport to empower disabled people, see Burton & Kagan (2006) and Oliver (2004). Excellent overviews of the general extent of poverty and material insecurity in the UK can be obtained from the United Nations General Assembly Human Rights Council (2018) and Armstrong (2017).

> *of local authority spending cuts. Lisa's options have shrunk even further with the recent retraction of her disability benefits by an unsympathetic assessor.*

In this section we look at three initiatives that differ in terms of scale and organisational status, while sharing a mental health focus. First, we consider an ambitious attempt, backed by the British Psychological Society's Division of Clinical Psychology (DCP), to rethink the concept of mental ill health. Second, we describe a small set of initiatives, fostered within a single mental health service, that were designed to produce incremental yet enduringly positive changes to its culture. Finally, we discuss the work of a small, self-organising group of psychologists who have spoken out against the damaging psychological consequences of neoliberal policies.

It will help to contextualise these initiatives with respect to the history of UK clinical psychology in relation to mental health. At the birth of the profession in the 1950s, there were only a few dozen clinical psychologists in the UK. All were answerable to the far more institutionally powerful and better-paid profession of psychiatry. Their chief roles were to audit the equilibrium of those described as mentally ill and the abilities of those called mentally subnormal, and to think up new diagnostic tests for both groups (Pilgrim & Treacher, 1982).

However, as the profession grew in size and confidence, it began to develop psychological interventions. For the majority who endorsed mainstream psychological perspectives, this meant gaining status and authority that would allow them to collaborate with psychiatrists on equal terms. But for a significant minority, a tradition gradually emerged, that now stretches back half a century, whereby they challenged biomedical psychiatry.

These challenges started in the late 1960s with the involvement of some UK clinical psychologists in the nascent therapeutic community movement. Here, for the first time, people on long-stay wards were encouraged to find meaning in their personal troubles. Previously, they had been taught to regard their distress as the consequence of biologically based mental disorders. Much of this labour was inspired by the writings of dissident psychiatrist R.D. Laing and colleagues at Kingsley Hall in London, who sought to apply the insights of European existentialist and phenomenological thinkers to help people described as schizophrenic (Ingleby, 1983).

By the 1980s, the dissolution of the large hospitals and the rise of 'care in the community' meant that the therapeutic community movement stalled. However, in the more dispersed mental health services that now predominate, some determined groups of clinical psychologists have continued trying to humanise mental health treatment. In recent years, they have forged alliances with the small but growing numbers of psychiatrists who share their concerns (Double, 2006). Mental health professionals from both specialisms have highlighted the poor quality of the evidence base for ECT, and the evidence associating it with sometimes fatal adverse consequences (Read et al., 2019). They have emphasised the similarly poor evidence for most drug treatments, including those described (dishonestly, since they have no such specific effects (Moncrieff, 2020)) as anti-psychotics and antidepressants. They have also noted the damaging effects of these therapies and the longstanding failure of many services to listen to the views of those who have become dependent on them (Holmes et al., 1999). Others have argued for the abolition of the concept of mental illness, and for its replacement with less stigmatising and more accurate concepts (Coles et al., 2013; Hallam, 2018; Holmes, 2010).

Even some mainstream clinical psychologists have sought to provide analyses of healthcare institutions with a view to making them more benign and empowering for those who use them. A good example in NHS mental health services over the last decade is the successful promotion of a trauma-informed ethos. This acknowledges that severe distress is rooted in abusive experience, and adjures health professionals to take care, rather than control, by learning to listen to and work alongside sufferers in recognition that they are experts in their own experience of distress.[5]

This twin focus on biography and hurt is strongly informed by the arguments and complaints of mental health service users. It led clinical psychologists, notably Lucy Johnstone and Rudi Dallos (2013) to promote psychological formulation as an alternative to psychiatric diagnosis. Formulation can be characterised as thinking together with the distressed person, to help them understand their difficulties in light of their struggles with the people around them and with their wider circumstances. The aim is to explore how seemingly baffling psychiatric symptoms might actually represent concerted efforts to survive and cope.

For instance, the apparently groundless and irrational beliefs that psychiatry calls paranoia can begin to make sense when the sufferer tells – perhaps for the first time – how they grew up as a despised academic failure, the butt of many jokes. These beliefs may make even more sense when their holder describes how they now get by, in a flat that wants for comfort and privacy, in a graffiti- and crime-saturated neighbourhood where 'everyone keeps to themselves'. Such a history, allied with such dismal and threatening

---

5. For a general overview, see Fenney (2019). For a guide to current plans for the development of trauma-informed public health services in the UK over the next decade, see NHS England (2019). For a discussion of this approach in relation to women specifically (as the largest 'minority' mental health service user group), see, for example, Wilton & Williams (2019).

present circumstances, would be enough to make most people wary that others are out to get them.

Experiences of paranoia can attract a range of stigmatising psychiatric diagnoses, including schizophrenia. Instead, formulation aims to construct a potentially respectful narrative. Ideally, this narrative is co-created by the health professional and the distressed person, perhaps with the help of the latter's family and friends. It provides a viable explanation for the person's distress, and in so doing points to forms of intervention that may be of assistance. Nevertheless, formulation is not wedded to any particular therapeutic school. In principle, it leaves therapist and client free to choose the most suitable healing techniques (Johnstone & Dallos, 2013).

In 2019, there were more than 20,000 clinical psychologists practising in the UK. Many, though by no means all, dealt primarily with mental health concerns. While the majority aligned themselves with mainstream psychological perspectives, some were more open to experimentation and questioning. Clinical psychology has created a cumulative body of theory, research and practice that is increasingly accepted in services and that includes more radical approaches as well as those firmly of the mainstream. Formulation, for example, is now part of mainstream clinical psychology, taught on most training courses and often seen as central to mental health practice. The three initiatives we will now describe are all informed by, and contribute to, this still unfolding history.

Rethinking mental illness

The Western diagnostic system that is being busily exported across the globe regards mental health problems as disturbances of mind. More fundamentally, it regards them as the product of abnormalities in brain systems, structures or circuits – even though there is no good evidence for this. But this view not only lacks scientific support; it is also parochial. Across much of the world, in societies traditional and modern, disruptions of mood or wellbeing are seen as bodily unease. They are understood as signifying a breakdown in the tormented person's ability to belong and mesh with the people and places that count most. In many Asian, Southern European and African societies, it is literally more sensible to speak of melancholic or malevolent atmospheres and places than of one's own feelings of misery (Fuchs, 2013, 2016; Prinz, 2012; Watters, 2010). Madness, sorrow and bewilderment amount to the sufferer's sudden homelessness, both in their own physicality and in the familiar situations and relationships that once guided and all but defined them. Overall, people in many non-Western cultures appear more open to explanations of conduct and feelings that tap into larger systems of family, community and social class (Throop, 2008; Prinz, 2012).

At first glance, this way of seeing things might seem antique, even alien. It is too often dismissed by Anglo-American mental health practitioners as the product of naïvety and poor self-awareness, as confirmation of a shortfall in what they call mental health literacy.[6] This outlook is nevertheless mirrored in what many Western people say about their experience of distress, when anyone bothers to question them with sensitivity, patience and – above all – without a predetermined diagnostic or therapeutic agenda (Johnstone, 2022).

This viewpoint also reflects what health researchers have consistently found about the complex causes of mental health problems in post-industrialised societies. It is now well established that emotional (and often physical) wellbeing require freedom from violence, duress and indebtedness. They also depend on the *presence* of many ingredients: a meaningful occupation, close affiliations imbued with respect and trust, secure housing, and space and time for privacy and leisure. And all these things depend, in the last analysis, on everyone enjoying a solid income and protection from want (Wilkinson & Pickett, 2018). Yet in the UK and the US, the heartlands of neoliberalism, personal indebtedness is at record levels. Less than a third of households are free from financial insecurity, and close to a fifth of the population live in poverty (Dorling, 2018). Again, there are well-evidenced material reasons why neoliberal policies are associated with increased levels of personal malaise.

It is in this context that, in 2018, the British Psychological Society published the Power Threat Meaning Framework (PTMF) (Johnstone & Boyle, 2018). The PTMF is a substantial work that offers a detailed clinical and philosophical alternative to the psychiatric account of mental disorder. It begins by recognising that functional psychiatric diagnosis is conceptually flawed and unreliable. To a considerable extent, this is because reliable evidence for the abnormalities held to underpin these diagnoses has not been found. Decades of generously funded research, using increasingly sophisticated technologies (genome scanning, brain imaging) has failed to find any consistent biological aspects to these so-called mental illnesses. As psychiatry puts it – on those occasions when it does not simply gloss over this fundamental challenge to its own legitimacy – there are no biomarkers for the functional psychiatric diagnoses. In the 2013 press release marking the launch of the fifth edition of the international *Diagnostic and Statistical Manual of Mental Disorders* (*DSM-5*) (APA, 2013), psychiatrist David Kupfer (chair of the committee that produced this latest version of the 'bible' of psychiatric diagnosis) said:

---

6. See the thought provoking and disturbing discussions of some of the consequences of the misapplication of Western constructs across the world in Watters (2010) and Cohen (2018).

> In the future, we hope to be able to identify disorders using biological and genetic markers… Yet this promise, which we have anticipated since the 1970s, remains disappointingly distant. We've been telling patients for several decades that we are waiting for biomarkers. We're still waiting. (Kupfer, 2013)

To acknowledge that there are no biomarkers is, in effect, to acknowledge that there is no evidence that these diagnoses actually represent illnesses in the medical sense. With this established, the PTMF provides an explanatory meta-framework for distress that doesn't depend on notions of psychiatric illness.

Unlike some alternatives to diagnosis, the PTMF includes biology – it recognises that distress, like all experience, is biologically instantiated (Fisher, 2009; see also Chapter 6). But, unlike diagnosis, the PTMF doesn't treat biology as primarily causal of distress. Instead, it locates the origins of distress in threats that arise in a world structured by unequal power relations: a world where meanings are not freely chosen but must be constructed in and from frequently toxic combinations of events and circumstances. In this way, the PTMF seeks to transcend the many false dualisms – between mind and body, self and world, feeling and logic – that underpin the psychiatric concept of mental illness. By contrast, the PTMF holds that all of us are rooted in our own past and in our current social world, and no more separable from our history and surrounds than a turtle from its shell.

When it comes to understanding distress, the PTMF swaps the psychiatric demand for a diagnosis with four questions. These questions are not meant to be asked literally in therapeutic encounters. Rather, they are guides to reasoning and exploration, pointers that might structure a series of beneficial conversations, and deeds. The questions are:

- *'What has happened to you?'* – in other words, 'How has power operated in your life?'
- *'How did it affect you?'* – 'What kind of threats has it posed?'
- *'What sense did you make of it?'* – 'What did you understand the meaning of these situations and experiences to be?'

And the last and most important question:

- *'What did you have to do to survive?'* – 'What kinds of actions and thoughts did you devise and use to shield you – as the carapace that doctors describe, misguidedly, as your psychiatric symptom?'

By working through the implications of these questions, the PTMF proposes the identification of tentative, provisional patterns of distress. These patterns emerge because we have broadly shared biological capacities, and because we experience similar kinds of threats and challenges. Nevertheless, they are fundamentally different from psychiatric diagnosis in a number of ways. Unlike diagnoses, the patterns overtly include culture and meaning. And rather than naming supposed illnesses that people supposedly have, the patterns describe things people find themselves experiencing or doing. This is overtly recognised in the titles of the patterns, which include 'Surviving rejection, abandonment and loss' and 'Surviving defeat'.

As a conceptual framework, the PTMF is close to the position that we take in this book. From our perspective, it could usefully have developed a more substantial critique of mainstream psychology and its association with neoliberalism. Similarly, both the PTMF's own materialism and its challenge to individualism could perhaps have been more prominently worked through. We would also have liked to see some critical scrutiny of the evidence base for psychological treatment. But with these caveats in mind, the PTMF is a landmark document that holds considerable potential for future positive developments.

A questioning psychology

As a BPS publication, the PTMF has had a relatively high profile. Nevertheless, as our history of UK clinical psychology suggested, small groups of fortunately placed and resourced practitioners have, for many years, worked more subtly to foster creative ways of working. In some cases, this has involved deliberately creating and then strengthening a niche within NHS services, which are still largely dominated by psychiatry.

The adult mental health clinical psychology service in Nottingham, for instance, sought to foster a more thoughtful approach to mental health work. Its efforts were informed by the insights of community and critical psychologists who eschew the authoritarianism of many mental health interventions and question their tendency to blame sufferers for their woes. Community and critical psychology rejects the cult of the expert practitioner seeking to cure a putative mental illness. Instead, it promotes working alongside those who experience distress. One aim is to identify what is harmful as well as helpful about current treatments. It looks outward, to the social and economic world, as the primary source of both causes and remedies for people's difficulties (Kagan et al., 2019; Orford, 2008).

This approach can find common cause with the humanistic values that underpin psychiatric nursing and social work. It can also appeal to those medical practitioners who look to the all but forgotten traditions of community psychiatry (Bracken, 2002). At the same time, assumptions about the reality of mental illness, the value of diagnosis and the need to coerce the mad into accepting treatment are embedded within the mental health treatment system[7] – much as the doctrine of the Holy Trinity is embedded in the Catholic Church. Clearly, to entice colleagues in mental health work into questioning such fundamental beliefs is a long-term task.

Recognising this, clinical psychologists in Nottingham developed opportunities for discussion, thinking and debate around the meanings of distress – in staff supervision sessions and in more formal training and case work discussions with nurses, social workers and other professionals. A key aim was to encourage the idea that help, to be effective, must not only focus on what the person was thinking and feeling. It also needed to consider what changes in their circumstances might help them to progress. These changes might include everything, from family relationships, housing and community support, to employment, income and education (Diamond, 2013).

To help pave the way for this wider approach, the psychologists created a series of publications called *Bite Size*. These concise and pithy summaries of psychologically informed practice are co-authored with service users and other mental health professionals. Presented in a double-sided A4 leaflet format, *Bite Size* accessibly summarises theories, research and debates in the mental health field. Their consistent focus is on what this might mean for the lay reader, and particularly for service users wishing to make sense of their own distress. In a rolling programme that has spanned more than 50 editions, *Bite Size* features topics like 'Making Sense of Psychiatric Drugs'; 'Employment and Mental Health', which explores the connections between work and wellbeing, and 'Power and Decision-Making on Acute Wards', which shows how those detained in hospital can have more say over their own treatment and care.[8]

Like samizdat literature,[9] and competing with the glossy advertising leaflets of the pharmaceutical companies, copies of *Bite Size* are placed in waiting areas, coffee rooms and staff pigeonholes. Their intended readership is mental health workers, service users and their friends and families. For many who come across them, this is probably the first time they have encountered a health service-sponsored publication that encourages debate about the harmfulness and doubtful efficacy of routine psychiatric treatments and about the poor science behind psychiatric diagnosis.

---

7. For compelling analyses of how this might come about, see Burstow (2015) and Johnstone (2022). For an exploration of how mental health services without the use of psychiatric diagnoses might one day look, see National Hearing Voices Network (2018).

8. www.criticalvaluesbasedpracticenetwork.co.uk/clinical-psychology-bite-size/

9. Samizdat was the name given to clandestine literature self-published by dissidents under the former communist regimes of Eastern Europe.

Bite Size is intended to support a culture of enquiry. It exemplifies a commitment to continuous training and education informed by open debate and conviviality (Illich, 2001a). In the same vein, psychologists have worked with their colleagues, and with people who had used mental health services, to create open workshops and seminars. Rather than delivering pre-packaged training modules dominated entirely by expert perspectives, this meant democratically exploring key issues. The training sessions had titles such as 'Psychosis Revisited'; 'Working Therapeutically on Acute Psychiatric Wards'; 'Fostering User-Involvement in Mental Health Services'; 'CBT in the Real World' (a critical look at this ubiquitous therapy), and 'Sexuality and Mental Health', an early attempt to acknowledge how, for those who do not fit dominant sexual norms, distress and recovery are often intertwined with oppression and empowerment (Das Nair & Fairbank, 2012; Houghton, 2016).

Such a culture of enquiry requires more than just the introduction of new ideas; it needs a structure to sustain it. The Nottingham clinical psychologists therefore facilitated clinical meetings in which health professionals were encouraged to think about and plan their work together. These meetings took a much broader viewpoint than that implied by the language of 'caseloads' and 'service delivery'. Practitioners were asked to consider the historical and social context of both the service and the communities that it served. They were invited to consider what the helpful and unhelpful aspects of their work might be from the viewpoint of those communities and service users. Then they would be asked to think about the challenges that they and the service faced, and about the resources, strengths and coping methods on which they could draw in trying to meet their service goals (Diamond, 2014).

In clinical work, it is all too easy to rely on ideas and concepts that are well worn and comfortable. The same goes for some whom clinicians seek to help, who may embrace the identity and apparent explanatory certainty offered by a psychiatric diagnosis, or welcome the myth that they can be fundamentally remade by psychological treatment. In consequence, practice can become stale as psychologists slip, unawares, into the role of a blind servant of institutional power: thinkers, to be sure, but ones whose ideas no longer stray far outside the lines implicitly or explicitly drawn by managers and policy makers.

An essential element of a culture of enquiry, therefore, is to make time and space for discussing and thinking about ideas from beyond the mainstream. In Nottingham, conferences and seminars were organised around the theme of working psychologically in medically dominated workplaces. Often, these initiatives challenged psychiatric concepts by promoting alternative accounts of the meanings of distress (Das Nair & Fairbank, 2012). But this was no one-dimensional critique of biomedicine. Some of these gatherings also examined the limitations of talking treatment, and what those limitations might mean.

And there was a recurring focus on the ethical and political harms implied by the unquestioning national roll-out of CBT in the form of the Improving Access to Psychological Therapies (IAPT) programme in England (Houghton, 2005).

The Nottingham psychologists also facilitated supportive groups for service users and their families that encouraged open debate about psychiatric medication (Keenan, 2009). In addition, public forums were marshalled to bring 'hidden' controversies into the open (Keenan & Coles, 2012). These forums gently questioned the approved viewpoints promulgated by the mass media and the treatment system – in regard, for example, to the validity of the schizophrenia concept, the efficacy of cognitive therapy and other brand-name psychological cure-alls, and to the personal and societal consequences of the enforced drugging of service users outside of the hospital (under Community Treatment Orders). Service user accounts that acknowledged the influence of history, environments and social resources on experiences of psychological disturbance were also promoted. These and many other topics were opened up for lively questioning. They showed that the realities of distress, and of caring for those afflicted by it, are tangled, complicated and – above all – rooted in the sufferer's world. None of these elements can be reduced to numbers, care packages and measured outputs without grossly distorting what actually occurs.

Speaking out

Prevailing political agendas influence as well as reflect public attitudes. They also shape the health professions, including psychology. If an engineer is aiming to control and predict the behaviour of an electric motor, no one is likely to see this as having political or ethical consequences. Conversely, as soon as a psychologist aims to control and predict human behaviour, their efforts already have an inescapable ethical and political dimension. It follows that, if psychology is to have a social conscience, it must take a more active role in speaking out against injustices. Sometimes this may mean speaking up for values that do not always sit comfortably with professional advancement, or with the spirit of the times.

This brings us to our third mental health initiative, which is a particularly striking example of psychologists acting on this duty to sometimes speak uncomfortable truths. We are referring to an excellent briefing paper on the psychological effects of the British government's decade-long programme of ideologically driven, economically damaging spending cuts – austerity, as ministers and their media allies prefer to call it.

The briefing paper (McGrath et al., 2016) was authored in 2016 by a small group who initially called themselves Psychologists Against Austerity, but later became Psychologists for Social Change. In clear language that should be understandable even to politicians, the paper highlights the damaging psychological effects of the steady retrenchment of government spending on social care, housing, disability benefits and other public goods. It compiles evidence to demonstrate that these policy choices, which have already blighted the lives of more than a quarter of the population, are also storing up problems for the future. Many parents, the paper suggests, will be exhausted through overwork and low pay, and this will inevitably limit their capacity to create an emotionally secure family life for their children.

The paper identifies five specific varieties of psychological damage made more prevalent by policies of so-called austerity: humiliation and shame, fear and distrust, instability and insecurity, isolation and loneliness, and finally – and fittingly – entrapment and powerlessness. These domains of experience, which would have been familiar to 19th-century novelists like Balzac and Dickens, are recast as 'ailments'. The paper proposes that they are indicators of problems in society, of weakened social cohesion and the ingraining of economic and spiritual impoverishment into the lives of future generations. To combat these ailments, 'Social policy should work towards a more equitable and participatory society, to facilitate individual wellbeing, resilient places, and strong communities' (McGrath et al., 2016, p.46).

As we have seen, the indicators of a psychologically healthy society include agency, security, connection, meaning and trust. Politicians and policy makers often claim to want to nurture wellbeing. This briefing paper demonstrates how crucial it is that they therefore consider the psychological effects of what they are seeking to impose. Unfortunately, stated aspirations to foster positive outcomes all too often have scant regard for, or even knowledge of, the day-to-day experiences of the many who have to live with their results.

Conclusion

Humans are above all creatures of flesh and feeling, vulnerably intertwined with their world. If we want to ease or prevent their psychological difficulties it is this world that needs to be diagnosed and corrected, rather than those it has harmed. This chapter has shown how applied psychology can offer fresh perspectives on psychological problems by concentrating on the circumstances and environments that create and maintain them. In doing so, applied psychology suggests alternatives to neoliberalism, which insists we must simply be competitive and market driven. The alternatives discussed replace this narrow outlook with a view of human life as interdependent and founded on a shared understanding of our vulnerability. In doing so, they suggest ways forward to a more humane world.

Arguably, the need for such alternatives has never been greater. With respect to mental health, the aspiration to help those in distress to recover and return to productive living has become an important goal of services (Pilgrim & McCranie, 2013). Reports acknowledge the social roots of malaise and misery, and the value of non-medical responses – especially prevention (CEP Mental Health Policy Group, 2006; Mental Health Foundation, 2016). And yet, in their recommendations, these same documents often downplay or ignore what they have acclaimed. Likewise, in both the prison service and services for people with learning disabilities, laudable aspirations and proclamations of values are all too frequently undercut by the grim reality of under-resourced institutions staffed by poorly paid workers.

As we suggested earlier, power is central to these initiatives, just as it is to our social materialist approach. The ability to transform environments – in prisons or learning disability services – is a function of power, as was the ability to transform ways of working in the Nottingham mental health service. The PTMF identifies the operation of power as central to experiences of distress, while the briefing paper on so-called austerity starkly describes the baleful psychological consequences of a particular use of political power. All of this is helpful.

At the same time, with respect to power it is important to also recognise the limitations of these initiatives. In truth, the more humane and potentially efficacious initiatives being trialled by forensic psychologists are unlikely to become established unless supported by caring citizens, social movements and, ultimately, politicians (McGarvey, 2018). In learning disability services, PBS could be made to 'work' – but only as part of a whole-system approach to the enablement of people with learning disabilities and of those who care for them. Yet this appears unlikely under a government still intent on pursuing neoliberal policies. In mental health, the inextricable links that the PTMF makes between distress and power could underpin radical changes. Yet the PTMF has encountered opposition from psychiatrists, mainstream psychologists and others invested in diagnostic approaches. Likewise, the initiatives in Nottingham's mental health service were dependent on enlightened management and a critical mass of like-minded staff not wedded to mainstream approaches. In the face of the greater power that impacted the service under so-called austerity, not all of these arrangements were possible to sustain.

Distal power, then, is not some abstract force that operates at a distance or only affects others. Its influence is not reducible to the proximal sphere of family, friends and employment, where it most visibly plays out. Distal powers arrange and produce dynamics of proximal power. The psychological is already thoroughly intertwined with the social and material circumstances within which it arises. And these circumstances, arranged by power relations and smoothed by the operation of interest, are what impel feelings, prompt memories, produce habits and foster dominant ways of speaking. The next chapter will consider how this perspective can inform practice in two arenas: psychological therapy, and political activism.

Chapter 9

Within and beyond psychology

In the previous chapter we summarised a small set of institutional or organisational initiatives that break from the psychological mainstream and so have positive potentials. Yet we also described how these initiatives, for the most part, are not fully established and accepted. The dominant majority within psychology – the mainstream – remains complicit in the harms of neoliberalism. Mainstream psychology promotes individualism and subjectivism, and conceals its partiality with claims of positivist neutrality. This facilitates neoliberal policies, supports managerialist practices and deflects attention from the social and material roots of psychological problems.

The inescapable conclusion seems to be that psychology, at least in its mainstream incarnation, is more of an obstacle to social change than a resource to facilitate progress. And to the extent that the other helping professions (predominantly psychiatry and social work) either draw upon mainstream psychology or have similar tendencies to locate problems within individuals, they too are problematic.

In previous years, this seems to have been more widely recognised. One unfortunate (yet understandable) effect of the recent massive cuts to social and mental health services is that they have encouraged some mental health service users to defend existing practices – for example, psychiatric diagnosis – rather than campaign for something better. For example, an article in *Asylum* magazine, written by an anonymous service user, criticised the Power Threat Meaning Framework because its challenge to psychiatric diagnosis might be used by benefits agency assessors to refuse to recognise a claimant's need for financial support (A Service User, 2018). They argue:

> Policy and practice are very different, so although welfare policies may not state that assessors look for particular diagnoses, in reality they do... Equivocal and diluted PTMF descriptions would not be

good enough, especially when compared with authoritative medical descriptions (mental and physical) in others' reports. This is not about a psychological dependence on diagnosis, it's about trying to materially stay alive, ensuring mental health professionals provide information in an effective way but more importantly, what the culture of the department demands. (p.14).

Service user contributors to the influential Mental Elf blog[1] also frequently endorse or argue for psychiatric diagnostic categories, on similar grounds.

But in the 1960s and 1970s, when critique was often more vociferous and perhaps more consistent, workers in the helping professions were sometimes described as softcops.[2] Just as uniformed police maintain a social order that benefits the already rich and powerful, went the argument, so do softcops. The uniformed police do this by exerting legal power and physical force. Softcops, by contrast, maintain the social order by monitoring its boundaries, identifying and 'treating' those who transgress, and all the while camouflaging this oppressive activity as fundamentally benevolent. It's for your own good, say the softcops, we're only trying to help. You simply have to accept that your cognitive processes are distorted. Just be more mindful, accept what you cannot change, and be grateful for what you already have.

In this chapter we present some suggestions for mental health work and for social change. Along the way, we question whether psychologists can only ever be softcops. Just as some fortuitously placed psychologists have managed to foster helpful organisational and institutional initiatives, so some ways of working psychologically can potentially address people's distress, and can support positive social action. In what follows we demonstrate how these psychological practices can be rooted in the social materialist psychology we have begun to describe.

In the first section, 'Coercive bullying tactics', we consider psychological practices in therapy supplied by psychologists in mental health services. This is followed by a short section discussing innovative ways of working psychologically with small groups ('Beyond traditional therapy'), and then by a discussion of community psychology. After that ('Woke'), we discuss the use of psychological practices within political groups and campaigns, and consider examples of political campaigning within psychology. The chapter ends with some very brief reflection on the book and on ourselves.

---

1. www.nationalelfservice.net/mental-health/

2. Today the helping professions include many clinical and counselling psychologists, but in the 1970s consisted mostly of psychiatrists and social workers. The term 'softcop', which circulated in the radical political milieu of this time, was subsequently popularised by the title of Caryl Churchill's Foucauldian-inspired play, *Softcops*, first produced in the early 1980s.

Coercive bullying tactics

A service user on a mental health forum used to post insightfully about his weekly sessions of what he called 'coercive bullying tactics', or CBT.³ We have seen that, as the exemplary brand of psychological therapy today, CBT is oversold: Chapter 3 described its conceptual incoherence, while the questionable evidence for its efficacy was detailed in Chapter 4. In contemporary mental health settings, CBT is all too frequently delivered by under-resourced people working in overstretched, target-driven services. And in the case of IAPT, engagement with CBT is linked to access to benefits. In addition, and as we proposed earlier (Chapter 5), there is also something about the very form of therapeutic practice favoured by CBT that can itself foster unhelpful interactions. Consider this, from a book of 'persuasive arguments' for CBT practitioners (emphasis in original):

> When clients ask for your advice on how to tackle their problems, some of them may say at the next session 'Your advice didn't work' and thereby attempt to undermine your credibility, or wait for you to come up with another suggestion because they expect you to carry the responsibility for their change. It is understandable why you might become defensive... Instead, immediately ask the client 'Well, why didn't you make my suggestion work?' or 'What did *you* do that prevented my ideas from working?' In other words, make *the client* responsible for not showing any improvement. (Heenan & Dryden, 2002, p.4)

Coercive bullying tactics, indeed. When psychologists conduct individual therapy in the CBT mode, both their professional situation and the practice they deploy could encourage them to act as softcops. But we want to suggest that there are ways of approaching individual therapy, informed by social materialist psychology, that can be more helpful.

To be perfectly clear, we are certainly not suggesting that all of the deep-rooted structural causes of distress can be addressed by providing individual therapy, one client after another, as though we will all live forever. We are not proposing that therapy can take the place of political change, or offering therapy as a universal panacea, the answer to all ills. And we are absolutely, definitely *not* advocating Social Materialist Therapy™. Instead, we have two much more modest goals: first, to show how our psychology can help explain why individual therapy sometimes does work, and second, to illustrate how our social materialism can foster a kind of sensibility within therapeutic practice that may make progress more likely.

---

3. We have not named this person because we had no way of contacting them to seek their consent.

First, we have shown that psychological therapy is nowhere near so effective as advocates frequently claim. We have described how the evidence base is flawed and how, overall, therapeutic efficacy is difficult to demonstrate. At the same time, it is undoubtedly the case that some people do benefit from therapy. Indeed, it has long been said that those most likely to benefit bear a particular set of characteristics. If you are fortunate enough to be Young, Attractive, Verbal, Intelligent and Successful – YAVIS – therapy is more likely to be of assistance.

YAVIS originated in a 1964 book by William Schofield (reprinted more recently as Schofield, 1986). Today we might be tempted simply to say 'white, middle-class and articulate'. Alternatively, we might seek further specificity by using the multifaceted concept of 'social graces' from systemic family therapy.[4] Here, to strike a balance between specificity and brevity, we will focus solely on YAVIS characteristics.

Schofield argued that clients with these characteristics are more inclined to be 'psychologically literate', to share their therapist's belief in the power of self-reflection, and therefore to collaborate with the zeal needed to attain a better result. It seems plausible that, in some instances, this is exactly what happens. Indeed, a growing research literature on the harmful effects of therapist blindness to cultural and ethnic difference between themselves and their clients underlines the importance of common understanding. At the same time, our social materialist psychology reveals another, more immediate, more pervasive and more concrete set of reasons why such clients are disproportionately likely to show therapeutic gains.

Younger people simply have more years remaining in which to engage with life chances and opportunities (even though these opportunities are currently more restricted than for previous generations). Socially, there is an expectation that young people will experiment, try things out, mature and develop: their social position (if not their material situation) affords them some power to change (Kagan, 2013). Because they are still maturing and orienting themselves toward life, this can give therapy more actual social and relational opportunities to work with. At the same time, toxic habits and traumatic memories have had less time to become engrained, and so might be easier to resolve.

Conventionally attractive people, meanwhile, have reserves of beauty: a source of influence and interpersonal power, and a potential resource that can smooth interactions, create opportunities, and encourage approaches from others (Hakim, 2011; Schilling, 2003). Likewise, those with good verbal skills

---

[4]. Social graces are constellations of characteristics such as gender, geography, race, religion, age, ability, appearance, class, culture, education, ethnicity, employment, sexuality, sexual orientation and spirituality.

will be better able to use language to re-story difficult or damaging experiences, both to themselves and with others. They will also be better at negotiation and self-presentation in relationships, interviews and other important situations.

Similarly, those blessed with at least average intelligence will also find re-storying easier, as well as being able to deploy their abilities in the labour market, and use them to make more-or-less competent everyday decisions. Some forms of intelligence – wittiness, for example – also facilitate social relationships. And, of course, those who have been successful in life – through their own efforts, or by the accident of birth – will already have greater social status, more power, and more resources: all of which can be used as levers for turning therapeutic reflections into tangible personal change in the world beyond the consulting room. Some, too, will have internalised deep-rooted feelings of confidence, borne of consistent material security, that can mitigate against the worst extremes of misery.

So social materialist psychology helps explain why being YAVIS is therapeutically helpful. It also casts further light on why poorer and minority ethnic clients seem to be more likely to drop out of therapy and to find it disappointing (Kim & Cardemil, 2012; Kearney, 2018; Sue & Sue, 2012).[5] But, like so many other important influences on distress, YAVIS features cannot be freely chosen. We cannot make ourselves young or attractive or any other of these characteristics by mere acts of will. Both clients and therapists can only ever work with the embodied, social and material powers and resources actually available to them. Here are two examples of how psychologists can sometimes help clients make use of these powers and resources in ways that combat their distress.

Hilary's story

Hilary's story exemplifies our contention that psychology has predominantly focused on the internal world of thoughts and feelings, while also demonstrating how a social materialist perspective can shift this focus.

> *Hilary attended a weekly psychodynamic support group for four years. Then she explained that she had to leave because of work commitments, and besides didn't feel she was getting much from the group. It may well have been that the interests of the services were prioritised here. In*

---

5. A further reason why minority ethnic and working-class clients (two groups that significantly intersect in British and US society) might be more prone to disengage from talking therapy are the greater logistical obstacles that they often face in attending their appointments, notably including transport and childcare issues, as all three of these publications acknowledge.

> *subsequent individual sessions, while she missed the company of group members, Hilary confirmed that the invasive, damaging, self-harming obsessions she had lived with for 20 years had not changed at all. Hilary was also in debt, and in part withdrew from the therapy group to increase her hours at work. She was trapped financially, dependent on her long-term partner, caught in domestic circumstances with their relationship moribund. None of these factors had been discussed in the therapy group, and nor had the abusive childhood she suffered. It was crucial, then, to clarify Hilary's feelings and memories. Embarrassed by her own self-destructive behaviour and trapped by financial pressures, Hilary was socially isolated. Her only solace was walking her dog. Hilary's habits had narrowed as she was stripped of economic, interpersonal power.*

All too often, psychotherapy focuses almost entirely on the individual. It assumes that psychological processes are simply internal, somehow residing wholly within the person. This is arguably an example of psychology putting its own interests first, in an ill-informed way. For Hilary, this had meant talking about her feelings in the psychotherapy group. Clarifying and understanding the significance of emotions is certainly crucial to wellbeing. However, this is much more likely to be meaningful when emotions are connected with actions, and are set in their social, material and historical circumstances: outsight, not insight. In the individual sessions, Hilary described the desperation and struggle she faced trying to reduce her debts. She talked about the material and emotional entrapment she confronted as a nightmare repeat of her abusive childhood. Her relative lack of influence over her situation – her disempowerment – informed how she understood her frantic efforts to establish control by inflicting self-harm. Habits had formed that were both relieving and ensnaring, restricting any possible consideration of new interests.

Tentatively, the possibility of developing social contacts was raised. Eventually, Hilary struck up conversations with another dog walker, who later became a trusted friend. She also began to make social media contact with other folks in similar circumstances – a source of comfort, reassurance and encouragement. Then, over time, she started to apply for alternative employment. From a social materialist perspective, therapeutic attention was switched away from the supposedly individual internal realm to the world of social contacts and material resources – the real public world, with its possibilities of experiencing respect and valued, trusted engagement.

Of course, more typical psychological concepts were also considered. Following further clarification of Hilary's memories and of the ways she talked about herself, behavioural routines were discussed, the meanings of her feelings of anxiety were reflected upon, and the ubiquitous concept of confidence was deconstructed. But all of these were always understood within a social, material and historical framework that recognised the impress of forces that mitigate against wellbeing.

Through this process, Hilary was able, over time, to increase influence over her life, develop affiliations and acquire a sense of value, purpose and meaning. This came from finding a more rewarding, slightly better paid job, from striking up friendships, and from making tentative plans for a more independent future. Hilary's work became more secure and provided valuable experiences of meaning and acceptance by others through her supportive, caring role with elderly folk. Regarding the key reason for referral, Hilary now avoided the destructive cycle of self-harming. She recognised the possibility of occasionally resorting to such harmful behaviours but said that the intense and overwhelming urge to harm herself, as a desperate recourse to relief and control, was no longer there. Hilary was last seen at a six-month follow up appointment; the encouraging developments had consolidated, and she remained hopeful of establishing permanent changes. We can see that attending to Hilary's interests, while tentatively connecting with social and material opportunities, gave her the possibility to consider new interests and potential future access to at least some forms of power.

Joe's story

Neoliberal culture espouses values of independence and individualism. However, quite conveniently, it overlooks the impress of social institutions and structural inequalities that mitigate against these same values of self-reliance. This dilemma lies at the heart of Joe's story.

> *At 25, Joe considered life had already passed him by. He came from an early disrupted family home and, bullied and threatened throughout adolescence, he had missed his rite of passage into adulthood. Now he felt suspended in a meaningless state and was contemplating suicide.*
>
> *Initially, therapy clarified Joe's history and his isolated social circumstances. Joe described how feelings of fear and anxiety rendered future options seemingly impossible, making the very notion of 'having a life', in the present or the future, meaningless. Indeed, Joe was disconnected from any meaningful social contact, and spent most of his time alone, in his room. While therapy was a comfort, it became clearer and clearer that the chance to secure peer acceptance, to join a community, and to acquire a shared identity would be more helpful.*

> But Joe could only see one option, and attempted to take his own life. He was found in a remote setting by the police and then admitted to a psychiatric ward under section. Joe was trapped by his feelings and memories, and this resulted in power being stripped away from him.
>
> On the ward, Joe felt angry and resentful that his attempt to kill himself had been thwarted. Simultaneously, his long-standing fears resulted in his feeling isolated and imprisoned. Attempts by staff to support Joe were spurned, because they were perceived as insensitive and patronising. Here we can see the familiar occurrence of clashes of interests between services and people hoping to be helped by them. So, when Joe was then left alone by the ward staff for most of the day, it was the other relatively young men and women on the ward who struck up conversations with him.
>
> At first apprehensive, Joe gradually accepted their offers of company. Initially dismissing their offers to socialise, in a very short time Joe came to respect and value their acceptance of him. It wasn't that long before Joe, witnessing discourtesies shown by staff towards his new acquaintances, felt compelled to speak up at ward meetings. This in turn furthered the respect and standing he was getting from his fellow service users. Joe not only started to develop interests, but also to use several subtle forms of power. Before long, Joe developed a friendship with one particular person, which some months later evolved into a trusting intimate relationship. Somewhat ironically, in this most unlikely of settings, Joe now experienced acceptance by his peer group. He contributed a respected, valued role, and at the same time learned to trust and enjoy an intimate relationship.

The impoverished environment of Joe's early years and the marginalisation and bullying he encountered in his teens had left no opportunities for him to engage with life in meaningful ways. Therapeutically, clarifying the impact of such social and material influences is crucial on several levels. It sets the scene, enabling each of us to piece together the origins of our distress. At the same time, it counters prevailing dominant explanations, be they psychiatric or psychotherapeutic, that emphasise inner faults or limitations residing within: it invalidates coercive bullying tactics. Over time, clarifying the impact of social and material forces can help people to feel open to the possibility of future alternative settings beyond the limited experiences hitherto encountered.

Despite the hugely significant improvements in Joe's mental health that occurred during his time on the ward, reports cautioned against the very source of Joe's growing social ease. Rather than noting the encouraging increases in activities, social contact and general ability to interact, ward staff reported concerns that Joe was acting inappropriately. To some extent, staff were justifiably concerned about Joe's unwillingness to engage with them, while readily engaging with the other younger folk on the ward. However, what can also be seen is the impress of social institutions: a psychiatric ward attempting to exert softcop power, and in so doing adding to the alienation previously experienced by Joe.

Nevertheless, Joe was discharged relatively soon after striking up friendships on the ward. He has continued to stay in touch with several people and, alongside his partner, has made significant improvements in visiting and engaging in social events. Opportunities are arising to develop his interests, and as he experiences his new interpersonal power, there may be opportunities to form new habits. Joe is now looking for employment so, with luck, will improve his economic power. Joe has even said that, in retrospect, 'being sectioned was the best thing that ever happened to me'. In the rather unlikely circumstances of a psychiatric admission ward, Joe had the good fortune to experience a form of social contact with peers that embraced feelings of trust and respect.

From a social materialist perspective, Joe gained feelings of confidence and acceptance by experiencing actual solidarity and a collective sense of belonging. For the first time, he was able to talk things over with peers, while also being respected and valued by them. Over time and with the supportive company of friends, Joe managed to leave his home and joined a number of social groups. While still experiencing some anxiety, he no longer felt a prisoner in his own home and, most importantly, no longer considered that life was happening elsewhere and without him. No amount of conversations with Joe that were focused solely on the dubious concepts of self-confidence or self-esteem would have ever achieved such outcomes. The intervention here largely involved clarifying, supporting and encouraging a social dynamic that emerged independently.

These two examples – Hilary and Joe – both show how it is possible to provide helpful individual therapy informed by social materialist thinking. Again, this is not a matter of technique, of following a set of instructions, of applying a template or sticking to a formula. We are not suggesting this orientation is exclusive to a social materialist psychology.[6] Rather, it simply and more transparently involves being sensitive to the real constraints, difficulties and potentials of clients, using social materialist concepts to understand their psychological aspects, and working with people to help them use any powers and resources they actually have at their disposal.

---

6. In systemic approaches, for example, John Burnham's 'problems, possibilities, resources, restraints' model can also fulfil a similar function. See: www.cfssw.org/sites/default/files/atoms/files/problems_possibilities_resources_restraints_a_versatile_pprractice_map_by_john_burnham.pdf

Beyond traditional therapy

So individual therapy can sometimes be helpful, despite both its limitations and its over-selling. But the high profile attached to its practices can sometimes mean that useful alternatives are overlooked. One set of innovative alternatives that are compatible with social materialist psychology were formulated in a book by clinical psychologist Guy Holmes (2010).

Holmes' book describes a number of novel initiatives aimed at bringing groups of people together in everyday settings, typically with shared interests, to comment on and learn from one another. The groups were facilitated gently and unobtrusively. Participants were encouraged to suspend their assumptions, and to view other group members, whether colleagues or peers, as equals. As Holmes puts it:

> I encourage everyone to offer ideas, thoughts, reflections, personal stories 'out to the group' where we might each hold them 'suspended in front of us'; where we can 'play' with and critique ideas (not critique the person who offered them); where we can see how they interact with and perhaps challenge some of our own beliefs and ways of seeing ourselves and the world. And at some point (perhaps during or at the end of the session) we might allow ourselves to absorb some of these new ideas. (2010, p.24)

Groups were set up to discuss topics such as toxic mental environments, thinking about medication, and understanding ourselves and others. In a group called 'Black Dog', collective critiques of the concept of depression were shared, and explanations for why people experience profound misery (including responses to oppression) were considered. There was also a writing group.

At its heart, this approach is about 'doing things with, rather than to or for, other people' (Holmes, 2010, p.3). Rather than focusing on therapy, it emphasises the importance of people coming together, in non-institutional settings, recognising they have similar interests in real matters of life, and supporting and learning from one another. While not set up as therapy groups, from a social materialist perspective, they were therapeutic because they promoted wellbeing by encouraging feelings of empathy and belonging in a non-stigmatised way; because they fostered outsight, and (to some extent) because they provided safe spaces where new possibilities and different ways of being – alternative stories and perspectives, new habits of reacting – might be rehearsed. The groups exemplify an open, real world-oriented and modest approach to psychology, including a reflexivity that encourages us to be more open and explicit about our failures as well as successes.

Community psychology

In addition to working with individuals and small groups, clinical psychologists can work at a community level. This, too, can be compatible with a social materialist approach. Community psychology aspires to promote better environments and greater opportunities for equality. Simultaneously, the approach is committed to justice and freedom. Community psychology promotes the prevention of distress and the development of wellbeing by using shared, collective resources and creating joint initiatives. In part it is a response to mainstream psychology, which as we have seen is premised on concepts and practices that locate both the origins of and the proposed solutions to distress almost entirely within the individual.

Instead, community psychology recognises the importance of the many interlocking social and material circumstances that individuals find themselves in. These include relationships, families, friendships, and societal, educational and occupational settings. All of these settings are enmeshed with each other, and threaded through by cultural, political and ideological beliefs, practices and ways of speaking (discourses) – and by their related forms of power and influence (Orford, 2008; Prilleltensky, 1997). This means that salient principles of community psychology include working with communities as well as individuals; encouraging collaborative, participative involvement of individuals and communities; promoting strengths; acknowledging the significant influences of housing, income and social circumstances, as well as histories; emphasising prevention; a commitment to devolving professional power; recognising social injustices, and engaging in action to overcome pathologies in services.

Whereas mainstream psychology pays scant attention to the political, ideological and cultural circumstances within which it operates (with the consequence that it often reproduces their assumptions), community psychology acknowledges the over-arching influence of distal powers (Burton & Kagan, 2005; Martin-Baro, 1994; Montero & Sonn, 2009). Indeed, an important source for community psychology is the liberation theology, psychology and community education and participation scholarship of Central and Latin America – particularly the work of Martin-Baro, a Jesuit who lived and worked among the oppressed peoples of El Salvador (Martin-Baro, 1994). He identified three basic principles for community psychology. First, from the voices of the oppressed, ways can be fostered to seek truth. Second, by creating new psychological practices, we can transform both people and societies in ways that acknowledge their denied potential. And third, by de-centring psychology's preoccupation with its own scientific status (in other words, by rejecting positivism in favour of a more sophisticated way of using and analysing evidence), we can encourage it to devote itself to the problems of oppressed majorities.

For Martin-Baro, what he called de-ideologisation – helping people to better understand the nature and effects of the social circumstances in which they live – was critically important if psychology was to be taken seriously: the discipline could not and cannot remain impartial in the face of injustice. He called for a psychological praxis that is transforming and liberating – one that encourages grassroots movements to come together, sharing their experiences and knowledge and developing ways to overcome the oppressive powers that constrain their lives. This, Martin-Baro argued, should be a pressing engagement for psychology.

Another important influence on community psychology is the work of Brazilian educator and philosopher Paolo Freire (Freire, 1993). Freire critically assessed established educational settings and their associated practices, and argued that much of the current educational system serves to train people to fit into the existing social order: there is no such thing as a neutral education. Under capitalism, Freire said, education can be compared to banking, because its scope of action is largely restricted to 'receiving, filing and storing the deposits' of knowledge (Freire, 1993, p.53).

To counter this, Freire advocated the need to first 'unlearn' what is accepted as current established knowledge. He encouraged people and communities to come together and, through mutually supportive conversations, question the sources of historical domination and oppression over their lives. Through these discussions, people engaged in a process he called 'conscientization': raising awareness of how their lives are structured and distorted by the demands of capitalism, and realising their own collective power to begin changing their circumstances. Freire also argued that truly human knowledge emerges only through invention and re-invention, through restless, impatient, hopeful enquiry with the world and with each other. Such a process of 'critical pedagogy', he proposed, could create both frameworks and structures for transformational change, and offer liberation from extant forms of oppression.

In different ways, then, both Freire and Martin-Baro question the role and purpose of mainstream psychology, pointing to its ideological function and its complicity with various forms of oppression. Both their analyses show how psychology can potentially be so much more than a tool for softcops, and how, instead of individualism and subjectivism, it can offer engagement, participation, education and action. Yet we should never underestimate the determination of the rich and powerful to preserve the existing order of injustices and inequalities that benefits them. In 1989, Martin-Baro (along with colleagues, a rectory worker and a family member) was assassinated by a

Salvadorean death squad funded and trained by the US.[7] In the ensuing years, the numerous community initiatives in Brazil inspired by Freire's teachings have been unable to prevent the rise of an extreme right-wing government, as populist as it is repellent.

While community psychology does not exist as a profession in the UK, the past three decades have witnessed many projects that draw on its principles and from which practitioners might learn. Most have been undertaken by either NHS clinical psychologists or psychologists in academic settings, working alongside communities seeking ways to prevent or mitigate distress in the localities in which they work and live. Initiatives have focused on identifying inner-city neighbour health concerns (Bostock, 1998); the NHS and community psychology (Bostock & Diamond, 2005; Diamond, 1998); child and family neighbourhood projects (Harris, 2014); men's health issues (Melluish & Bulmer, 1999); research participation (Fals-Borda, 1987); employment, health and housing issues (Fryer, 1992; Fryer, & Fagan, 2003); women's health and co-operative support systems (Holland, 1992; Kagan et al., 2005); housing & health (Edge et al., 2004; Kagan, 2007), and mental health and community groups (Holmes, 2010). While these examples need to be understood within the particular local contexts where they took place (because their successes and failures occurred within the communities where they were initiated), looking across them it is possible to elicit some general principles. These include:[8]

- supporting people with similar experiences to come together
- sharing key information and advice about activist networks and resources, for example, and recognising that some of it may be missing, neglected, or suppressed
- creating spaces for reflection and dissension that help local people develop *their own* accounts of their struggles.

As ever, though, caution is required. While impoverished and stigmatised communities can harbour strengths and resources invisible to onlookers, they can also be prone to civic indifference and to internal conflict, extending even – or especially – to how they view their collective problems. One thing that such polities *do* often share is a history of political mismanagement and official neglect, giving their constituents good reason to mistrust well-meaning

---

7. See https://theconversation.com/liberation-psychology-why-an-idea-from-the-salvadorean-struggle-is-relevant-today-94432

8. For those wanting to learn more about community psychology theory and praxis, two excellent sources are *Critical Community Psychology: Critical action and social change* (Kagan et al., 2019) and *Psychology of Liberation: Theory and applications* (Montero & Sonn, 2009).

outsiders who see themselves as agents of change.⁹ When practitioners fail to listen and to understand, they are unlikely to secure the communal participation and ownership that should be the hallmarks of their work. Indeed, the success of a given project may depend on unusually well-placed and perhaps charismatic individuals, ready to confront entrenched power. And, as we have argued throughout this book, none of us can altogether ignore an appeal – or a threat – to our own interests. In a competitive world where funding for community projects is scarce, how comfortable can it ever be for the psychologist to argue with the king who pays the shilling?¹⁰

Moreover, it is all too easy for collaboration to slide into appropriation and control, when professionals start to claim hard-won local expertise as their own. This hazard was first highlighted by the social philosopher Ivan Illich (2001b), when he called for prudence and humility from would-be helpers. In the subsequent decades, many incisive analyses of community interventions across the world suggest the persistence of this problem (Cooke & Kothari, 2001; Davis, 2006; Earnshaw, 2008). More fundamentally, some critics argue that the quality of outcome research in the field seldom sustains the assertions of the practitioners, or of the communities that they claim to represent.¹¹

With these cautions firmly in mind, community psychology offers a framework of values and a set of priorities and practices that could enable psychologists to understand some of the tensions that persist in their work. It also opens up possibilities for working beyond the reactive, reductionist role currently promoted as psychological practice (Kagan & Burton, 2001). We wonder what a psychology might look like that embraced these values while moving away from a focus on the individual and notions of independence

---

9. Lisa McKenzie's *Getting By*, an ethnography of life on a impoverished housing estate in Nottingham, UK, offers some powerful and nuanced insights (McKenzie, 2015). See, also, Hanley's *Estates. An intimate history* (2008) for a revealing biography that shows how the experience of growing up on a working-class housing estate can shape the psychology of the most resilient of individuals and families, and Robins' *Tarnished Visions* (1993) for a gripping report of how painful divisions within a community cannot always be resolved through the agency of a grassroots project, no matter how credible and humane.

10. For a perhaps unusually forthright discussion of the conflicts of interest that paid professionals can face in the field of community work, see, for instance, Melluish & Bulmer (1999). See also the thoughtful discussion of community psychology by Holmes in Chapter 9 of Moloney's (2013) *The Therapy Industry*.

11. Wide-ranging political and methodological critiques of the research adduced to demonstrate the success of community interventions by community psychologists and professionals of varying stripes – deploying the same kinds of concepts and methods as those deployed by many community psychologists – can be found, for example, in Davis's (2006) *Planet of Slums*, Epstein's (2019) *Psychotherapy and the Social Clinic in the United States* and his (2010) *Democracy Without Decency*. More specifically, some community psychologists focus on helping communities to rebuild or strengthen the mutual connections or 'social capital' that define them by a process of education, persuasion, inspiration or bargaining – that is, by invoking each participant's capacity for 'rational choice'. However, this approach is dubious, because it downplays the influence of context, habit, tradition and history within civic life. For a fuller discussion, see, for instance, Chaiklin (2011) and McLean et al. (2002).

and free will – a psychological practice that focused on relationships, social structures, political awareness and interdependence.

Woke

Earlier (Chapter 6) we discussed Mark Fisher's argument (2009) that, today, consciousness of alternatives to neoliberalism has been deflated. Not only is it difficult to imagine alternatives to neoliberalism, Fisher said; we simply don't realise the massive extent to which we have already restricted our imaginations.

For the most part, Fisher's argument still rings true. But we also noted the encouraging signs that recently things are, slowly, changing for the better, and that a new, progressive generation of young people now seems to have been formed. These political developments are going hand in hand with changes in consciousness, to the extent that a word to describe these changes has now risen to prominence. The term 'woke' was first used by African-Americans in the 1960s to describe awareness of issues of justice and racial equality.[12] Since 2014, the 'Black Lives Matter' movement has popularised 'woke', and it is now increasingly used to refer to personal awareness of structural causes of social and political injustice.

More recently, 'woke' has also been used in a pejorative sense (particularly online) to describe moralising tendencies associated with so-called identity politics. We reject any such moralising gestures or privileging of identities divorced from circumstances, while also rejecting this perversion of the term's meaning. We use 'woke' only in the original sense of an expansion of awareness associated with a structural analysis of oppression and meaningful political action.

In this sense, the spread of the term reflects how knowledge of the possibility of alternatives to neoliberalism is currently growing. With it, we are seeing a renewed recognition that political change has a psychological dimension. This, in turn, raises the question of whether psychological practices can help achieve or maintain changes in political consciousness. Can woke, in its original sense of increased understanding of the experiential effects of

---

12. Minority black cultures have long emphasised the importance of remaining conscious of oppression and structural discrimination, as a necessary counter to racism. The autobiography of UK rapper and activist Akala (2018), *Natives: Race and class in the ruins of empire*, describes how black people in London set up Saturday schools to overcome the effects of racism in education. And at the level of culture, consider (to take just one example) the opening monologue from a 1979 live recording of Misty in Roots: 'When we trod this land we walked for one reason. The reason is to try to help another man to think for himself. The music of our art is Roots Music. Music which recalls history, because without the knowledge of your history you cannot determine your destiny. Music about the present, because if you're not conscious about the present you're like a cabbage in this society. Music which tells about the future – and the judgement which is to come.' See https://midnightpunk.wordpress.com/2017/03/05/misty-in-roots-live-from-the-counter-eurovision-79/

power and uneven social structures, be deliberately sustained and nurtured? At least some activists seem to think that the answer to this question is 'yes' (Plan C, 2017). They have been experimenting with a political-psychological practice called 'consciousness raising'.

Consciousness raising groups first emerged from the women's movement, as part of the second wave of feminism at the end of the 1960s. Small groups of women began meeting regularly to discuss their lives, relationships and experiences. In these discussions, what had initially appeared to the women as individual issues, such as relationship difficulties, were revealed as shared problems, with institutional or systemic origins. In the words of one woman:

> We assume that our feelings are telling us something from which we can learn... that our feelings mean something worth analyzing... that our feelings are saying something *political*, something reflecting fear that something bad will happen to us or hope, desire, knowledge that something good will happen to us. (Sarachild, 1973)

So, while consciousness-raising groups were established as primarily political rather than psychological initiatives, frequently they took a psychological focus and engaged in (quasi-therapeutic) psychological practices. Perhaps unsurprisingly, then, their influence has already seeped across into the discipline. Clinician Sue Holland's 'From Social Abuse to Social Action' framework (Holland, 1992) reversed the above process by initially meeting women individually and then, after 10 sessions, introducing them into groups to encourage support and practical initiatives (e.g. co-operatives for education, food, social support). Likewise, a qualitative research method in psychology called 'memory work' formalises a practice of collective discourse analysis that is closely related to, and was inspired by, experiences in consciousness-raising groups.[13] In community psychology, Freire's process of conscientization has at least some similarities with consciousness raising.

Today, some of the functions of these groups can be partially fulfilled by social media. In the wake of the acquittal of the killer of Trayvon Martin in 2012, Twitter hashtags associated with Black Lives Matter rose to prominence and began to be widely shared. Similarly, the spread of #MeToo from late 2017 onwards raised awareness of the prevalence of sexual assault among all women. While this is certainly valuable, our social materialist perspective suggests that regular, face-to-face, small-group meetings, in the manner of consciousness-raising groups, can also be helpful. This is especially the case if

---

13. For the original account of the method and its results see Haug (1987) *Female Sexualisation: A collective work of memory*. For a more recent methodological description, see Willig (2001), *Introducing Qualitative Research in Psychology*.

meetings are fairly quickly closed to new people, so that membership becomes stable.

From a social materialist perspective, we would emphasise how small, inclusive and democratic face-to-face meetings can be effective at generating *enduring* feelings of acceptance, empathy and trust. While social media interactions can facilitate such feelings online, the embodied presence of other group members can sustain this shared sociality in ways that are difficult for social media to achieve. These enduring shared feelings, in turn, can counter the angst-ridden individuality of neoliberalism, and are necessary sources of sustenance and reassurance if people are to engage in determined political action.

Whether online or face-to-face, group discussions can reveal the structural character of difficult or shaming experiences; they can provide outsight, or clarification. They can help members understand their experiences in ways that allocate due responsibility to structural or societal influences. As a result, individuals may be able to reconfigure their memories as matters of (for example) class injury, sexism or racial discrimination, rather than personal failing. At the same time, groups can engender confidence in the validity of arguments and feelings that run counter to the mainstream. Knowing that you are not alone in reasoning and feeling as you do is reassuring. If the group is also specifically aligned to a particular political issue or campaign, as were women's consciousness-raising groups, it can benefit from shared interest in addressing this issue. Simultaneously, the solidarity the group provides can itself be a source of collective power with which to campaign and raise issues.

There are also other ways in which broadly psychological ideas and practices, informed by and compatible with social materialism, can contribute to political activity. For example, one of us contributed towards bringing together a city-wide forum of people in Nottingham with an interest in mental health: the Nottingham Mental Health Alliance. The Alliance held monthly meetings in community centres for many years, with the aim of supporting one another over concerns about current mental health services and promoting future meaningful provision. Bringing a broad range of experiences and interests, Alliance members offered one another encouragement and advocacy. Most importantly, the Alliance created a public, independent space for the expression of experiences and ideas that otherwise remained unheard.

In practice, the Alliance developed various interests. It took an active role in contributing to proposed mental health legislation, campaigning for improvements to psychiatric wards and promoting user involvement in numerous settings. Discussions in Alliance meetings encouraged some people to try out a self-help group for people hearing voices, a discussion group on medication, and a psychiatric survivors support group. The Alliance also organised a national conference highlighting the crucial contribution from people with lived experiences of mental health difficulties to our understandings of distress. Subsequently, several additional conferences were organised that encouraged perspectives and experiences that questioned dominant discourses in mental health (Coles et al., 2013).

While all these endeavours are modest attempts to promote alternative accounts to the dominant oppressive roles in mental health services, we argue that it is essential for psychology to acknowledge and act on the tensions that exist when working in such environments. If the profession of psychology is to be taken seriously in the future, it must incorporate within the discipline the ability to bring about open spaces that encourage reflective, critical perspectives that will, over time, enable constructive means to promote dignity, justice and equality.

And finally… the Midlands Psychology Group

Throughout this book we have acknowledged the critically important function and effect of interest. As we have seen, interest describes how we are pulled by social and material circumstances to act or speak in certain ways because doing so might be to our own advantage. This is how interest smooths the operation of power. We believe that acknowledging and reflecting on interest is essential for psychology to retain intellectual rigour, and to develop (relative) freedom from the established order. It is necessary if we are not to simply reproduce ideas and customs that maintain inequalities and injustices. We encourage all psychologists to retain an element of critical reflection in their work that opens up intellectual and practical spaces for ideas beyond current concepts (Diamond, 2008).

So, in closing this book, it seems fitting to briefly reflect on ourselves. Writing this book has been very challenging – perhaps more than some of us anticipated at the start. It turns out that collectively writing a book-length manuscript is exponentially more difficult than producing a journal paper in that way! At the same time, it has developed our collective thinking and our joint skills of researching, writing and debating. Emotionally, it has brought us closer together.

It has also helped us to appreciate that, in effect, the Midlands Psychology Group itself functions, in part, as a consciousness-raising group. In the group, we share difficult experiences, as well as joy. We have opportunities to reflect on our many collective privileges – not to castigate or make ourselves feel guilty, but to increase our awareness. We gain strength and confidence from checking out our arguments and ideas with each other, and from having our feelings validated. We discuss important psychological questions, in between drinking tea and coffee and eating biscuits. And we bemoan the state of the world, while frequently laughing at ourselves and each other. The death of David Smail in 2014 was a great loss, but at that difficult time the group itself was a source of considerable solace. In short, we each have an interest in the group: it supports us in our individual working lives; it encourages us to question oppressive practices and to be suspicious of glib solutions, and it provides a valuable source of power since, when we speak and write in its name, we know that we do not do so alone.

For many years, then, the Midlands Psychology Group has helped us, its members, to sustain and develop a distinct psychological and political perspective. Women's consciousness-raising groups were local, small, democratic and self-organising. They often sprang from personal relationships among women (who initially met in work, at college, or at the school gates, dropping off their children). The Midlands Psychology Group similarly sprang from a small number of personal relationships – in our case, mostly initially facilitated by David Smail. Our group has self-organised outside of the institutions – psychology services, academic departments – where we work. This has partly happened through necessity (pressure of time), but also out of growing recognition that only by meeting outside of the workplace can we transcend its many impositions. It has been self-organising and democratic (we have no hierarchy), if perhaps not entirely local (currently we are spread across the East and West Midlands, and Dublin).

So we would like to end with a plea. If you have found this book useful, by all means share and discuss it with others. Use it in your practice if you are a psychologist, social worker or counsellor. Share it with others if you are a student of psychology. And use it to reflect if your primary interest has been to better understand your own experiences.

But please, don't stop there.

Because we want to emphasise that anyone could do what we have done. You too can seek out like-minded others to form a group. You too can gain solace, confidence and comfort from meeting with trusted others. You can learn to collectively self-organise – to arrange meetings, take notes, agree actions. You can form a group that educates its members about each other's values and ideas, that questions taken-for-granted truths, and that begins to identify viable alternatives. In those ways, you too can work towards a better psychology, and a better world.

Chapter 10

Postscript: WTF 2020

In this book, we have argued that social and material circumstances, arranged in relations of power, are the primary influences on psychology. We have explained how these power relations are associated with the ideology of neoliberalism, and shown how mainstream psychology is not only compatible with but actively benefits from this ideology.

We were in the final stages of writing this book at the end of 2019 when the first reports began to emerge from China of a new and deadly coronavirus. By March 2020, Covid-19 had spread across the world, causing thousands of deaths and prompting governments to initiate lockdowns to slow the rate of infection and prevent health services being overwhelmed. In the UK, lockdown was accompanied by levels of state intervention unprecedented in recent decades, including a government scheme to pay 80% of the wages of workers whose jobs were suspended or furloughed.

Some saw these levels of state intervention, and in particular the furlough scheme, as signalling the end of neoliberalism. So, does this mean that all we have said about neoliberalism in this book is now irrelevant? In this postscript we explain why this is far from the case.

Writing about the Covid-19 pandemic is peculiarly difficult. As we write, the pandemic is still ongoing, so we do not have the clarity of hindsight. And while hundreds of peer-reviewed papers have been published about coronavirus from the medical and biological sciences, social scientific and psychological papers are so far mostly lacking. The government has promised an inquiry into the handling of the pandemic but (as of now) this will not even begin for many months. So a complete and authoritative assessment of the economic, political, health and social impacts of the pandemic is yet to be conducted. It nevertheless seems clear that the UK has not done well, and that this is largely due to many years of so-called austerity and to continuing commitments to certain elements of neoliberal ideology.

During the first lockdown from March 2020, there was considerable speculation that the coronavirus pandemic would produce enduring and positive social and economic changes. The environmental impact of greatly reduced traffic was widely noted in approving terms, accompanied by calls for more permanent changes (Muhammad et al., 2020). Commentators also hypothesised that the pandemic could cause a permanent shift towards homeworking (Hern, 2020), reconfigure the travel industry on a more sustainable footing (Dunford, 2020), and perhaps even create a new working class (Khazan, 2020).

In economic terms, the government scheme to fund 80% of the wages of workers temporarily unable to work was seen as highly significant. State intervention on this scale - amounting to the temporary nationalisation of much of the economy – is fundamentally at odds with neoliberalism. With this in mind, sociologist and political economist Will Davies described the pandemic as 'the sort of world-making event that allows for new economic and intellectual beginnings'. Characterising the government scheme as 'astonishing', he noted that, 'Such unthinkable measures are suddenly possible – and that sense of possibility may not be easily foreclosed again' (Davies, 2020a).

This renewed sense of possibility was amplified by a surge in community activism and solidarity. Early in the pandemic, people began gathering outside their homes at 8pm every Thursday evening to applaud NHS staff and other essential workers. For some, this weekly ritual engendered momentary, shared feelings of solidarity and compassion. Relatedly, epidemiologists Richard Wilkinson and Kate Pickett (2020) noted approvingly the rise in community cohesion signalled by local WhatsApp groups, more and friendlier casual conversations with passers-by, and the overwhelming response to a call for volunteers to assist the NHS in supporting the vulnerable. These responses, they said, were typical of more equal countries rather than the grossly unequal UK.

Such widespread community level changes have obvious potentials to support political action. As an article on an activist website rhetorically asked: 'With 1,500 mutual aid groups set up in a matter of days, will things ever be the same again?' (Rosa, 2020). For many commentators, sadly, it seems that the answer to this hopeful question is, 'No – but they could easily get worse.'

While the social cohesion mobilised to combat the pandemic had positive aspects, as the first lockdown began to be eased in June 2020 it was already being predicted that:

> Social bonds and common purpose are likely to be a short-lived experience. We can already see that the poor, the insecurely employed and those in essential employment are exposed. Public transport was quickly over-filled and is likely to boost infection rates. The right-wing

press baited school workers worried about returning to their jobs. (Atkinson, 2020)

The coronavirus itself is blind, unprejudiced, insensate, barely able even to meet most criteria for life (Brown, 2016), but the human world in which it circulates, reproduces and mutates is structured by entrenched hierarchies of inequality that regulate its spread, moderate its effects, and influence the strategies deployed to combat it. As restrictions started being lifted it was observed that:

> Teleworking professionals and people with personal drivers clamoured loudest for the mass to get back to work and restore a tanking economy that risked lower investor returns. There has been a strong sense of class that thrives on the labour and risks of the weakest. (Atkinson, 2020)

With respect to the supposed break with neoliberalism, political theorist Alex Doherty (2020) reminds us that the 2008 financial crash failed to derail this ideology. At that time, too, massive state intervention (the bailouts provided to the banking sector) prevented capitalism from collapsing. Yet once the immediate crisis was over, neoliberal ideology quickly re-emerged. In a similar vein, he suggests, the Johnson government's funding of 80% of workers wages was explicitly time-limited:

> ... in order to swiftly return to 'normal' and wean the public off their 'addiction' to state support. The government's frustrated desire to curtail the furlough scheme, and the clear opposition to implementing a universal basic income, indicate a commitment to maintaining the core of neoliberal welfare policy. This means opposing generous, non-means-tested payments, which neoliberals view as detrimental to fostering entrepreneurial activity and disciplining the workforce. (Doherty, 2020)

Indeed, Doherty went on to note the disturbing possibility that the coronavirus pandemic could be used to further legitimate the designation of some groups and populations, migrants for example, as 'disposable'. As he put it:

> In a context of ballooning national debt, where migrant populations are being treated as vectors of disease, it's not difficult to see how an exclusionary neoliberal politics that supports investment in certain populations and disinvestment in others could gain traction. (Doherty, 2020)

History shows that there is clear potential for the Covid-19 pandemic to function in this manner. Fear of foreigners has long been justified on the grounds that they are 'dirty', the bearers of disease and impurity. In fact, fear in general tends to be associated more frequently with nationalist and protectionist tendencies than with progressive agendas (Wodak, 2015). Notably, former US president Donald Trump consistently characterised Covid-19 as a 'Chinese virus', while Hungary's extreme nationalist leader Victor Orban said:

> We are fighting a two-front war... one front is called migration and the other one belongs to the coronavirus. There is a logical connection between the two as both spread with movement. (Earle, 2020)

In this context, even something as superficially harmless and uplifting as the Thursday 8pm round of applause for NHS and other frontline workers had more sinister connotations. Not only was it swiftly co-opted by advertisers and cynically colonised by politicians known more for their hostility to the NHS; not only did it gloss over failures to provide adequate personal protective equipment for frontline staff, and adequate pay and appropriate resources; for some, it might also have functioned as a rehearsal of exclusionary, nationalist sentiments (Davies, 2020b).

To see this nationalism at work, consider how the centrality to the government of the NHS (as *brand*, totem, symbol, rather than well-funded service) was signalled, quite literally, by the slogan 'Stay home, protect the NHS, save lives'. Consider, too, how 100-year-old war veteran Tom Moore's NHS fundraising was lauded by the tabloid press, honoured by the Queen, and led to his birthday being marked by a fly-past of World War II fighter planes. Both examples show the profundity of the ideological work going on: to deflect attention from the death rates and the government's failures; to foster the illusion that a decade of so-called austerity had not significantly damaged the NHS (Lawrence et al., 2020); to engender and reinforce organisations of feeling that associate heroism, pride and courage with icons of nationalism rather than the efforts and sacrifices of ordinary people.

Some predict that the coronavirus pandemic could have other long-term adverse consequences. Author Naomi Klein is known for writing about the 'shock doctrine'. This is the thesis that the rich and powerful exploit crises (and sometimes engineer them) to accomplish economic and social changes that, in ordinary times, would be seen as unacceptable. Applying this insight to the coronavirus pandemic, Klein presents evidence that technology-sector billionaires such as Eric Schmidt, chair and major shareholder of the company that owns Google, are using the pandemic to legitimate and advance high-tech initiatives that will increase their profits even further (Klein, 2020). Her argument is not that technology should have no part to play in resolving the pandemic; rather, that the crisis is allowing the rich and powerful to circumvent democratic checks and balances and to avoid scrutiny of proposed new surveillance infrastructures with profound human rights implications. Similarly, there have been predictions that billionaire venture capitalists will exploit the crisis, and the political and material changes it has wrought, to further bypass or even undermine the power of nation states (Slobodian, 2020).

Whatever the eventual truth of such predictions, it is already apparent that Covid-19 will have a massive economic impact, and that the under-25s will be particularly adversely affected (Major & Machin, 2020). The furlough scheme alone had cost an estimated £100 billion by December 2020 (Wallace et al., 2020). To this must be added the costs of lost tax revenue, increased unemployment, and delayed or cancelled investment, particularly in sectors such as hospitality, travel and higher education. So, government debt will massively increase in the coming years, making more savage cuts to public spending likely.

Conclusion

Where does all this leave us?

In terms of politics, the future is undecided. It seems safe to say, though, that whatever happens in the coming years will at the very least be shaped by neoliberalism: just as the background to the pandemic was shaped by it; just as the government's coronavirus response was shaped by it, and just as the pandemic's distribution of illness and mortality, such that poorer, disadvantaged, black and minority ethnic people were disproportionately affected, was cumulatively shaped by decades of neoliberal policy decisions.

Neoliberalism was never entirely new – it was always a rejuvenation or intensification of certain aspects of existing capitalism. In the coming years, government rhetoric about 'levelling up' (driven by interest in maintaining newly recruited Conservative voters, especially in the north of England) might well drive some small changes to economic policy, some minor geographical reshuffling of government departments, and some token investment in infrastructure projects outside of London. But the government is not about to ditch capitalism for a more thoroughly equitable, less exploitative economic model. Nor is it likely to make big businesses and the very wealthy foot most of the bill for the pandemic.

Besides, and as we have shown, neoliberal ideology has proved very useful to the rich and powerful. So they are unlikely to entirely reject it now, simply because other strategies were also needed during the pandemic. Hence we expect still to see tendencies toward privatisation, emphases on individualism and personal responsibility, and practices of scapegoating marginalised and disadvantaged groups. The use of psychological techniques, methods and knowledge – exemplified by work in behavioural economics and the social policy strategies pioneered by the Conservative government's so-called 'nudge unit' or Behavioural Insights Team – also seems likely to continue.

Overall, it seems inevitable that, without determined resistance, UK government policies will continue to increasingly favour the rich and powerful. Inequality will grow, exploitation will intensify, and climate change will continue to accelerate. Yet these actualities will be denied, downplayed and excused. Our collective interests in resolving them will be prevented from coalescing by 'culture wars' that work primarily on identities. The prospect of regaining a collective sense of purpose founded in shared social and economic interest – glimpsed during the Corbyn years and experienced briefly by some during the pandemic – will once again recede. Should this occur, then the mass of ordinary people will pay the price. Increased misery, decreased life expectancy, sharpened social divisions and a climate crisis considerably nearer to the point of no return will be amongst the costs.

Ultimately, whether these outcomes occur is a matter for political struggle, not speculation. Achieving a more equitable future will be challenging but is far from impossible. Nearly 80 years ago the Beveridge report concluded that a decent society could only be achieved by eradicating the 'five giants' of want, disease, ignorance, squalor and idleness (Timmins, 1995). Today, in the shadow of Covid-19, the provision of health, education, housing, meaningful occupation and access to resources for all are still essential constituents of a decent civil society. With this in mind, the disproportionate impact of Covid-19 on the under-25s could further accelerate their progressive radicalisation, helping build a critical mass for change (Milburn, 2020).

Finally, in terms of this book, all this shows that, while social and material circumstances are important drivers of psychological phenomena, their influence is consistently recruited by interests manipulated by the operation of power (the continued dominance of capitalism requires continuous effort). It shows how the reality we experience is a social and material reality: a dynamic hybrid simultaneously constituted from feelings, language and memory (and the habits that organise them), as well as from material, cultural and historical actualities. And this reality is contested, such that the dominant meanings of its material elements – viruses, mortality rates, election results, wealth inequalities, health inequalities, homelessness – are the emergent, somewhat unstable outcomes of power dynamics.

So, any psychology that does not take account of power and interest is incomplete. But in order to adequately consider power and interest, we must consider *both* the feelings, language, memories and habits that transmit their influence *and* the social and material circumstances that they reflect, and that those in power are always trying to arrange for their own benefit.

If the task is to build on the key lessons of the Covid pandemic and work toward a more equal and sustainable society, we must focus our attention unwaveringly on the world around us – and especially on the rich and powerful and the harmful systems that they uphold. Living as we do on an unstable and fast-changing planet, this effort will face not just the enmity of these privileged groups and those who pursue common cause with them, but the contingencies of time, place, environmental upheaval and technological change. In such circumstances the pursuit of outsight cannot guarantee the creation of a better world, but it would be a good start.

The Midlands Psychology Group
June 2021

Appendix 1

Draft manifesto for a social materialist psychology of distress

This draft manifesto was written in 2011–2012, after our group had been meeting for approximately eight years. In many ways, it is the foundational document in which most of the material for this book was first articulated. It distils the essence of ideas that we had been debating, discussing, formulating and writing about during this time.

It was very much a group co-production in which all of our voices are clearly present – including that of David Smail, who was central to its completion. It was published in 2012, in the *Journal of Critical Psychology, Counselling and Psychotherapy* (12(2), pp.93–107). Following publication, and some of the subsequent interest expressed and feedback received, we decided to take on the challenge of producing a more comprehensive version. Ultimately, that led to this book.

When reading the draft manifesto, you will notice that it contains (in summary form) many of the core arguments made here. However, in the book we locate those arguments more explicitly with respect to neoliberalism and its consequences. This may help readers to relate their own lived experience – as persons, as workers, as distressed people – to the more abstract ideas presented in the manifesto. We hope that this strengthens our arguments and makes them more convincing.

We reprint it here, in its entirety, with kind permission of the journal editor, Craig Newnes.

Draft manifesto for a social materialist psychology of distress

This paper explains the shared background and working practices of the authors; identifies the main assumptions of a social materialist psychology, and sets out a manifesto showing what it might mean to consider distress from a social materialist perspective.

What follows is aimed in part, but not exclusively, at people in the Psy professions who seldom have any other vocabulary in which to talk about these issues outside of psychiatry on the one hand, and talking therapy on the other. The article marshals a wide range of theory and research on the kinds of misery that get treated by mental health professionals.

We are a group of psychologists: clinical, counselling and academic. We have been meeting regularly since 2003. We call ourselves social materialist psychologists. This is not necessarily a formally worked-out philosophical stance. Most psychology is individual and idealist. It takes the individual as a given unit of analysis, and treats the social as a somewhat optional and often uniform context. And, in what is still at root a Cartesian move, it treats the material world as straightforwardly present, but simultaneously subordinate to the immaterial cognitions by which we reflect upon it.

It is by contrast to this that our psychology is social materialist. Social because we affirm the primacy of the social, of collectivity, relationality and community, because we acknowledge that individuals are thoroughly social: ontogenetically, in their origins, and continuously and non-optionally during their existence. And material because we acknowledge that the cognitions by which we reflect upon the world do not simply float free of its affordances, character and properties. Cognition is both social and material, rooted in the ring-fenced metacognitive resources we have acquired, the embodied capacities it recruits, and the resources and subjective possibilities our world supplies (Johnson, 2007; Tolman, 1994; Vygotsky, 1962).

By social materialist psychology, then, we do not mean to imply a mere inverse reflection of the mainstream, a negation, a futile rush to its polar opposite. Individuals exist, but their experiences are thoroughly social, at the very same time as they are singular and personal. And cognitions occur, but their relation to the material world is neither determinate nor arbitrary. Our social materialist psychology is therefore aligned – in sentiment, if not content – with other contemporary initiatives that similarly refuse the naïve separations of individual and social, experience and materiality: psychosocial studies, studies of subjectivity, process philosophy, the turns to language and to affect. In each of these perspectives (and more besides) we find resources, echoes and inspirations.

We write as we act: collectively. In this, we align ourselves with a tradition of psychologists (Curt, 1994), political theorists and activists (The Free Association, 2011), writers and artists (Home, 1991) who reject in practice the notion that ideas are simply the achievement of individuals. At a moment when collectivity, solidarity and mutual trust are so sorely needed, this simple act may take on significances beyond the pages within which it appears.

This manifesto is unfinished, a work in progress, a direction rather than a destination. We hope you find the ideas useful. Moreover it may inspire you to join with like-minded others, and spend time sharing ideas and interests as we continue to do.

1. Persons are primordially social and material beings

Before anything else, we are feeling bodies in a social world (Csordas, 1994; Merleau-Ponty, 2002; Schutz, 1970). Primordially, experience consists of a continuous flux of bodily feedback, or feeling. This feedback – which is the raw stuff of consciousness itself (Damasio, 1999) – reflects our embodied, material situation (hot, tired, hurting etc). It situates us in a particular setting, and furnishes an ongoing sense of our bodily potentials: an embodiment. This feedback is also continuously social (influenced by the changing social relations of the lived moment) and socialised (somewhat habitual, shaped by the impress of prior experience). Bodily feedback, in the form of feelings, is the most elemental stuff of our being human.

However, the ineffability of the body means that the centrality of feeling often eludes reflection (Langer, 1967). Consequently, the most prominent component of thought itself is frequently what Vygotsky (1962) called inner speech. This running commentary on our own and others' actions has social origins: its cognitive aspects are secondary to the social, discursive relations that engendered it. It is also largely retrospective, serving to stabilise or represent what has just occurred. In doing so it can serve as a tool to guide our own (and others') actions, and in this way have some relatively limited influence on future circumstances.

Bodily, despite our somewhat fuzzy edges, we are discrete individuals. But this individuality is relationally and socially produced: ontogenetically, in the fusion of egg and sperm; developmentally, in the experience-dependent construction of important neural assemblies (Schore, 2001); and psychologically, through relations and interactions that inculcate the implicit habits and beliefs of selfhood. Because social relations shape our being, experience is not only specific to a particular trajectory of relational and familial social participation, it is also reflective of our epoch (Elias, 1978), class (Bourdieu, 1984), gender (Fine, 2010; Young, 1990) and – no doubt – other important social divisions.

This is not a denial of individuality. No one else will occupy precisely the same circumstances as you, with exactly the constellation of bodily capacities with which you are endowed: for this reason, we are each unique. But this uniqueness is constituted from elements of the same flesh, the same social relations, the same material organisations of tools, objects, locations and institutions, the same cultural resources, artefacts and norms, the same discursive signs and symbols. Uniqueness and individuality are thoroughly social and material accomplishments.

2. Distress arises from the outside inwards

Distress is not the consequence of inner flaws or weaknesses. All mainstream approaches to 'therapy' locate the origin of psychological difficulty within the individual, usually as some kind of idiosyncracy of past experience. A morally neutral 'normality' may thus be seen as having become 'neurotically' distorted via, for example, unconscious personal desires or errors of personal judgment (e.g. over-generalization of negative experiences). Certainly this is the way we often experience our distress since such experience is inevitably interior. But experience and explanation are two very different things. Professional therapy tends to presume that both the causes and the experience of distress are interior, since this affords the therapist a legitimate ground of intervention: individuals can be worked on in ways that social and material circumstances cannot. Individuals thus quickly learn to see themselves as in some way personally defective when in fact their troubled experience arises from a defective environment (Smail, 2005).

Neither is distress the consequence of cognitive errors, or failures to process information correctly. Those therapeutic approaches that do not attribute distress to some kind of personal emotional defect (however acquired) often point instead to 'cognitive' failure. The possibility that individuals, through no fault of their own, have drawn the wrong conclusions from unfortunate eventualities may at least have the advantage of absolving them from the odour of blame or personal shortcoming that tends often to waft around more 'psychodynamic' approaches. Again, this kind of view allows the therapist an apparently legitimate field of operation in re-working the person's cognitive processes. It does so, however, at the expense of a truly convincing account of human learning. There is, surely, enough evidence of what a distressing place the world can be for us to avoid the necessity of concluding that the distress we experience is somehow mistaken (Smail, 2001a, 2005).

So-called 'individual differences' in susceptibility to distress are largely the consequences of prior socialization. The fact that some of us seem to survive adverse experience unscathed while others are thrown into confusion or despair may be taken as pointing to 'interior', personal qualities: 'self-esteem', 'willpower', or most recently 'resilience'. However, it is far easier, and more credible, to point to the embodied advantages someone has acquired over time from the social/material environment than it is to postulate essentially mysterious and unanalysable personal qualities that originate from within. To mistake the gifts of providence for personal virtues is an all-too-common category mistake, and one that psychotherapies do little to rectify.

3. Distress is produced by social and material influences

Social and material influences are typically complex and multiple. None of them are either necessary causes or sufficient causes, but the more that they intersect the more likely clinical distress becomes. They include trauma, abuse and neglect; social inequality, (organised in hierarchies of class, gender, ethnicity, sexuality and disability); and, somewhat more randomly, accidents, disability, severe illness and 'life events'.

For example, there is convincing evidence that we are more likely to experience diagnosable distress if we have experienced traumatic events, including abuse and neglect. Read, van Os, Morrison & Ross's (2005) meta-analysis suggests that at least 60–70 per cent of people experiencing visual or auditory hallucinations were subject to physical or sexual abuse in childhood. This body of evidence has received much less attention than the dominant psychiatric view that portrays distress as a consequence of biological or genetic influences.

Similarly, social inequalities that exclude or marginalise contribute significantly to the potential for distress. Poverty, impoverished housing and diet, threatening environments, limited resources, restricted choices, demeaning or poorly-paid employment, discrimination, oppression and scapegoating all cause distress. People born in working class areas to parents in manual labour are 8 times more likely than controls to be given a diagnosis of schizophrenia as adults (Harrison, Gunnell, Glazebrook, Page, & Kwiecinski, 2001). Being born to poorly educated parents doubles the risk of being given a diagnosis of depression; if neither parent is in skilled or professional employment the risk is tripled (Ritsher, Warner, Johnson & Dohrenwend, 2001). Non-white ethnic minorities in the UK are more likely to be given a diagnosis of schizophrenia, but only if they live in majority-white areas (Boydell et al., 2001). Women are roughly twice as likely as men to be given diagnoses of depression or anxiety disorder; in part, this is seemingly due to domestic violence (Garcia-Moreno, Jansen, Ellsberg, Heise & Watts, 2005). Distress is consistently associated with markers of social inequality such as unemployment, low income and impoverished education, in countries including the UK, USA, Canada, Australia and the Netherlands (Melzer,

Fryers & Jenkins, 2004). Wilkinson & Pickett (2009) have amassed extensive evidence showing that in societies where the gap between the richest and poorest is greater the prevalence of many health problems is higher.

We are more likely to experience distress the more our experiences are invalidated and the more isolated we become from one another. Equally, the further we are from supportive, nurturing relationships, the more that invalidation and isolation will engender distress. People stripped of ameliorative influences such as a loving, supportive family and friends; comfortable, safe environments; and the trust, support and solidarity of others, are increasingly likely to experience diagnosable distress. In other words, the effects of trauma, social inequality and life events contingently interact with the less visible, less quantifiable effects of parenting, friendship, nurturing and caring. This is one reason why 'the same' event causes distress in some, but not others.

4. Distress is enabled by biology but not primarily caused by it

Harré (2002) distinguishes between enabling and causing. All experience is enabled by the biological capacities which constitute our embodiment in the material world. For example, your experience of reading this paragraph is enabled by the musculature of your head, body and eyes, the light-sensitive cells of your retinas, the cortical pathways and neural assemblies that relay, collate and interpret the signals that these cells generate, and so on. But these biological capacities did not cause you to read it.

This distinction is useful in relation to distress, not least because it accords very well with the evidence. For a very small number of organic diagnoses (syphilis, respiratory or urinary tract infections in older adults, Korsakoff's syndrome, dementia), consistent biological causes of distress are known (although even these always interact with other influences). But for the overwhelming majority of functional diagnoses – schizophrenia, depression, generalised anxiety disorder, personality disorder and so on – there is no such consistent evidence. Over a hundred years of extremely well-funded research using ever-more sophisticated technologies has so far failed to establish that any of these diagnoses denote biological diseases. In the words of eminent psychiatrist Kenneth Kendler (2005, p.434–5): 'We have hunted for big, simple, neuropathological explanations for psychiatric disorders and have not found them. We have hunted for big, simple, neurochemical explanations for psychiatric disorders and have not found them. We have hunted for big, simple genetic explanations for psychiatric disorders, and have not found them.'

But this does not mean that biology should be largely ignored, as is so often the case in social science and (predominantly cognitive) psychology. Embodied capacities lend shape and texture to distress, by enabling activities and by co-constituting perceptions, thoughts and feelings. This means we should strive to understand how distress is produced by the adverse socialization of embodied, biological capacities, rather than by their impairment, disease or failure. This massively complex interdisciplinary undertaking will draw upon anthropology, social science, neuroscience, psychology and other disciplines. Despite some suggestive recent accounts (Schore, 2001) we have barely begun to conduct such research, nor address the many methodological and conceptual difficulties it will encounter (Cromby, 2007; Newton, 2007; Rose, 1997).

5. Distress is influenced by biological variation to the extent that this variation provides non-specific capacities

Some biologically enabled capacities may facilitate people's transactions with the world and so help protect them from some forms of psychological distress or self-doubt. It may thus be an advantage to possess conventional physical beauty, sporting prowess, musical ability, unusual intellectual ability, and so on. More important, perhaps, (perceived) lack of such gifts may undermine a person's self-worth and render them more susceptible to distress.

An example: less conventionally-attractive people encounter a more hostile social environment, have less chance of developing friendships and social skills, and experience fewer rewards (O'Grady, 1982). Meta-analyses by Langlois et al. (2000) suggest that conventional beauty – in children and adults - is associated with more favourable judgements by and treatment by others. Farina et al. (1977) found that female psychiatric inpatients were judged less conventionally attractive than women selected from either a shopping centre or a university, and Napoleon, Chassin, & Young (1980) showed that mental health service users were judged less attractive than high or middle income – but not low income – controls.

Another example: sensitivity to others is a trait that might have a genetic component. Ordinarily this trait is adaptive, associated with maintaining good relationships, being a better employee, functioning well in groups, and so forth. But when someone with this trait is placed in a traumatic or abusive environment, the trait becomes maladaptive because it means that the effects of this toxic environment are felt more keenly. Tienari's (1991) adoption study found that, even amongst people with a family history of difficulties, the experiences associated with a psychotic-spectrum diagnosis emerged only in the context of unfavourable family dynamics.

This perspective is consonant with current molecular genetic research, which typically finds that effects are small, non-specific, produced by multiple DNA sequences, and always dependent upon environmental mediation (Joseph, 2006; Rose, 1997). Biological factors can influence susceptibility to distress, but this is not simply a matter of objective biological advantage which inevitably orders people along some or other dimension of human 'excellence'. The value placed upon biological capacities is always a social valuation, and their effects always depend upon social and material circumstances.

6. Distress does not fall into discrete categories or diagnoses

The quaint notion that distress can be neatly partitioned into robust categories reflects the mistaken belief that it is caused by organic diseases or impairments. If distress is understood instead as a kind of socially and materially inculcated experience, there is no reason to presume that we should be able to classify it in this way.

This may be why psychiatric diagnosis is notoriously both unreliable and invalid. Evidence of unreliability is provided by the lives of service recipients, who frequently receive different diagnoses during their contact with services. Further evidence comes from studies showing that, even in reliability trials where normal variation is artificially constrained (by video presentations, special training and broad categories), psychiatrists frequently disagree about the 'correct' diagnosis (e.g. Bentall, 2003, 2009; Pilgrim & Rogers, 2010; van Os et al., 1999). Evidence that diagnosis is invalid comes from studies of comorbidity which show that patients who meet the criteria for one diagnosis most likely meet the criteria for at least one other (e.g. Boyle, 2002; Brady & Kendall, 1992; Dunner, 1998; Maier & Falkai, 1999; Sartorious, Ustun, Lecrubier, & Wittchen, 1996; Timimi, 2011). Other evidence comes from studies of symptom profiles which show (for example) that the symptoms of people given a diagnosis of bipolar disorder do not cluster separately from those of people given a diagnosis of schizophrenia (Bentall, 2003). Because psychiatric diagnosis is neither reliable nor valid, all of its claimed benefits – in respect of aetiology, treatment, prognosis, service planning, inter-professional communication, reassurance to service users and their families – are compromised.

As a kind of experience, distress is on a continuum and continuously responsive to all other experiences. Its intrinsic variability is reflective of the great complexity of our social and material worlds, the many interacting, mediated contingencies that co-constitute our experience, and the primordially socialised embodiments each of us have acquired. Nevertheless, since we all occupy the same planet and belong to the same species, there are also similarities in our experiences of distress. These reflect shared embodied capacities: to feel sad when abandoned, to feel angry when insulted, to feel ashamed about sadness or frightened of anger; to get so overwhelmed by such mixtures of feeling that our very perceptions of the world get distorted (Cromby & Harper, 2009). They also reflect similar – but never 'the same' – experiences of power relations, social relations, material circumstances, and the contingent, mediated affordances they yield.

7. Distress is an acquired, embodied way of being in the world

Cognitive psychology studies processes such as memory, perception, reasoning, and judgement, and has influenced recent attempts within clinical psychology to explain and develop interventions for distress. These attempts are broadly based on the assumption that distress is caused by some problem or dysfunction with 'normal' cognitive processes: for example, within cognitive therapy, depressed mood is attributed to errors in reasoning such as 'overgeneralisation'. Therapy attempts to help correct such errors, and so restore normal psychological functioning. However, this approach overemphasizes individual psychology, and particularly consciousness; conflates (social and material) causes with (cognitive) effects; downplays bodily processes; and almost completely neglects those social and material causes of distress external to the person and their proximal situation. It also fails to address the ways in which cognitive psychology is itself an ideological construction, rather than a naturally-scientific field investigating independently-existing phenomena (Bowers, 1990; Sampson, 1981; Shallice, 1984).

Conversely, psychiatry tends to construe clinical distress as akin to a medical disease and focuses upon diagnosing and treating (usually with drugs) so called 'mental illnesses': depression, schizophrenia etc. Although this acknowledges the body as the site of distress, it fails to adequately address the ways in which bodily manifestations of emotional distress are produced by, and consistently responsive to, social and material circumstances. Instead, psychiatry traces distress back to biological impairments and dysfunctions for which there is no credible, reliable and consistent evidence (Lynch, 2004).

Core to most psychological therapies is the development of 'insight'. For example, in cognitive therapy the therapist 'helps' the client become aware of cognitive processing errors, with the aim of helping to correct them. Research in neuroscience and social psychology, however, has shown that much of our experience, including emotional arousal, is not necessarily available to conscious introspection (Kahneman & Tversky, 1982; Schwitzgebel, 2011; Wilson & Dunne, 2004). Hence, when individuals from Western cultures are asked to talk about feelings of low mood they usually offer accounts that emphasise individual inadequacy and guilt, whereas those from non-Western cultures offer very different accounts (Fancher, 1996; Kleinman, 1986; Watters, 2010). Rather than providing reliable, accurate, direct accounts of experience, introspection is always mediated by cultural norms and linguistic resources that regulate what and how we can notice and report.

It is frequently difficult for us to make sense of, or explain to others, how we feel and why we feel the way we do. Complex feeling states are often triggered involuntarily in response to subtle environmental features, related to past events that have been forgotten, or that we do not connect with our current experience (Damasio, 1999; Kagan, 2007; Le Doux, 1999). We are often unaware of the many social factors that influence us: due to their complexity, or sometimes – in the case of advertising, tabloid media or politician's speeches – the conscious manipulation of feelings by those in positions of power, with the intention of concealing such manipulation (Caldini, 1994; Freedland, 2012; Jones, 2011). Perhaps one of the useful aspects of therapy is the opportunity to try to make connections between events, past and present, and the feelings they evoke.

Both psychiatric and mainstream psychological explanations of distress are at best partial, at worst ideological, because they fail to capture the way in which experience is shaped over time by a social world that is frequently oppressive. The acquisition of what could be described as an affective 'default' position is sensibly interpreted by the person as reflecting the way the world is, has been, and will always be. This enduring, embodied aspect of distress means it is very difficult for us to change the way we experience ourselves and our world.

8. Social and material influence is always contingent and mediated

The ability to act is always contingent on the particular social, material and embodied resources available. In turn, the effects of these actions are not simply dependent on our intentions. They are also a function of the intentions and actions of others, and of the variable capacities and affordances of the (constantly changing) social and material world.

Bradley (2005) offers a startling example: stepping out and knocking a cyclist off his bike. In one circumstance, the man is largely unhurt and cycles away; in another, he is knocked into the path of an oncoming vehicle and killed. Intrinsically unpredictable combinations of interlocking factors (choices about where and when to travel; velocities, trajectories and reactions of cyclist, driver and walker; traffic flow and density; road and pavement layout) mean that three lives continue much as before in the first circumstance but are radically transformed in the second.

Contingency necessarily means that social and material influences are always mediated. They are in constant flow and exchange with each other and with the human characteristics and resources (habits, perceptions, affects, discourses, narratives) by which we understand and respond to them. Vitally, this does not mean that social and material influence is random: the contingencies and mediations by which it gets enacted are always already structured in relays of power. Nevertheless, power's influence therefore necessarily has an 'on average' character (cf. Bourdieu, 1977; Young, 1990). This means there are always potentials for movement, always immanent moments of becoming and change, even within what seem to be the most frozen and static regimes (Stephenson & Papadopoulos, 2007).

Adequate psychological accounts of causality therefore need to be multiple, complex and open-ended: they need to recognise the radical indeterminacy of social interaction (Shotter, 1993), the probabilistic character of social influence (Archer, 1995), and the influence of culture as a mutable system of normative guiding principles (Harré, 2002). But mainstream psychology is preoccupied with mechanistic notions of causality: consequently, it tends to read these indeterminacies, probabilities and norms in ways that consistently subordinate social and material circumstance to immaterial cognition. Social and material influence is therefore downplayed, in favour of individualistic conceptualisations against which these real influences typically appear only as mere context. When elaborated, this understanding provides further reasons why 'the same' events seemingly impact differently upon different people.

9. Distress cannot be removed by willpower

An at least tacit notion of 'willpower' inhabits just about every theory of psychotherapy. Having been led, one way or another, to confront their personal failings, mistakes, or cognitive errors, it is assumed that patients can make the necessary correction by an act of will. If not, they are being uncooperative, 'resistant', etc. Never explicitly theorized, the notion of willpower lurks within such concepts as 'insight' and is typically assumed as an obvious, everyday human faculty that can be called on by all in extremis. Willpower constitutes a mysterious, interior moral force that cannot be measured or demonstrated – because, whatever its social utility, it doesn't exist (Smail, 2001a). To assume that it does, and to call upon patients to demonstrate it, can be positively cruel.

This does not mean that we are necessarily unable to choose a given course of action, nor that we are constrained to perform actions against our desires. 'Freedom', 'will' and 'power' are necessary and valid concepts. 'Willing' means choosing this or that; 'freedom' means having the power to choose this or that. Whether or not we have the power to exercise our will depends upon the availability of the necessary social and material resources. Will and power are two distinct capacities: without resources, exercise of will is impossible.

So there is no immaterial force called willpower upon which we can call. The personal powers that make the exercise of will possible may be concurrently present in the world, or they may be acquired historically – embodied – from engagement with it. I will not be able to speak French (to 'will' a sentence in French) if I have not studied and practised the language sufficiently for it to become an embodied skill. Similarly, I will not be able to behave confidently in a given circumstance if I have not acquired and embodied the kind of experiences which engender the appropriate confidence. Most therapies, whether explicitly or not, invoke boot-strap-pulling as a vehicle of change, but boot-strap-pulling is no substitute for the necessary personal power (Smail, 2005).

10. Distress cannot be cured by medication or therapy

Distress is not an 'illness', so cannot be 'cured'. It is not bad genes, faulty cognitions or the Oedipus complex, but misfortune and the widespread abuse of power that mire so many in madness, addiction or despair. These are not symptoms of illness: they are states of being that encapsulate how most of us might respond to chronic adversity. The most widely cited evidence bases for psychiatric medication and talking therapy are overly-optimistic catalogues of error and bias, featuring inadequate recruitment and blinding procedures, unreliable clinical outcome measures of limited real life significance, and the selective publication of favourable results (Angell, 2004; Epstein, 2006; Kirsch, 2010). The more rigorous the study and the longer the post-treatment followup, the harder it is to demonstrate any superiority for the clinical treatment over dummy, placebo or alternative (Westen & Morrison, 2001). Neither drugs nor psychological therapies are magic bullets aimed at specific symptoms: whatever effects they have upon body and mind are quite general. The one reliable finding is that emotionally warm and attentive practitioners are more appreciated and get better results - an observation that applies equally to politicians, salespeople and prostitutes.

Indeed, the expectation that therapy or medication might 'cure' is itself harmful. Psychiatric drugs are marketed and prescribed relentlessly – cures for supposed chemical imbalances said to afflict up to a quarter of the population (Busfield, 2010). Likewise, the jargon and practices of over 400 schools of psychological therapy have invaded almost every corner of daily life: from the products of a lucrative 'self-help' industry to the running of schools, universities, business, clinics and prisons. The UK government's Improving Access to Psychological Therapies (IAPT) programme promises to make psychological treatment 'available to all', as prophylactic for distress and happiness bromide: therapy on an industrial scale.

But the majority of psychoactive drugs cause mental and physical harm, especially with long-term use (Breggin, 1991; Moncrieff, 2006; Whitaker, 2010). The over prescribing of so-called anti-psychotics has unleashed an epidemic of psychosis throughout the world, as dependency upon (and withdrawal from) medication has almost everywhere been mistaken for 'mental illness'. Whilst the talking therapies appear more benign, too often they are just a more insidious form of control, fostering the illusion that misery is an internal failure or breakdown, awaiting correction from an expert (Illouz, 2008; Parker, 2007). And – when medication or therapy frequently fails to generate the profound changes that were implicitly promised – we then become those who simply cannot be cured.

11. Medication and therapy can make a difference, but not by curing

Sometimes, medication can usefully anaesthetize the distressed to their woes, yielding brief bubbles of respite or clarity. During these short, chemically induced holidays from their misery, those with the resources may initiate life changes that alleviate their problems and establish positive future trajectories. But whether this occurs is a function, not simply of the medication, but of the resources and circumstances within which it is ingested: consequently, medication can also make things worse (Moncrieff, 2008).

Therapy can also help, though again not by 'curing'. Understood generically, therapy provides comfort (you are not alone with your woes), clarification (there are sound reasons why you feel the way you do) and support (I will help you deal with your predicament) (Smail, 2001b). In an atomised, fragmented, time-poor society, where solidarity and collectivity are derided, time limited, and relationships consistently infected with a toxic instrumentalism, these are valuable, compassionate functions.

At its best, psychological therapy can help the sufferer to understand distress, not as a (more or less wilful) failure of insight, motivation or learning, but as the inevitable result of living in a noxious world. Moreover, both medication and therapy can help people make better use of the powers and resources already available to them. Both may draw attention to unrecognized resources (e.g., solidarity with others); make it feel permissible to use available powers and resources; change the ways that people use available powers and resources; or explicitly support people to cease viewing themselves as 'the problem'.

With the exception of iatrogenic poisoning and disciplinary self-regulation, neither therapy nor medication has any other significant influence.

12. Successful psychological therapy is not primarily a matter of technique

When therapy succeeds it seems to be primarily a matter of two kinds of influence: on the one hand relationality (ordinary human compassion and understanding); on the other, coincidence with social and material and circumstances and resources.

In the therapy literature is it well established that the clients who do best are generally young, attractive, verbal, intelligent and successful – YAVIS (Pilgrim, 1997). By contrast, the people whose needs are described as 'complex' and requiring long-term treatment are usually the poorest (Davies, 1997; Hagan & Donnison, 1999). Where people have (or can obtain) more resources then they will have more scope to act upon whatever insights they might have gained.

It is also well-established in this literature that so-called 'non-specific factors' are a consistent predictor of good outcomes: in other words, that the therapist and client are able to establish a good relationship (Mair, 1992; Norcross, 2010). Indeed, unlike professional therapists, service users frequently declare the most ordinary aspects of therapy the most helpful: listening, understanding, respectfulness.

Despite this, therapy is mostly presented as a matter of technique. CBT, psychoanalysis, and almost all other schools of therapy appear as specialist technologies of subjectivity, skilled interpersonal practices founded on specific assumptions, locked in place by particular theories and evidence bases. In a thoroughly commodified society it is perhaps understandable that some practitioners will want to have branded, marketable products, just as in a professionalised culture some will want to identify themselves as bearers of highly specialised knowledge and skills. Like everyone else, therapists must earn a living, so it is only to be expected that interest should influence how they present themselves and their work. Nevertheless, doing so distracts attention from the actual causes of distress by bolstering the belief that it is a mysterious state amenable only to professional help; it disables friends and family, who may feel that they could not possibly understand; and it negates the contribution of community, solidarity and trust. The presentation of therapy as specialised technique cheapens and oversells psychology itself; leads to resources being wasted comparing the marginal differences between this brand and that; and deflects effort and attention from the very real opportunities for psychological research and insight that are supplied by the highly privileged situation of the therapeutic encounter.

References

Angell, M. (2004). *The truth about drug companies: How they deceive us and what to do about it.* New York: Random House.

Archer, M. (1995). *Realist social theory: The morphogenetic approach.* Cambridge: Cambridge University Press.

Bentall, R. (2003). *Madness explained.* London: Allen Lane/Penguin.

Bentall, R. (2009). *Doctoring the mind: Why psychiatric treatments fail.* Harmondsworth: Penguin.

Bourdieu, P. (1977). *Outline of a theory of practice* (R. Nice, Trans.). Cambridge: Cambridge University Press.

Bourdieu, P. (1984). *Distinction.* London: Routledge.

Bowers, J. (1990). All hail the great abstraction: Star wars and the politics of cognitive psychology. In I. Parker & J. Shotter (Eds.), *Deconstructing social psychology.* London: Sage Publications.

Boydell, J., Van Os, J., McKenzie, K., Allardyce, J., Goel, R., McCreadie, G. et al. (2001). Incidence of schizophrenia in ethnic minorities in London: Ecological study into interactions with environment. *British Medical Journal, 323*, 1336–38.

Boyle, M. (2002). *Schizophrenia: A scientific delusion?* (2nd ed.). London: Routledge.

Bradley, B. (2005). *Psychology and experience*. Cambridge: Cambridge University Press.

Brady, E. & Kendall, P. (1992). Comorbidity of anxiety and depression in children and adolescents. *Psychological Bulletin, 111*(2), 244–55.

Breggin, P. (1991). *Toxic psychiatry*. New York: St. Martins Press.

Busfield, J. (2010). 'A pill for every ill'. Explaining the expansion in medicine use. *Social Science and Medicine, 70*, 934–41.

Caldini, R. (1994). *Influence: The psychology of persuasion*. New York: Morrow.

Cromby, J. (2007). Integrating social science with neuroscience: Potentials and problems. *Biosocieties, 2*(2), 149–70.

Cromby, J. & Harper, D. (2009). Paranoia: A social account. *Theory and Psychology, 19*(3), 335–61.

Csordas, T. (Ed.). (1994). *Embodiment and experience: The existential ground of culture and self*. Cambridge: Cambridge University Press.

Curt, B. (1994). *Textuality and tectonics: Troubling social and psychological science*. Buckingham: Open University Press.

Damasio, A.R. (1999). *The feeling of what happens: Body, emotion and the making of consciousness*. London: William Heinemann.

Davies, D. (1997). *Counselling in psychological services*. Buckingham: Open University Press.

Dunner, D.L. (1998). The issue of co-morbidity in the treatment of panic. *International Clinical Psychopharmacology, 13*(Apr), S19–24.

Elias, N. (1978). *The history of manners: The civilising process* (Vol 1). (E. Jephcott, Trans.). Oxford: Basil Blackwell.

Epstein, W. (2006). *The civil divine: Psychotherapy as religion in America*. Nevada: University of Nevada Press.

Fancher, R. (1996). *Cultures of healing: Correcting the image of American mental health care*. San Francisco: W.H. Freeman & Co.

Farina, A., Fischer, E., Sherman, S., Smith, W., Groh, T. & Mermin, P. (1977). Physical attractiveness and mental illness. *Journal of Abnormal Psychology, 86*, 510–517.

Fine, C. (2010). *Delusions of gender*. London: Icon Books.

Freedland, J. (2012, January 28). Bash the poor and wave the flag – how this Tory trick works. *The Guardian*. http://gu.com/p/354a2

Garcia-Moreno, C., Jansen, H.A.F.M., Ellsberg, M., Heise, L. & Watts, C. (2005). *WHO multicountry study on women's health and domestic violence against women*. Geneva: World Health Organisation.

Hagan, T., & Donnison, D. (1999). Social power: Some implications for the theory and practice of cognitive behaviour therapy. *Journal of Community and Applied Social Psychology, 9*, 119–35.

Harré, R. (2002). *Cognitive science: A philosophical introduction*. London: Sage Publications.

Harrison, G., Gunnell, D., Glazebrook, C., Page, K. & Kwiecinski, R. (2001). Association between schizophrenia and social inequality at birth: case-control study. *British Journal of Psychiatry, 179*, 346–50.

Home, S. (1991). *The assault on culture: Utopian currents from Lettrism to class war*. Edinburgh: AK Press.

Illouz, E. (2008). *Saving the modern soul: Therapy, emotions and the culture of self-help*. Berkeley: University of California Press.

Johnson, M. (2007). *The meaning of the body: Aesthetics of human understanding*. Chicago: University of Chicago Press.

Jones, O. (2011). *Chavs: The demonisation of the working class*. London: Verso.

Joseph, J. (2006). *The missing gene: Psychiatry, heredity and the fruitless search for genes.* New York: Algora.

Kagan, J. (2007). *What is emotion?* New Haven & London: Yale University Press.

Kahneman, D. & Tversky, A. (Eds.). (1982). *Judgement under uncertainty: Heuristics and biases.* Cambridge: Cambridge University Press.

Kendler, K. (2005). Towards a philosophical structure for psychiatry. *American Journal of Psychiatry, 162,* 433–40.

Kirsch, I. (2010). *The emperor's new drugs: Exploding the antidepressant myth.* New York: Basic Books.

Kleinman, A. (1986). Social origins of distress and disease: Depression, neurasthenia, and pain in modern China. *Current Anthropology, 24*(5), 499–509.

Langer, S. (1967). *Mind: An essay on human feeling* (Vol. 1). Baltimore: The Johns Hopkins University Press.

Langlois, J., Kalakanis, L., Rubenstein, A., Larson, A., Hallam, M. & Smoot, M. (2000). Maxims or myths of beauty? A meta-analytic and theoretic review. *Psychological Bulletin, 126*(3), 390–423.

Le Doux, J. (1999). *The emotional brain.* London: Phoenix.

Lynch, T. (2004). *Beyond Prozac: Healing mental distress.* Ross-on-Wye: PCCS Books.

Maier, W. & Falkai, P. (1999). The epidemiology of comorbidity between depression, anxiety disorders and somatic diseases. *International Clinical Psychopharmacology, 14,* S1–6.

Mair, K. (1992). The myth of therapist expertise. In W. Dryden & C. Feltham (Eds.), *Psychotherapy and its discontents.* Buckingham: Open University Press.

Melzer, D., Fryers, T., & Jenkins, R. (2004). *Social inequalities and the distribution of the common mental disorders.* Hove: Psychology Press.

Merleau-Ponty, M. (2002). *Phenomenology of perception* (C. Smith, Trans.). London: Routledge.

Moncrieff, J. (2006). Why is it so difficult to stop psychiatric drug treatment? It may be nothing to do with the original problem. *Medical Hypotheses, 67*(3), 517–23.

Moncrieff, J. (2008). *The myth of the chemical cure: A critique of psychiatric drug treatment.* London: Palgrave.

Napoleon, T., Chassin, L., & Young, R. (1980). A replication and extension of 'Physical Attractiveness and Mental Illness'. *Journal of Abnormal Psychology, 89,* 250–3.

Newton, T. (2007). *Nature and sociology.* London: Routledge.

Norcross, J. (2010). The therapeutic relationship. In B. Duncan, S. Miller, B. Wampold & M. Hubble (Eds.), *The heart and soul of change: Delivering what works in therapy.* Washington: APA Books.

O'Grady, K. (1982). Sex, physical attractiveness and perceived risk for mental illness. *Journal of Personality and Social Psychology, 43*(5), 1064–71.

Parker, I. (2007). *Revolution in psychology.* London: Pluto Press.

Pilgrim, D. (1997). *Psychotherapy and society.* London: Sage.

Pilgrim, D. & Rogers, A. (2010). *A sociology of mental health and illness.* Maidenhead: Open University Press/McGraw Hill Education.

Read, J., van Os, J., Morrison, A.P. & Ross, C.A. (2005). Childhood trauma, psychosis and schizophrenia: a literature review with theoretical and clinical implications. *Acta Psychiatrica Scandinavica, 112,* 330–50.

Ritsher, J.E.B., Warner, V., Johnson, J.G. & Dohrenwend, B.P. (2001) Inter-generational longitudinal study of social class and depression: a test of social causation and social selection models. *British Journal of Psychiatry, 178* (suppl 40), s84–s90.

Rose, S. (1997). *Lifelines: Life beyond the gene*. Oxford: Oxford University Press.

Sampson, E.E. (1981). Cognitive psychology as ideology. *American Psychologist*, 36(7), 730–43.

Sartorious, N., Ustun, T. B., Lecrubier, Y. & Wittchen, H.U. (1996). Depression co-morbid with anxiety: results from the WHO study on psychological disorders in primary health care. *British Journal of Psychiatry, Suppl.* 30(Jun), 38–43.

Schore, A. (2001). The effects of early relational trauma on right brain development, affect regulation, and infant mental health. *Infant Mental Health Journal*, 22(1), 201–269.

Schutz, A. (1970). *On phenomenology and social relations*. Chicago: University of Chicago Press.

Schwitzgebel, E. (2011). *Perplexities of consciousness*. Cambridge, MA: MIT Press.

Shallice, T. (1984). Psychology and social control. *Cognition*, 17, 29–48.

Shotter, J. (1993). *Conversational realities: Constructing life through language*. London: Sage Publications.

Smail, D (2001a). *The nature of unhappiness*. London: Robinson.

Smail, D. (2001b). *Why therapy doesn't work*. London: Robinson.

Smail, D. (2005). *Power, interest and psychology: Elements of a social materialist understanding of distress*. Ross-on-Wye: PCCS Books.

Stephenson, N. & Papadopoulos, D. (2007). *Analysing everyday experience: Social research and political change*. London: Palgrave Macmillan.

The Free Association. (2011). *Moments of excess: Movements, protest and everyday life*. Oakland, CA: PM Press.

Tienari, P. (1991). Interaction between genetic vulnerability and family environment: the Finnish adoptive family study of schizophrenia. *Acta Psychiatrica Scandinavica*, 84(5), 460–465.

Timimi, S. (2011). *The myth of autism: Medicalising men's and boys' social and emotional competence*. London: Palgrave.

Tolman, C. (1994). *Psychology, society, subjectivity: An introduction to German Critical Psychology*. London: Routledge.

van Os, J., Gilvarry, C., Bale, R., van Horn, E., Tattan, T., White, I. et al. (1999). A comparison of the utility of dimensional and categorical representations of psychosis. UK700 Group. *Psychological Medicine*, 29(3), 595–606.

Vygotsky, L.S. (1962). *Thought and language* (E. Hanfmann & G. Vakar, Trans.). Cambridge, MA: M.I.T. Press.

Watters, E. (2010). *Crazy like us: The globalisation of the American psyche*. New York: Free Press.

Westen, D. & Morrison, K. (2001). A multi-dimensional meta-analysis of treatments for depression, panic and generalised anxiety disorder: an empirical examination of the status of empirically supported therapies. *Journal of Consulting and Clinical Psychology*, 69(6), 875–899.

Whitaker, R. (2010). *Anatomy of an epidemic*. New York: Random House.

Wilkinson, R. & Pickett, K. (2009). *The spirit level: Why equality is better for everyone*. Harmondsworth: Penguin.

Wilson, T. & Dunne, E. (2004). Self knowledge: Its limits, value and potential for improvement. *Annual Review of Psychology*, 581–593.

Young, I.M. (1990). *'Throwing like a girl' and other essays in feminist philosophy and social theory*. Bloomington: Indiana University Press.

Appendix 2

Establishing and maintaining a group

If you are reading this, the chances are you might be interested in setting up a group like ours. It's likely also that you are a clinical or counselling psychologist/trainee, or have something to do with psychology. If so, you are probably already familiar with the processes of establishing and maintaining groups. So, in this short appendix, we will not describe groups in general – we will describe how our own group was established. We will explain some of the activities we shared and describe some of the early decisions we took that helped to shape and stabilise what became the Midlands Psychology Group (MPG).

The first meetings from which the MPG emerged were initiated by David Smail around 2002. From the outset, those who took part shared the feeling that the workplace offered relatively few opportunities to think honestly about theory and practice in psychology. What we wanted was to find space and time outside the work context where we could discuss, debate, consider and share information in a constructive and mutually supportive atmosphere. Inevitably, this meant meeting in the evening.

One of the first things we did was circulate by email to the group a short description of ourselves, our backgrounds and interests, and a description of what we hoped to get from the group. After this we spontaneously (i.e. without knowing where we were going, and without having a destination or endpoint in mind) agreed in turn upon a series of three different activities, all of which helped to shape the emerging group.

First, we invited external speakers to come along and talk with us and share their ideas and information. These included critics of therapy and social constructionist or critical psychologists. The speakers would talk to us for up to an hour, and this would be followed by an hour or so of discussion.

Second, we circulated journal papers and book chapters, chosen by group members, that we thought might be of interest to others. These readings would be shared by email up to a month before the meeting so that everyone had plenty of time to read them. We would then have a meeting of up to two hours that began with the person who had chosen the reading briefly explaining the reasons for their choice and why they thought it was worth sharing. The great majority of the time would then be spent discussing the ideas that had been shared.

Third, we began writing together. Someone would develop a topic of concern and circulate their initial thoughts to the other members of the group by email. Everybody else would then comment and suggest amendments in turn. After everyone had contributed, we would then meet to discuss the final document. Our aim in doing this was explicitly not to critique each other's view, but to find, clarify and develop common ground. Also, at this point, our collective writing was not necessarily intended for publication: it was a vehicle for identifying common ground and acknowledging difference.

David knew that differences of opinion often prevent large groups from operating effectively (he saw this with the Psychology and Psychotherapy Association and its eventual demise). He was therefore keen for the MPG to remain small. This is why, instead of inviting others to join MPG, or accepting people's requests to join, we made the decision quite early that we would be a closed group. We decided that we had already invested a lot of time and emotional energy in the emerging group, and felt that keeping the group open had the potential to continually absorb more of that energy. Conversely, closing the group allowed us to further cement the trust and mutual empathy we had already begun to develop.

We have explicitly discussed the decision to close the group with regards to David's ideas about how therapy works (when it does). A small group that has reserves of trust and empathy has considerable potential to provide comfort (meeting with like-minded people), clarification (reporting and analysing, in honest detail, experiences from clinical practice and everyday life), encouragement (helping each other identify and use available resources to improve their situations and those of the people they work with), and solidarity (acting and writing collectively, sharing frustrations, forging alliances, and finding ways to go on).

More than this, we were also aware that writing and acting collectively was a way of acquiring power – that as a collective we could speak with more authority than any one of us could do alone. Membership of the group made us feel more powerful, more secure, and more confident in our ideas. At the same time, having an identity as a group and writing collectively in its name allowed us to acquire power, by making it clear that our words were not spoken in isolation but instead were endowed with the authority, judgement and expertise of multiple speakers who were all in agreement.

It is only with hindsight that we have begun to realise the extent to which – as we explain in Chapter 9 of this book – the MPG in fact functions as a kind of consciousness-raising group. Indeed, with hindsight we can see that the process we went through in establishing the group had many parallels with descriptions of how consciousness-raising groups can be set up (although there are also some differences, most notably – and amusingly – that our process was arguably less 'therapeutic' in character). If you are interested in setting up your own group, then, in addition to this appendix, you may also wish to look at, and adapt, the excellent guide to consciousness-raising groups by the activist network Plan C.[1]

---

1. www.weareplanc.org/blog/c-is-for-consciousness-raising/

References

Adair-Stantiall, A. & Needs, A. (2018). Steps to an ecology of human functioning for forensic psychology. In G. Akerman, A. Needs & C. Bainbridge (Eds.), *Transforming environments and rehabilitation: A guide for practitioners in forensic settings and criminal justice* (pp. 7–30). Routledge.

Adams, G., Estrada-Villalta, S., Sullivan, D. & Markus, H.R. (2019). The psychology of neoliberalism and the neoliberalism of psychology. *Journal of Social Issues, 75*(1), 1–28.

Ahn, H. & Wampold, B.E. (2001). Where oh where are the specific ingredients? A meta-analysis of component studies in counseling and psychotherapy. *Journal of Counseling Psychology, 48*(3), 251–257.

Akala (2018). *Natives: Race and class in the ruins of empire*. Two Roads/Hodder & Stoughton.

Allagui, I, & Kebler, J. (2011). The Arab spring and the role of ICTs. *International Journal of Communication, 5,* 1435–1442.

Allen, K. (2009). *Ireland's economic crash: A radical agenda for change*. The Liffey Press.

Allen, K. & O' Boyle, B. (2013). *Austerity Ireland: The failure of Irish capitalism*. Pluto Press.

American Psychiatric Association. (APA). (2013). *Diagnostic and statistical manual of mental disorders* (5th ed.) (*DSM-5*). APA.

American Psychological Association. (n.d.). Scientist-practitioner model. *APA Dictionary of Psychology.* https://dictionary.apa.org/scientist-practitioner-model

Anderson, M. (2003). Embodied cognition: A field guide. *Artificial Intelligence, 149*(1), 91–130.

Anderson, T., Lunnen, K.M. & Ogles, B.M. (2010). Putting models and techniques in context. In L. Duncan, S.D. Miller, B.E. Wampold & M.A. Hubble (Eds.), *The heart and soul of change: Delivering what works in therapy* (pp.143–166). American Psychological Association.

Armstrong, S. (2017). *The new poverty*. Verso.

A service user. (2018). Will the Power Threat Meaning Framework help survivors on welfare? *Asylum, 25*(3), 14. https://asylummagazine.org/2018/09/asylum-magazine-volume-25-no-3-autumn-2018/

Athanasiou, A., Hantzaroula, P. & Yannakopoulos, K. (2008). Towards a new epistemology: The 'affective turn'. *Historein, 8,* 5–16.

Atkinson, P. (2014). Lies, damned lies, and IAPT statistics. *Self and Society, 41*(1–2), 18–19.

Atkinson, R. (2020, June). UK coexists with coronavirus. *Le Monde Diplomatique.*

Aubrecht, K. (2012). The new vocabulary of resilience and the governance of university student life. *Studies in Social Justice, 6*(1), 67–83.

Baldwin, P. (1992). *The politics of social solidarity: Class bases of the European Welfare State, 1875–1975*. Cambridge University Press.

Ball, S.J. (2009). Privatising education: Privatising education policy, privatising educational research: Network governance and the competition state. *Journal of Education Policy, 24*(1), 83–99.

Barlow, D.H. (2010). Negative effects from psychological treatments: A perspective. *American Psychologist, 65*(1), 13–20.

Barr, B., Kinderman, P. & Whitehead, M. (2015). Trends in mental health inequalities in England during a period of recession, austerity and welfare reform 2004 to 2013. *Social Science & Medicine, 147*, 324–331.

Barr, N. (2004). *The economics of the welfare state* (4th ed.). Oxford University Press.

Bartley, M. (1990). Do we need a strong program in medical sociology? *Sociology of Health and Illness, 12*(4), 371–390.

Bates, Y. (Ed.). (2005). *Shouldn't I be feeling better by now? Client views of therapy.* Palgrave Macmillan.

Bausell, R.B. (2007). *Snake oil science: The truth about complementary and alternative medicine.* Oxford University Press.

BBC News (2017, September 14). Jacob Rees-Mogg: Food banks 'rather uplifting'. *BBC News.* www.bbc.co.uk/news/uk-politics-41264965

BBC News Reality Check Team (2019, June 19). Tory leadership: How much has social care been cut? *BBC News.* www.bbc.co.uk/news/health-48690733

Beck, A.T. (1952). Successful outpatient psychotherapy of a chronic schizophrenic with a delusion based on borrowed guilt. *Psychiatry: Interpersonal & Biological Processes, 15*(3), 305–312.

Beck, A.T. & Weishaar, A.T. (1989). Cognitive therapy. In A. Freeman, K. Simon, L. Beutler & H. Arkowitz (Eds.), *Comprehensive handbook of cognitive therapy* (pp.21–36). Plenum Press.

Beck, J.S. (1995). *Cognitive therapy: Basics and beyond.* Guilford Press.

Becker, D. (2013). *One nation under stress: The trouble with stress as an idea.* Oxford University Press.

Behavioral Tech (n.d.). *What is Dialectical Behavior Therapy (DBT)?* https://behavioraltech.org/resources/resources-for-clients-families/

Bell, E.C., Marcus, D.K. & Goodland, J.K. (2013). Are the parts as good as the whole? A meta-analysis of component studies treatment studies. *Journal of Consulting and Clinical Psychology, 81*(4), 722–736.

Benish, S., Imel, Z.E. & Wampold, B.E. (2008). The relative efficacy of bona fide psychotherapies of post-traumatic stress disorder: A meta-analysis of direct comparisons. *Clinical Psychology Review, 28*(5), 746–758.

Bennett, T., Dodsworth, F., Noble, G., Poovey, M. & Watkins, M. (2013). Habit and habituation: Governance and the social. *Body & Society, 19*(2–3), 3–29.

Berger, P. & Luckmann, T. (1966). *The social construction of reality: A treatise in the sociology of knowledge.* Penguin.

Berman, J.S. & Norton, N.C. (1985). Does professional training make a therapist more effective? *Psychological Bulletin, 98*(2), 401–407.

Bhaskar, R. (2008). *A realist theory of science.* Routledge.

Bilet, T., Olsen, T., Anderson, J.R. & Martinsen, E. (2020). Cognitive behavioural group therapy for panic disorder in a general clinical setting: A prospective cohort study with 12–31 years follow-up. *BMC Psychiatry.* https://doi.org/10.1186/s12888-020-02679-w

Billig, M. (2013). *Learn to write badly: How to succeed in the social sciences.* Cambridge University Press.

Billig, M. (2015). John Shotter, uniqueness and poetics: Parallels with Ernst Cassirer. In T. Corcoran, T, & J. Cromby (Eds.), *Joint action: Essays in honour of John Shotter* (pp.10–27). Routledge.

Bisson, J., Roberts, N., Andrew, M., Cooper, R. & Lewis, C. (2013). Psychological therapies for chronic post-traumatic stress disorder (PTSD) in adults. *Cochrane Database of Systematic Reviews, 12.*

Blackman, L., Cromby, J., Hook, D., Papadopoulos D. & Walkerdine, V. (2008). Creating subjectivities. *Subjectivity, 22,* 1–27.

Bohart, A.C. & Tallman, K. (2010). Clients: The neglected common factor in psychotherapy. In L. Duncan, S.D. Miller, B.E. Wampold & M.A. Hubble (Eds.), *The heart and soul of change: Delivering what works in therapy* (pp.83–111). American Psychological Association.

Bohdi, B. (2011). What does mindfulness really mean? A canonical perspective. *Contemporary Buddhism, 12*(1), 19–39.

Bostock, J. (1998). From clinic to community: Generating social validity in clinical psychology. *Clinical Psychology Forum, 121,* 2–6.

Bostock, J. & Diamond, R. (2005). The value of community psychology: Critical reflections from the NHS. *Clinical Psychology Forum, 153,* 22–25.

Bourdieu, P. (1991). *Language and symbolic power.* Polity Press.

Bowcott, O. (2016, October 11). Legal aid cuts creating two-tier justice system, says Amnesty. *The Guardian.* www.theguardian.com/law/2016/oct/11/legal-aid-cuts-two-tier-system-amnesty-international-law-justice

Bowers, J. (1990). All hail the great abstraction: Star Wars and the politics of cognitive psychology. In I. Parker & J. Shotter (Eds.), *Deconstructing social psychology* (pp.127–140). Sage Publications.

Boyle, M. (2002). *Schizophrenia: A scientific delusion?* Psychology Press.

Bracken, P. (2002). *Trauma: Culture, meaning and philosophy.* Whurr.

Bregman, R. (2020). *Humankind: A hopeful history.* Bloomsbury.

Brewer, C. & Lait, J. (1980). *Can social work survive?* Maurice Temple Smith.

Broadbent, A. (2019.) *Philosophy of medicine.* Oxford University Press.

Brown, N. (2016, May 10). Are viruses alive? *Microbiology Society.* https://microbiologysociety.org/publication/past-issues/what-is-life/article/are-viruses-alive-what-is-life.html

Brown, S.D. (1996). The textuality of stress: Drawing between scientific and everyday accounting. *Journal of Health Psychology, 1*(2), 173–193.

Brown, P. & Ross, C. (2020). Academic oversight in policy research: Questions arising from the Sex Offender Treatment Programme study. *Lancet Psychiatry, 7*(3): 224–226.

Brown, S. & Reavey, P. (2015). *Vital memory and affect: Living with a difficult past.* Routledge.

Brown, S.D. & Stenner, P. (2009). *Psychology without foundations: History, philosophy and psychosocial theory.* Sage Publications.

Brown, W. (2003). Neo-liberalism and the end of liberal democracy. *Theory & Event, 7*(1), 10.1353/tae.2003.0020

Brown, W. (2006). American nightmare: Neoliberalism, neoconservatism and de-democratisation. *Political Theory, 34*(6), 690–714.

Brown, W. (2015). *Undoing the demos: Neoliberalism's stealth revolution.* Zone Books.

Bruce, M.L., Takeuchi, D.T. & Leaf, P.J. (1991). Poverty and psychiatric status: Longitudinal evidence from the New Haven Epidemiologic Catchment Area Study. *Archives of General Psychiatry, 48*(5), 470–474.

Burkeman, O. (2017, July 28). Is the world really better than ever? *The Guardian.* www.theguardian.com/news/2017/jul/28/is-the-world-really-better-than-ever-the-new-optimists

Burnett, R. & Roberts, C. (Eds.). (2004). *What works in probation and youth justice.* Willan.

Burr, V. (2003). *Introduction to social constructionism.* Sage Publications.

Burstow, B. (2015). *Psychiatry and the business of madness. An ethical and epistemological accounting.* Palgrave Macmillan.

Burton, M. & Kagan, C. (2005). Liberation psychology: Learning from Latin America. *Journal of Community and Applied Social Psychology, 15*, 63–78.

Burton, M. & Kagan, C. (2006). Decoding valuing people. *Disability and Society, 21*(4) 299–313.

Butler, P. (2019, January 28). Deprived northern regions worst hit by UK austerity, study finds. *The Guardian*. www.theguardian.com/society/2019/jan/28/deprived-northern-regions-worst-hit-by-uk-austerity-study-finds#:~:text=Austerity%20cuts%20have%20fallen%20hardest,brunt%20of%20council%20spending%20cuts.

Butler, P. (2020, June 28). Disabled man starved to death after DWP stopped his benefits. *The Guardian*. www.theguardian.com/society/2020/jan/28/disabled-man-starved-to-death-after-dwp-stopped-his-benefits

Butler, P., Wintour P. & Gentleman, A. (2014). Tory peer forced to eat her words after claiming poor people can't cook. *The Guardian*. www.theguardian.com/society/2014/dec/08/poor-cannot-cook-peer-eats-words

Butt, R. (1981, May 3). Economics are the method: The object is to change the soul. *Sunday Times*. www.margaretthatcher.org/document/104475

Canguilhem, G. (2016). What is psychology? *Foucault Studies, 21*, 200–213.

Care Quality Commission. (2018). *Brief guide: Positive behaviour support for people with behaviours that challenge*. www.cqc.org.uk/sites/default/files/20180705_900824_briefguide-positive_behaviour_support_for_people_with_behaviours_that_challenge_v4.pdf

Carver, C.S., Scheier, M.F. & Segerstrom, S.C. (2010). Optimism. *Clinical Psychology Review, 30*, 879–889.

Cederstrom, C. & Spicer, A. (2015). *The wellness syndrome*. Polity Press.

Cederstrom, C. & Spicer, A. (2017). *Desperately seeking self-improvement: A year inside the optimization movement*. OR Books.

CEP Mental Health Policy Group. (2006). *The depression report: A new deal for depression and anxiety disorders*. London School of Economics.

Chaiklin, H. (2011). Attitudes, behavior and social practice. *Journal of Sociology and Social Welfare, 38*(1), 31–54.

Chakelian, A. (2019, October 8). Parliament's chaplain complained about 'stench' and security risk of Westminster Tube's homeless. *New Statesman*. www.newstatesman.com/politics/uk-politics/2019/10/parliament-s-chaplain-complained-about-stench-and-security-risk-westminster-tube

Chan, A.-W., Krleza-Jerić, K., Schmid, I. & Altman, D.G. (2004). Outcome reporting bias in randomised trials funded by the Canadian Institutes of Health Research. *Canadian Medical Association Journal, 171*(7), 735–740.

Chapman, S. (2015, September 11). Dear Richard Littlejohn: Please don't pretend that hunger and poverty are not real, right here, right now. [Blog.] *Huffington Post*. www.huffingtonpost.co.uk/sarah-chapman/foodbanks-richard-littlejohn_b_8123772.html

Charlton, B. (2000). Infostat, cargo-cult science and the policy sausage machine: NICE, CHI and the managerial takeover of clinical practice. In A. Miles, M.J.R. Hampton & B. Hurwitz (Eds.), *NICE, CHI and the NHS reforms: Enabling excellence or imposing control?* (pp.13–32). Aesculapius Medical Press.

Cherry, F. (1995). *The 'stubborn particulars' of social psychology: Essays on the research process*. Routledge.

Chomsky, N. & Herman, E.S. (1995). *Manufacturing consent: The political economy of the mass media*. Vintage Books.

Cialdini, R. (2008). *Influence: The science of persuasion*. William Morrow & Company.

Clarke, J. & Newman, J. (2012). The alchemy of austerity. *Critical Social Policy, 32*(3), 299–319.

Cloud, D. (2007). Corporate social responsibility as oxymoron: The case of Boeing. In S. May, G. Cheney & J. Roper (Eds.), *The debate over corporate social responsibility* (pp. 219–231). Oxford University Press.

Clough, P. & Halley, J. (Eds.). (2007). *The affective turn: Theorising the social.* Duke University Press.

Cobain, I. (2013). *Cruel Britannia: A secret history of torture.* Portobello Books.

Cohen, B.M.Z. (Ed.). (2018). *The Routledge international handbook of mental health.* Routledge.

Coles, S., Keenan, S. & Diamond, B. (Eds.). (2013). *Madness contested: Power and practice.* PCCS Books.

Collini, S. (2012). *What are universities for?* Penguin.

Cooke, B. & Kothari, U. (Eds.). (2001). *Participation: The new tyranny?* Zed Books.

Cooper, M. (2008). *Essential research findings in counselling and psychotherapy: The facts are friendly.* Sage.

Courea, E. (2019, June 19). Cuts to social care funding went too far, admits Jeremy Hunt. *The Times.* www.thetimes.co.uk/article/tory-leaders-debate-cuts-to-social-care-funding-went-too-far-admits-hunt-wsrrkmm7r

Cromby, J. (2004). Between constructionism and neuroscience: The societal co-constitution of embodied subjectivity. *Theory and Psychology, 14*(6), 797–821.

Cromby, J. (2011). The greatest gift? Happiness, governance and psychology. *Social and Personality Psychology Compass, 5*(11), 840–852.

Cromby, J. (2012a). Beyond belief. *Journal of Health Psychology, 17*(7), 943–957.

Cromby, J. (2012b). Feeling the way: Qualitative clinical research in the affective turn. *Qualitative Research in Psychology, 9*(1), 88–98.

Cromby, J. (2015). *Feeling bodies: Embodying psychology.* Palgrave.

Cromby, J. (2018). Ten suggestions for critical teaching in psychology. In C. Newnes & L. Golding (Eds.), *Teaching critical psychology: International perspectives* (pp.19–36). Routledge.

Cromby, J. (2019). The myths of Brexit. *Journal of Community & Applied Social Psychology, 29*(1), 56–66.

Crook, J. (2009). *World crisis and Buddhist humanism. End games: Collapse or renewal of civilization.* New Age Books.

Crowley, M., Tope, D., Chamberlain, L.J. & Hodson, R. (2010). Neo-Taylorism at work: Occupational change in the post-Fordist era. *Social Problems, 57*(3), 421–447.

Cuijpers, P. (2017). Four decades of outcome research on psychotherapies for adult depression: An overview of a series of meta-analyses. *Canadian Psychology, 58*(1), 7–19.

Cuijpers, P., Smit, F., Bohlmeijer, E., Hollon, S.D. & Andersson, G. (2010a). Efficacy of cognitive-behavioural therapy and other psychological treatments for adult depression: Meta-analytic study of publication bias. *British Journal of Psychiatry, 196*(3), 173–178.

Cuijpers, P., Van Straten, A., Bohlmeijer, E., Hollon, S. D. & Andersson, G. (2010b). The effects of psychotherapy for adult depression are overestimated: A meta-analysis of study quality and effect size. *Psychological Medicine, 40*(2), 211–223.

Curran, J., Parry, G.D., Hardy, G.E., Darling, J., Mason, A. & Chambers, E. (2019). How does therapy harm? A model of adverse process using task analysis in the meta-synthesis of service users' experience. *Frontiers in Psychology, 10,* 347.

Daguerre, A. & Etherington, D. (2014). Welfare reform in the UK under the Conservative-led Coalition government: Ruptures and continuities. *Economic and Social Research Council.* http://workfare.org.uk/images/uploads/docs/Welfare_Reform_in_the_UK_PubReady.pdf

Dahlstedt, M., Fejesb, A. & Schönninga, E. (2011). The will to (de)liberate: Shaping governable citizens through cognitive behavioural programmes in school. *Journal of Education Policy*, 26(3), 399–414.

Dalal, F. (2015). Statistical spin: Linguistic obfuscation: The art of overselling the CBT evidence base. *The Journal of Psychological Therapies in Primary Care*, 4, 1–25.

Dalal, F. (2018). *CBT: The cognitive behavioural tsunami: Managerialism, politics, and the corruption of science*. Routledge.

Damasio, A.R. (1999). *The feeling of what happens: Body, emotion and the making of consciousness*. William Heinemann.

Dardot, P. & Laval, C. (2013). *The new way of the world: On neoliberal society*. Verso.

Das Nair, R. & Fairbank, S. (2012). Mental health. In R. Das Nair & C. Butler (Eds.). (2012), *Mental health, intersectionality, sexuality and psychological therapies* (pp.185–212). John Wiley & Sons.

Davies, D. (1997). *Counselling in psychological services*. Open University.

Davies, W. (2015). *The happiness industry. How government and big business sold us well-being*. Verso.

Davies, W. (2020a, March 24). The last global crisis didn't change the world. But this one could. *The Guardian*. www.theguardian.com/commentisfree/2020/mar/24/coronavirus-crisis-change-world-financial-global-capitalism

Davies, W. (2020b, May 16). The Great British Battle: How the fight against coronavirus spread a new nationalism. *The Guardian*. www.theguardian.com/books/2020/may/16/the-great-british-battle-how-the-fight-against-coronavirus-spread-a-new-nationalism

Davis, M. (2006). *Planet of slums*. Verso.

Diamond, B. (1998). Stepping outside and not knowing: Community psychology and enduring mental health problems, *Clinical Psychology Forum*, 12, 40–42.

Diamond, B. (2008). Opening up space for dissension: A questioning psychology. In A. Morgan (Ed.), *Being human: Reflections on mental distress in society* (pp.174–189). PCCS Books.

Diamond, B. (2013). Rebuilding the house of mental health services with home truths. In S. Coles, S. Keenan & B. Diamond (Eds.), *Madness contested: Power and practice* (pp.317–331). PCCS Books.

Diamond, B. (2014). *The political economy of formulation: An account of practice*. DCP National Conference, Glasgow.

Dineen, T. (1998). *Manufacturing victims*. Dent.

Dixon, T. (2003). *From passions to emotions: The creation of a secular psychological category*. Cambridge University Press.

Doherty, A. (2020, May 16). Has the coronavirus crisis killed neoliberalism? Don't bet on it. *The Guardian*. www.theguardian.com/commentisfree/2020/may/16/state-intervention-agenda-dont-assume-neoliberalism-dead

Dorling, D. (2004). Prime suspect: Murder in Britain. In P. Hillyard, C. Pantazis, S. Tombs & D. Gordon (Eds.), *Beyond criminology: Taking harm seriously* (pp.178–192). Pluto Press.

Dorling, D. (2017). *The equality effect: Improving life for everyone*. New Internationalist Publications.

Dorling, D. (2018). *Injustice* (2nd ed.). Polity Press.

Double, D. (Ed.). (2006). *Critical psychiatry: The limits of madness*. Palgrave.

Double, D. (2019). Twenty years of the Critical Psychiatry Network. *British Journal of Psychiatry*, 214, 61–62.

Dragioti, E., Dimoliatis, I. & Evangelou, E. (2015). Disclosure of researcher allegiance in meta-analyses and randomised controlled trials of psychotherapy: A systematic appraisal. *BMJ Open, 5*(6), e007206. https://bmjopen.bmj.com/content/5/6/e007206

Driessen, E., Hollon, S., Bockting, C.L., Cuijpers, P. & Turner, E.H. (2015, September 30). Does publication bias inflate the apparent efficacy of psychological treatment for major depressive disorder? A systematic review and meta-analysis of US National Institutes of Health-Funded Trials. *PLoS One, 10*(9), e0137864. https://doi.org/10.1371/journal.pone.0137864

Duffy, S. (2013). *A fair society? How the cuts target disabled people.* Centre for Welfare Reform. www.centreforwelfarereform.org/uploads/attachment/354/a-fair-society.pdf

Dunford, J. (2020, May 28). 'Things have to change': Tourism businesses look to a greener future. *The Guardian.* www.theguardian.com/travel/2020/may/28/things-had-to-change-tourism-businesses-look-to-a-greener-future

Durham R.C., Guthrie M., Morton R.V., Reid D.A., Treliving L.R., Fowler D. & Macdonald, R.R. (2003). Tayside-Fife clinical trial of cognitive-behavioural therapy for medication-resistant psychotic symptoms. Results to 3-month follow-up. *British Journal of Psychiatry, 182,* 303–311.

Durlak, J.A. (1979). Comparative effectiveness of paraprofessional and professional helpers. *Psychological Bulletin, 86*(1), 80–92.

Eagleton, T. (1991). *Ideology: An introduction.* Verso.

Earle, S. (2020, April 16). The nationalist right feeds on fear. Coronavirus is its big chance. *The Guardian.* www.theguardian.com/commentisfree/2020/apr/16/nationalist-right-fear-coronavirus-infection-pandemic

Earnshaw, M. (2008). Communities on the couch. In D. Clements, A. Donald, M. Earnshaw & A. Williams. (Eds.), *The future of community (Reports of a death greatly exaggerated)* (pp.147–159). Pluto Press.

Edge, I. Stewart, A. & Kagan, C. (2004). Living poverty: Surviving on the edge, *Clinical Psychology, 38,* 28-31.

Edwards, D. & Potter, J. (1992). *Discursive psychology.* Sage Publications.

Ehrenreich, B. (2018, March 31). Why are the poor blamed and shamed for their deaths? *The Guardian.* www.theguardian.comlifeandstyle/2018/mar/31/why-poor-blamed-shamed-their-deaths-barbara-ehrenreich

Elkin, I., Shea, M.T., Watkins, J.T., Imber, S.D., Sotsky, S.M., Collins, J.F., Glass, D.R., Pilkonis, P.A., Leber, W.R., Docherty, J.P., Fiester, S.J. & Parloff, M.B. (1989). National Institute of Mental Health treatment of depression collaborative research program. *Archives of General Psychiatry, 46*(11), 971–982.

Elkin, L. (2003). Rosalind Franklin and the double helix. *Physics Today, (March),* 42–48.

Elliott, L. (2016, May 27). Austerity policies do more harm than good, IMF study concludes. *The Guardian.* www.theguardian.com/business/2016/may/27/austerity-policies-do-more-harm-than-good-imf-study-concludes

Elliott, L. (2019, February 1). This is about saving capitalism: The Dutch historian who savaged Davos elite. *The Guardian.* www.theguardian.com/business/2019/feb/01/rutger-bregman-world-economic-forum-davos-speech-tax-billionaires-capitalism

Elliott, L. & Wintour, P. (2010, June 22). Budget 2010: Pain now, more pain later in austerity plan. *The Guardian.* www.theguardian.com/uk/2010/jun/22/budget-2010-vat-austerity-plan

Ellis, D., Tucker, I. & Harper, D. (2013). The affective atmospheres of surveillance. *Theory & Psychology, 23*(6), 716–731.

Eltantawy, N. & Wiest, J.B. (2011). Social media in the Egyptian revolution: Reconsidering resource mobilisation theory. *International Journal of Communication, 5,* 1207–1224.

Epstein, W.M. (1995). *The illusion of psychotherapy.* Transaction.

Epstein, W.M. (2006). *The civil divine: Psychotherapy as religion in America.* University of Nevada Press.

Epstein, W.M. (2010). *Democracy without decency: Good citizenship and the war on poverty.* Penn State Press.

Epstein, W.M. (2013). *Empowerment as ceremony.* Transaction Publishers.

Epstein, W.M. (2018). *The masses are the ruling classes: Policy romanticism, democratic populism, and social welfare in America.* Cambridge University Press.

Epstein, W.M. (2019). *Psychotherapy and the social clinic in the United States: Soothing fictions.* Springer International.

Evaldsson, A.-C. (2003). Throwing like a girl? Situating gender differences in physicality across game contexts. *Childhood, 10*(4), 475–497.

Evans, S., Tsao, J.C.I., Lu, Q., Myers, C., Suresh, J. & Zeltzer, L.K. (2008). Parent-child pain relationships from a psychosocial perspective: A review of the literature. *Journal of Pain Management, 1*(3), 237–246.

Evans, T.M., Bira, L., Gastelum, J.B., Weiss, L.T. & Vanderford, N.L. (2018). Evidence for a mental health crisis in graduate education. *Nature Biotechnology, 36,* 282.

Fals-Borda, O. (1987). The application of participatory-action research in Latin America. *International Sociology, 2,* 329–347.

Farias, M. & Wikholm, C. (2015). *The Buddha pill: Can meditation change you?* Watkins.

Farlow, A. (2013). *Crash and beyond: Causes and consequences of the global financial crisis.* Oxford University Press.

Federal Ministry for Economic Affairs and Climate Action. (2022). *What is Industrie 4.0?* Federal Ministry for Economic Affairs and Climate Action. www.plattform-i40.de/PI40/Navigation/EN/Industrie40/WhatIsIndustrie40/what-is-industrie40.html

Fenichel, O. (1994). *The psychoanalytic theory of the neuroses.* W.W. Norton & Co.

Fenney, D. (2019). *Tackling poor health outcomes: The role of trauma-informed care.* The King's Fund. www.kingsfund.org.uk/search?search=tackling+poor+health+outcomes+trauma+informed

Ferguson, D. (2017, November 21). Working-class children get less of everything in education – including respect. *The Guardian.* www.theguardian.com/education/2017/nov/21/english-class-system-shaped-in-schools

Ferguson, I. (2007, December 18). Neoliberalism, happiness and wellbeing. *International Socialism, 117.* http://isj.org.uk/neoliberalism-happiness-and-wellbeing/

Ferneyhough, C. (2016). *The voices within: The history and science of how we talk to ourselves.* Profile Books.

Fine, M. (2012). Resuscitating critical psychology for 'revolting' times. *Journal of Social Issues, 68*(2), 416–438.

Finley, K. (2013, April 17). What if your boss tracked your sleep, diet, and exercise? *Wired.* www.wired.com/2013/04/quantified-work-citizen/

Fisher, M. (2009). *Capitalist realism: Is there no alternative?* Zero Books.

Fisher, S. & Greenberg, G. (1989). *The limits of biological treatments for psychological distress: Comparisons with psychotherapy and placebo.* Lawrence Earlbaum.

Ford, M. (2016). *The rise of the robots: Technology and the threat of mass unemployment.* Oneworld.

Forde, R.A. (2018). *Bad psychology: How forensic psychology left science behind.* Jessica Kingsley.

Foti, A. & Romano Z. (Eds.). (2004). Precarity. (Special issue.) *Greenpepper Magazine.*

Foucault, M. (1977). *Discipline and punish*. Penguin.

Foucault, M. (1988). Technologies of the self. In L. Martin, H. Gutman & P. Hutton (Eds.), *Technologies of the self* (pp.16–49). Tavistock Publications.

Fox, C. (2016). The snowflake factory. *The Spectator*. www.spectator.co.uk/2016/06/generation-snowflake-how-we-train-our-kids-to-be-censorious-cry-babies/

Fox, D., Prilleltensky, I. & Austin, S. (2009). *Critical psychology: An introduction*. Sage Publications.

Frank, J.D. (1961). *Persuasion and healing: A comparative study of psychotherapy*. John Hopkins University Press.

Freire, P. (1993). *Pedagogy of the oppressed*. Penguin.

Freud, S. (1973). *New introductory lectures on psychoanalysis*. Penguin.

Friedli, L. (2009). *Mental health, resilience and inequalities*. World Health Organization.

Friedli, L. & Stearn, R. (2015). Positive affect as coercive strategy: Conditionality, activation and the role of psychology in UK government workfare programmes. *Medical Humanities, 41*(1), 40–47.

Frost, N.D., Laska, K.M. & Wampold, B.E. (2014). The evidence for present centered therapy as a treatment for post-traumatic stress disorder. *Journal of Traumatic Stress, 27*(1), 1–8.

Fryer, D. (1992). Signed on at the 'Beroo': Mental health and unemployment in Scotland. *The Psychologist, 5,* 539–542.

Fryer, D. & Fagan, R. (2003). Towards a critical psychology perspective on unemployment and mental health research. *American Journal of Community Psychology, 32,* 89–96.

Fryer, D. & Stambe, R. (2014). Neoliberal austerity and unemployment. *The Psychologist, 27*(4), 244–249.

Fuchs, T. (2013). Depression, intercorporeality and interaffectivity. *Journal of Consciousness Studies 20,* 219–238.

Fuchs, T. (2016). Intercorporeality and interaffectivity. In C. Meyer, J. Streeck & S. Jordan (Eds.), *Intercorporeality: Emerging socialities in interaction* (pp.3–24). Oxford University Press.

Fukayama, F. (1989). The end of history? *The National Interest, 16,* 3–18.

Furedi, F. (2003). *Therapy culture: Cultivating vulnerability in an uncertain age*. Routledge.

Garland, D. (2002). *The culture of control: Crime and social order in contemporary society*. Oxford University Press.

Garthwaite, K. (2016). *Hunger pains: Life inside foodbank Britain*. Policy Press.

Gayle, D. (2019, August 3). Home secretary Priti Patel criticised over wish for criminals 'to feel terror'. *The Guardian*. www.theguardian.com/politics/2019/aug/03/priti-patel-home-secretary-wants-criminals-to-literally-feel-terror

Gergen, K.J. (1985). The social constructionist movement in modern psychology. *American Psychologist, 40*(3), 266–275.

Gigerenzer, G. (2004). Mindless statistics. *Journal of Socio-Economics, 33*(5), 587–606.

Gilbert, J. (2016, April 18). Why did 'working-class culture' disintegrate in the 1980s? A sort of reply to Paul Mason. *Open Democracy*. www.opendemocracy.net/uk/jeremy-gilbert/why-did-working-class-culture-disintegrate-in-1980s-sort-of-reply-to-paul-mason

Gilbert, P. (1992). *Depression: The evolution of powerlessness*. Lawrence Erlbaum Associates.

Gleitman, H., Gross, J. & Reisberg, D. (2010). *Psychology*. W.W. Norton & Co.

Godsi, E. (2004). *Violence and society: Making sense of madness and badness*. PCCS Books.

Goldacre, B. (2019). *All trials registered. All results reported*. +AllTrials. www.alltrials.net//wp-content/uploads/2013/09/What-does-all-trials-registered-and-reported-mean.pdf

Goldberg, S., Rousmaniere, T.G., Miller, S.D., Whipple, J. Nielsen, N.L., Hoyt, W.T. & Wampold, B.E. (2016). Do psychotherapists improve with time and experience? A longitudinal analysis of real world outcome data. *Journal of Counseling Psychology, 63*(1), 1–11.

Goodman, L.A., Rosenberg, S., Mueser, K. & Drake, R. (1997). Physical and sexual assault history in women with serious mental illness: Prevalence, correlates, treatment and future research directions. *Schizophrenia Bulletin, 23,* 685–697.

Gould, S.J. (1981). *The mismeasure of man.* Penguin.

Graeber, D. (2018). *Bullshit jobs: A theory.* Simon & Schuster.

Gregg, M. & Seigworth, G. (Eds.). (2010). *The affect theory reader.* Duke University Press.

Grierson, J. (2019, April 3). Abolish prison terms of under a year to ease safety crisis, say MPs. *The Guardian.* www.theguardian.com/society/2019/apr/03/abolish-prison-terms-of-under-a-year-to-ease-safety-crisis-say-mps

Guardian, The (n.d.). The Cambridge Analytica files. *The Guardian.* www.theguardian.com/news/series/cambridge-analytica-files

Gunnell, D., Kidger, J. & Elvidge, H. (2018). Adolescent mental health in crisis. *BMJ 361,* k2608.

Hagan, T. & Donnison, D. (1999). Social power: Some implications for the theory and practice of cognitive behaviour therapy. *Journal of Community and Applied Social Psychology, 9,* 119–135.

Hakim, C. (2011). *Honey money. The power of erotic capital.* Allen Lane.

Hallam, R. (2018). *Abolishing the concept of mental illness: Rethinking the nature of our woes.* Routledge.

Han, B-C. (2017). *Psycho-politics: Neoliberalism and new technologies of power.* Verso.

Hanley, B. (2008). *Estates: An intimate history.* Allen Lane.

Hanley, L. (2016). *Respectable: The experience of class.* Allen Lane.

Harper, D. & Speed, E. (2012). Uncovering recovery: The resistible rise of recovery and resilience. *Studies in Social Justice, 6* (1), 9–25.

Harré, R. (2002). *Cognitive science: A philosophical introduction.* Sage Publications.

Harris, C. (2014). The impact of austerity on a British council estate. *The Psychologist, 27*(4), 250–253.

Harvey, D. (2005). *A brief history of neo-liberalism.* Open University Press.

Hassiotis, A., Poppe, M., Strydom, A., Vickerstaff, V., Hall, I.S., Crabtree, J., Omar, R.Z., King, M., Hunter, R., Biswas, A., Cooper, V., Howie, W. & Crawford, M.J. (2018). Clinical outcomes of staff training in positive behaviour support to reduce challenging behaviour in adults with intellectual disability: Cluster randomised controlled trial. *British Journal of Psychiatry, 212*(3), 161–168.

Hattie, J.A., Sharpley, C.F. & Rogers, H.F. (1984). Comparative effectiveness of professional and paraprofessional helpers. *Psychological Bulletin, 95*(3), 534–541.

Haug, F. (1987). *Female sexualisation: A collective work of memory.* Verso.

Healy, D. (2013). *Pharmageddon.* University of California Press.

Hearn, A. (2008). Meat, mask, burden: Probing the contours of the branded 'self'. *Journal of Consumer Culture, 8*(2), 197–217.

Heenan, M. & Dryden, W. (2002). *Cognitive behaviour therapy: An A-Z of persuasive arguments.* Whurr Publishers.

Hern, A. (2020, March 13). Covid-19 could cause permanent shift towards home working. *The Guardian.* www.theguardian.com/technology/2020/mar/13/covid-19-could-cause-permanent-shift-towards-home-working

Hilbrecht, M., Shaw, S.M., Johnson, L.C. & Andrey, J. (2008). I'm home for the kids: Contradictory implications for work–life balance of teleworking mothers. *Gender, Work & Organization*, 15(5), 454–476.

HM Inspectorate of Prisons. (2015). *Annual report 2014 to 2015*. HM Inspectorate of Prisons. www.gov.uk/government/publications/hm-chief-inspector-of-prisons-annual-report-2014-to-2015

Hobfoll, S.E. (2001). The influence of culture, community, and the nested-self in the stress process: Advancing conservation of resources theory. *Applied Psychology*, 50(3), 337–421.

Hobfoll, S.E. & Lilly R.S. (1993). Resource conservation as a strategy for community psychology. *Journal of Community Psychology*, 21, 128–147.

Hochschild, A.R. (1983). *The managed heart: The commercialisation of human feeling*. University of California Press.

Hoffart, A., Hedley, L.M., Svanøe, K., Langkaas, T.F. & Sexton, H. (2016). Agoraphobia with and without panic disorder: A 20-year follow-up of integrated exposure and psychodynamic therapy. *The Journal of Nervous and Mental Disease*, 204(2), 100–107. https://doi.org/10.1097/NMD.0000000000000419

Holland, S. (1992). From social abuse to social action: A neighbourhood psychotherapy and social action project for women. In J. Ussher & P. Nicholson (Eds.). *Gender issues in clinical psychology* (pp.68–77). Routledge.

Holmes, G. (2010). *Psychology in the real world: Using community-based groups to help people*. PCCS Books.

Holmes, G., Newnes, C. & Dunne, C. (Eds.). (1999). *This is madness*. PCCS Books.

Homeless Link. (n.d.). *Rough sleeping – our analysis*. Homeless Link. www.homeless.org.uk/facts/homelessness-in-numbers/rough-sleeping/rough-sleeping-our-analysis

Hook, D. (2007). *Foucault, psychology and the analytics of power*. Palgrave.

Houghton, P. (2005). Stop the juggernaut. *Mental Health Today, February*, 22–25.

Houghton, P. (2016). Joining the debate around psychiatric medication. *Clinical Psychology Forum*, 286, 10–13.

Howard, A. (1998). *Challenges to counselling and psychotherapy*. Macmillan.

Hróbjartsson, A., Emanuelsson, A., Skou Thomsen, A.S. & Hilden, J. (2014). Bias due to lack of patient blinding in clinical trials. A systematic review of trials randomizing patients to blind and nonblind sub-studies. *International Journal of Epidemiology*, 43(4), 1272–1283.

Iacobucci, G. (2019). NHS prescribed record number of antidepressants last year. *BMJ*, 364(l1508). www.bmj.com/content/364/bmj.l1508

Illich, I. (2001a). *Tools for conviviality*. Marion Boyars.

Illich, I. (2001b). *Disabling professions*. Marion Boyars.

Iliffe, S. (2008). *From general practice to primary care: The industrialization of family medicine*. Oxford University Press.

Illouz, E. (2008). *Saving the modern soul: Therapy, emotions and the culture of self-help*. University of California Press.

Independent Living (n.d.). *PIP and ESA claims update*. Independent Living. www.independentliving.co.uk/advice/pip-esa-appeals/

Inequality.org. (n.d.). *Facts: Global inequality*. Inequality.org. http://inequality.org/global-inequality/

Ingleby, D. (1974). The job psychologists do. In N. Armistead (Ed.), *Reconstructing social psychology* (pp.314–328). Penguin.

Ingleby, D. (Ed.). (1983). *Critical psychiatry*. Penguin.

Jackson, C. & Rizq, R. (Eds.). (2019). *The industrialisation of care: Counselling, psychotherapy and the impact of IAPT*. PCCS Books.

Jacobson, N. & Truax, P. (1991). Clinical significance: A statistical approach to defining meaningful change in psychotherapy research. *Journal of Consulting and Clinical Psychology, 59*(1), 12–19.

James, O. (2008). *The selfish capitalist: Origins of affluenza*. Vermilion.

Jensen, J.A. (1994). An investigation of eye movement desensitization and reprocessing (EMDR) as a treatment for posttraumatic stress disorder (PTSD) symptoms of Vietnam combat veterans. *Behavior Therapy, 25*, 311–325.

Jensen, S.A. & Corralejo, S.M. (2017). Measurement issues: Large effect sizes do not mean most people get better – clinical significance and the importance of individual results. *Child and Adolescent Mental Health, 22*(3), 163–166. https://doi.org/10.1111/camh.12203

Jensen, T. (2014). Welfare commonsense, poverty porn and doxosophy. *Sociological Research Online, 19*(3), 3. https://doi.org/10.5153/sro.3441.

Jessop, B. (2002). *The future of the capitalist state*. Polity Press.

Johnson, M. (2007). *The meaning of the body: Aesthetics of human understanding*. University of Chicago Press.

Johnstone, L. (2022). *Users and abusers of psychiatry* (Classic ed.). Routledge.

Johnstone, L. & Boyle, M. with J. Cromby, J. Dillon, D. Harper, P. Kinderman, E. Longden, D. Pilgrim and J. Read (2018). *The Power Threat Meaning Framework: Towards the identification of patterns in emotional distress, unusual experiences and troubled or troubling behaviour, as an alternative to functional psychiatric diagnosis*. British Psychological Society.

Johnstone, L. & Dallos, R. (Eds.). (2013). *Formulation in psychology and psychotherapy: Making sense of people's problems*. Routledge.

Jones, G., Meegan, R., Kennett, P. & Croft, J. (2016). The uneven impact of austerity on the voluntary and community sector: A tale of two cities. *Urban Studies 53*(10), 2064–2080.

Jones, L. (2018a). Trauma informed care and 'good lives' in confinement: Acknowledging and offsetting adverse impacts of chronic trauma and loss of liberty. In G. Akerman, A. Needs & C. Bainbridge (Eds.), *Transforming environments and rehabilitation: A guide for practitioners in forensic settings and criminal justice* (pp.92–114). Routledge.

Jones, L. (2018b). *New developments in interventions for working with offending behaviour*. In A. Ward & D. Polescheck (Eds.), *The Wiley international handbook of correctional psychology* (pp.669–686). Wiley.

Jones, L.F. (2015). The Peaks unit: From a pilot for 'untreatable' psychopaths to trauma-informed milieu therapy. *The Prison Service Journal, 218*, 17–23.

Jones, O. (2011). *Chavs: The demonisation of the working class*. Verso.

Jonsson, U., Alaie, I., Parling, T. & Arnberg, F.K. (2014). Reporting of harms in randomized controlled trials of psychological interventions for mental and behavioural disorders: A review of current practice. *Contemporary Clinical Trials, 38*(1), 1–8.

Jopling, D. (2008). *Talking cures and placebo effects*. Oxford University Press.

Judt, T. (2010). *Ill fares the land: A treatise on our present discontents*. Allen Lane.

Kabat-Zinn, J. (1994). *Full catastrophe living: Using the wisdom of your body and mind to face stress, pain and illness*. Delta.

Kagan, C. (2007). Working at the edge: Making use of psychological resources through collaboration. *The Psychologist, 20*(4), 224–227.

Kagan, C. & Burton, M. (2001). *Critical community psychology praxis for the 21st century*. Paper presented to British Psychological Society conference, Glasgow, March.

Kagan, C., Burton, M., Duckett, P., Lawthorn, R. & Siddiquee, A. (2019). *Critical community psychology: Critical action and social change* (2nd ed.). Routledge.

Kagan, C., Castile, S. & Stewart, A. (2005). Participation: Are some more equal than others? *Clinical Psychology Forum 153*, 30–34.

Kagan, J. (2013). *The human spark: The science of human development.* Basic Books.

Kazmi, A. (2011, September 27). How anonymous emerged to occupy Wall Street. *The Guardian.* www.theguardian.com/commentisfree/cifamerica/2011/sep/27/occupy-wall-street-anonymous

Kearney, A. (2018). *Counselling, class and politics. Undeclared influences in therapy* (2nd ed.) G. Proctor (Ed.). PCCS Books.

Keenan, S. (2009, June 1). *Medication groups.* [Blog.] Critical Values-Based Practice Network. https://criticalvaluesbasedpracticenetwork.co.uk/medication-groups/

Keenan, S. & Coles, S. (2012). The art of debate. *Clinical Psychology Forum, 233,* 19–22.

Kelly, A.E. (2000). A self-presentational view of psychotherapy: Reply to Hill, Gelso, and Mohr (2000) and to Arkin and Herman (2000). *Psychological Bulletin, 126*(4), 505–511.

Khazan, O. (2020, April 15). How the coronavirus could create a new working class. *The Atlantic.* www.theatlantic.com/health/archive/2020/04/coronavirus-class-war-just-beginning/609919/

Kim, S. & Cardemil, E. (2012). Effective psychotherapy with low-income clients: The importance of attending to social class. *Journal of Contemporary Psychotherapy, 42*(1), 27–35.

Kings Fund. (2017). *Understanding NHS financial pressures: How are they affecting patient care?* Kiongs Fund. www.kingsfund.org.uk/publications/understanding-nhs-financial-pressures

Kirsch, I. (2010). *The Emperor's new drugs: Exploding the antidepressant myth.* Random House.

Klein, N. (2020, May 13). Naomi Klein: How big tech plans to profit from the pandemic. *The Guardian.* www.theguardian.com/news/2020/may/13/naomi-klein-how-big-tech-plans-to-profit-from-coronavirus-pandemic

Klein, N. (2008). *The shock doctrine: The rise of disaster capitalism.* Penguin.

Kupfer, D./American Psychiatric Association. (2013). *Chair of DSM-5 task force discusses future of mental health research.* https://www.madinamerica.com/wp-content/uploads/2013/05/Statement-from-dsm-chair-david-kupfer-md.pdf

Lambert, M.J. & Bergin, A.E. (1994). The effectiveness of psychotherapy. In A.E. Bergin & S.L. Garfield (Eds.), *Handbook of psychotherapy and behavior change* (4th ed.) (pp.143–189). Wiley.

Landin-Romero, R., Moreno-Alcazar, A., Pagani, M. & Amann, B. (2018). How does Eye Movement Desensitisation and Reprocessing Therapy work? A systematic review on suggested mechanisms of action. *Frontiers in Psychology, 9,* 1395.

Langer, S. (1967). *Mind: An essay on human feeling* (Vol. 1). The Johns Hopkins University Press.

Lawrence, F., Garside, J., Pegg, D., Conn, D., Carrell, S. & Davies, H. (2020, May 31). Covid-19 investigations: How a decade of privatisation and cuts exposed England to coronavirus. *The Guardian.* www.theguardian.com/world/2020/may/31/how-a-decade-of-privatisation-and-cuts-exposed-england-to-coronavirus

Lazzarato, M. (2012). *The making of the indebted man: An essay on the neoliberal condition.* MIT Press.

Lehrhaupt, L. & Meibert, P. (2017). *Mindfulness based stress reduction: The MBSR program for enhancing health and vitality.* New World Library.

Lewin, K. (1951). *Field theory in social science: Selected theoretical papers.* D. Cartwright (Ed.). Harper Row.

Lewis, S. (2018). A campaign for climate change: The role of therapeutic relationships within a climate of control. In G. Akerman, A. Needs & C. Bainbridge (Eds.), *Transforming* environments and rehabilitation: A guide for practitioners in forensic settings and criminal justice* (pp.115–131). Routledge.

Lilienfeld, S.O. (1996). EMDR treatment: Less than meets the eye. *Skeptical Inquirer, 20*(1), 25–31.

Lilienfeld, S.O. (2007). Psychological treatments that cause harm. *Perspectives on Psychological Science, 2*(1), 53–70.

Loewenthal, D. & Proctor, G. (Eds.). (2018). *Why not CBT? Against and for CBT revisited*. PCCS Books.

Longmore, R. & Worrell, M. (2006). Do we need to challenge thoughts in Cognitive Behavior Therapy? *Clinical Psychology Review, 27*(2), 173–187.

Lordon, F. (2014). *Willing slaves of capital: Spinoza and Marx on desire*. Verso.

Lovett, H. (1996). *Learning to listen: Positive approaches and people with difficult behaviour*. Paul H Brookes Publishing Company.

Luber, M. (n.d.). *A community of heart profile: Francine Shapiro*. Francine Shapiro Library. https://emdria.omeka.net/items/show/7635

Mair, G. (2004). The origins of *What Works* in England and Wales: A house built on sand? In G. Mair (Ed.), *What matters in probation* (pp.12–33). Willan Publishing.

Major, L.E. & Machin, S. (2020, May 28). *Covid-19 and social mobility*. Paper number CEPCOVID-19-004. LSE Centre for Economic Performance. https://cep.lse.ac.uk/_new/publications/abstract.asp?index=7024

Malli, M.A., Sams, L., Forrester-Jones, R., Murphy, G. & Henwood, M. (2019). Austerity and the lives of people with learning disabilities. A thematic synthesis of current literature. *Disability and Society, 33*(9), 1412–1435.

Marmot, M. (2010). *Fair society, healthy lives: Strategic review of health inequalities in England post-2010*. Department of Health.

Marsh, B. (2011, September 4). The great prosperity 1947–79/The great regression 1980–Now. *New York Times*. https://archive.nytimes.com/www.nytimes.com/imagepages/2011/09/04/opinion/04reich-graphic.html

Martin, E. (1995). *Flexible bodies: Tracking immunity in American culture from the days of polio to the age of AIDS*. Beacon Press.

Martin, L., Gutman, H. & Hutton, P. (Eds.). (1988). *Technologies of the self: A seminar with Michel Foucault*. Tavistock Publications.

Martin-Baro, I. (1994). *Writings for a liberation psychology*. A. Aron & S. Corne (Eds.). Harvard Press.

Mason, P. (2016, April 4). The problem for poor, white kids is that a part of their culture has been destroyed. *The Guardian*. www.theguardian.com/commentisfree/2016/apr/04/the-problem-for-poor-white-kids-is-that-a-part-of-their-culture-has-been-destroyed

Masson, J. (1984). *The assault on truth: Freud's suppression of the seduction theory*. Farrar, Strauss & Giroux.

Masson, J. (1985). *Against therapy*. Sphere.

Massumi, B. (1995). The autonomy of affect. *Cultural Critique, 31*, 83–109.

McGarvey, D. (2018). *Poverty safari: Understanding the anger of Britain's underclass*. Picador.

McGrath, L., Griffin, V. & Mundy, E. (2016). The psychological impact of austerity: A briefing paper. *Educational Psychology Research and Practice, 2*(2), 46–57.

McKenzie, L. (2015). *Getting by: Estates, class and culture in austerity Britain*. Policy Press.

McLean, S., Schultz, D. & Steger, B. (Eds.). (2002). *Social capital: Critical perspectives on community and bowling alone*. New York University Press.

McNamee, S. & Gergen, K.J. (1992). *Therapy as social construction.* Sage Publications.

McVeigh, K. (2015, November 12). Austerity a factor in rising suicide rate among UK men – study. *The Guardian.* www.theguardian.com/society/2015/nov/12/austerity-a-factor-in-rising-suicide-rate-among-uk-men-study#:~:text=Debt%2C%20austerity%20and%20 unemployment%20have,2008%2C%20according%20to%20new%20research

Meeks, J. (2015). *Private island: Why Britain now belongs to someone else.* Verso.

Melluish, S. & Bulmer, D. (1999). Rebuilding solidarity: An account of a men's health action project. *Journal of Community & Applied Social Psychology, 9*(2), 93–100.

Meltzer, H., Lader, D., Corbin, T., Goodman, R. & Ford, T. (2004). *The mental health of young people looked after by local authorities in Scotland.* The Stationery Office.

Mental Health Foundation. (2016). *Mental health and prevention: Taking local action for better mental health.* Mental Health Foundation.

Mews, A., Di Bella, A. & Purver, M. (2017). *Impact evaluation of the prison-based Core Sex Offender Treatment Programme.* Ministry of Justice. www.gov.uk/government/publications/impact-evaluation-of-the-prison-based-core-sex-offender-treatment-programme

Middleton, D. & Brown, S.D. (2005). *The social psychology of experience: Studies in remembering and forgetting.* Sage Publications.

Middleton, D. & Edwards, D. (1990). *Collective remembering.* Sage Publications.

Milburn, K. (2019). *Generation left.* Polity Press.

Milburn, K. (2020, June 1). The pandemic is changing how it feels to be free. *Novara Media.* https://novaramedia.com/2020/06/01/the-pandemic-is-changing-how-it-feels-to-be-free/

Mindfulness All-Party Parliamentary Group. (2015). *Mindful Nation UK: Report by the Mindfulness All-Party Parliamentary Group (MAPPG).* The Mindfulness Initiative.

Mishra, P. (2004). *An end to suffering: The Buddha in the world.* Picador.

Mollon, P. (2007). The NICE guidelines are misleading, unscientific, and potentially impede good psychological care and help. *Psychodynamic Practice, 15*(1), 9–24.

Moloney, P. (2013). *The therapy industry: The irresistible rise of the talking cure, and why it doesn't work.* Pluto Press.

Moloney, P. (2016). Mindfulness: The bottled water of the therapy industry. In R.E. Purser, D.F. Forbes, D.F. & A. Burke (Eds.), *Handbook of Mindfulness. Culture, context, and social engagement* (pp.269–292). Springer International.

Monbiot, G. (2017). *How did we get into this mess?* Verso.

Moncrieff, J. (2013). *The bitterest pills: The troubling story of anti-psychotic drugs.* Palgrave Macmillan.

Moncrieff, J. (2017). *Inconvenient truths about antipsychotics should not be swept under the carpet: A response to Goff et al.* [Blog.] Joanna Moncrieff. https://joannamoncrieff.com/2017/05/08/inconvenient-truths-about-antipsychotics-should-not-be-swept-under-the-carpet-a-response-to-goff-et-al/

Moncrieff, J. (2020). *A straight talking introduction to psychiatric drugs* (2nd ed). PCCS Books.

Montero, M. & Sonn, C.S. (Eds.). (2009). *Psychology of liberation: Theory and applications.* Springer Science.

Moore, P. & Robinson, A. (2016). The quantified self: What counts in the neoliberal workplace. *New Media & Society, 18*(11), 2774–2792.

Morgan, A. (2008). The authority of lived experience. In A. Morgan (Ed.), *Being human: Reflections on mental distress in society* (pp.54–70). PCCS Books.

Morris, N. (2013, July 3). Demand for food banks has nothing to do with benefits squeeze, says Work Minister Lord Freud. *Independent.* www.independent.co.uk/news/uk/politics/

demand-for-food-banks-has-nothing-to-do-with-benefits-squeeze-says-work-minister-lord-freud-8684005.html

Muhammad, S., Long, X. & Salman, M. (2020). COVID-19 pandemic and environmental pollution: A blessing in disguise? *Science of The Total Environment, 728*, 138820.

Munder, T., Brutsch, O., Leonhart, R., Gerger, H. & Barth, J. (2013). Researcher allegiance in psychotherapy research: An overview of reviews. *Clinical Psychology Review, 33*(4), 501–511.

Mutch, A. (2003). Communities of practice and habitus: A critique. *Organization Studies, 24*(3), 383–401.

Mute (2005). The precarious issue. *Mute 1*(29). https://www.metamute.org/editorial/magazine/mute-vol-1-no.-29-%E2%80%93-precarious-issue

Nafstad, H.E. (2002). The neo-liberal ideology and the self-interest paradigm as resistance to change. *Radical Psychology, Spring*.

National Collaborating Centre for Mental Health. (2009). *Borderline personality disorder: The NICE guideline on treatment and management*. British Psychological Society/The Royal College of Psychiatrists.

National Collaborating Centre for Mental Health. (2010). *Depression: The treatment and management of depression in adults (updated edition)*. British Psychological Society/The Royal College of Psychiatrists.

National Collaborating Centre for Mental Health. (2014). *Psychosis and schizophrenia in adults. Treatment and management. National clinical guideline number 178*. National Collaborating Centre for Mental Health.

National Hearing Voices Network. (2018). *The Mental Health Act: An alternative review*. National Hearing Voices Network.

National Institute for Clinical Excellence. (2005). *Post-traumatic stress disorder*. National clinical practice guideline 26. NICE.

National Institute for Health and Care Excellence. (2015). *Challenging behaviour and learning disabilities: Prevention and interventions for people with learning disabilities whose behaviour challenges*. NICE guideline 11. NICE. www.nice.org.uk/guidance/ng11

National Institute for Health and Care Excellence. (2017). *Developing NICE guidelines: The manual*. NICE. www.nice.org.uk/process/pmg20

National Institute for Health and Care Excellence. (2018). *Post-traumatic stress disorder. [D] Evidence reviews for psychological, psychosocial and other non-pharmacological interventions for the treatment of PTSD in adults*. NICE.

Nelson, F. (2015, April 3). David Cameron should not be afraid to talk about food banks. *Daily Telegraph*. www.telegraph.co.uk/news/general-election-2015/11511944/David-Cameron-should-not-be-afraid-to-talk-about-food-banks.html

NHS England (2019). *The NHS long term plan*. NHS England. www.longtermplan.nhs.uk/wp-content/uploads/2019/08/nhs-long-term-plan-version-1.2.pdf

Nightingale, D.J. & Cromby, J. (1999). *Social constructionist psychology: A critical analysis of theory and practice*. Open University Press.

Norcross, J.C., VandenBos, G.R. & Freedheim, D.K. (Eds.). (2011). *History of psychotherapy: Continuity and change* (2nd ed.). American Psychological Association.

Nordt, C., Warnke, I., Seifritz, E. & Kawohl, W. (2015). Modelling suicide and unemployment: A longitudinal analysis covering 63 countries, 2000–11. *The Lancet, 2*(3), 239–245.

Norton, P.J. & Price, E.C. (2007). A meta-analytic review of adult cognitive-behavioral treatment outcome across the anxiety disorders. *Journal of Nervous and Mental Disease, 195*(6), 521–531.

Nylander, P.-A., Lindberg, O. & Bloom, A. (2011). Emotional strain and emotional labour amongst Swedish prison officers. *European Journal of Criminology, 8*(6), 469–483.

O'Hara, M. (2015, October 6). Cut off: How austerity relates to our mental health. *New Statesman.* www.newstatesman.com/politics/welfare/2015/10/cut-how-austerity-relates-our-mental-health

Oliver, M. (2004). If I had a hammer: The social model in action. In C. Barnes & G. Mercer (Eds.). *Implementing the social model of disability: Theory and research* (pp.18–31). The Disability Press.

Olson, G. (2013). *Empathy imperiled: Capitalism, culture, and the brain.* Springer.

O'Mahony, S. (2019). *Can medicine be cured? The corruption of a profession.* Head of Zeus.

Open Democracy (2013, December 10). *Campaign guide – NHS cuts and closures.* Open Democracy. https://www.opendemocracy.net/en/ournhs/campaign-guide-nhs-cuts-and-closures/

Open Science Collaboration. (2015). Estimating the reproducibility of psychological science. *Science, 349*(6251), 943. www.science.org/doi/10.1126/science.aac4716

Orford, J. (2008). *Community psychology: Challenges, controversies and emerging consensus* (2nd ed). John Wiley.

Orlinksy, D. (2010). Foreword. In L. Duncan, S.D. Miller, B.E. Wampold & M.A. Hubble (Eds.), *The heart and soul of change: Delivering what works in therapy* (pp.i-xxii). American Psychological Association.

Orne, M.T. (1962a). Implications for psychotherapy derived from current research on the nature of hypnosis. *The American Journal of Psychiatry, 118,* 1097–1103.

Orne, M.T. (1962b). On the social psychology of the psychological experiment: With particular reference to demand characteristics and their implications. *American Psychologist, 17,* 776–783.

Papadopoulos, D. (2018). *Experimental practice: Technoscience, alterontologies, and more-than-social movements.* Duke University Press.

Parker, I. (2007). *Revolution in psychology.* Pluto Press.

Parker, I., Georgaca, E., Harper, D., McLaughin T. & Stowell-Smith, M. (1995). *Deconstructing psychopathology.* Sage Publications.

Pearce, S.H.S. & Cheetham, T.D. (2010). Diagnosis and management of vitamin D deficiency. *BMJ, 340*(b5664). https://doi.org/10.1136/bmj.b5664

Peck, T. (2017, April 20). Theresa May struggles to answer when confronted live on TV about nurses going to foodbanks. *The Independent.* www.independent.co.uk/news/uk/politics/video-theresa-may-struggles-to-answer-when-confronted-live-on-tv-about-nurses-going-to-foodbanks-a7710066.html

Peev, G. (2011, April 5). Coalition is inflicting cuts Mrs Thatcher 'could only have dreamt of', says environment minister. *Mail Online.* www.dailymail.co.uk/news/article-1373350/Coalition-inflicting-cuts-Margaret-Thatcher-dreamt-says-Greg-Barker.html

Pilgrim, D. (2008a). Abnormal psychology: Unresolved ontological and epistemological contestation. *History and Philosophy of Psychology, 10*(2), 11–21.

Pilgrim, D. (2008b). 'Recovery' and current mental health policy. *Chronic Illness, 4,* 295–304.

Pilgrim, D. (2009). CBT in the British NHS: Vague imposition or imposition of vagueness? *European Journal of Psychotherapy & Counselling, 11*(3), 323–339.

Pilgrim, D. (2015). *Understanding mental health: A critical realist exploration.* Routledge.

Pilgrim, D. (2018). Happiness: CBT and the Layard thesis. In D. Loewenthal & G. Proctor (Eds.), *Why not CBT? Against and for CBT revisited* (pp.52–66). PCCS Books.

Pilgrim, D. & McCranie, A. (2013.) *Recovery and mental health: A critical sociological account.* Palgrave Macmillan.

Pilgrim, D. & Treacher, A. (1982). *Clinical psychology observed*. Routledge.

Plan C (2017, February 17). *Towards acid communism*. [Blog]. Plan C. www.weareplanc.org/blog/towards-acid-communism/

Plomin, J. (2019, May 22). Whorlton Hall hospital abuse and how it was uncovered. *BBC News*. www.bbc.co.uk/news/health-48369500

Potter, J. & Wetherell, M. (1987). *Discourse and social psychology: Beyond attitudes and behaviour*. Sage Publications.

Power, K., McGoldrick, T., Brown, K., Buchanan, R., Sharp, D., Swanson, V. & Karatzias, A. (2002). A controlled comparison of eye movement desensitization and reprocessing versus exposure plus cognitive restructuring versus waiting list in the treatment of post-traumatic stress disorder. *Clinical Psychology and Psychotherapy, 9*(5), 299–318.

Power, M. (1999). *The audit society: Rituals of verification*. Oxford University Press.

Prilleltensky, I. (1990). On the social and political implications of cognitive psychology. *The Journal of Mind and Behaviour, 11*(2), 127–136.

Prilleltensky, I. (1997). Community psychology: Reclaiming social justice. In D. Fox & I. Prilleltensky (Eds.), *Critical psychology: An introduction* (pp.166–184). Sage.

Prinz, J. (2012). *Beyond human nature. How culture and experience shape our lives*. Allen Lane.

Purser, R. (2019). *McMindfulness: How mindfulness became the new capitalist spirituality*. Random House.

Purser, R.E., Forgers, D. & Burke, A. (2016). Preface. In R.E. Purser, D.F. Forbes, D.F. & A. Burke (Eds.), *Handbook of mindfulness. Culture, context, and social engagement* (pp.v-xxv). Springer International.

Rapley, M. (2004). *The social construction of intellectual disability*. Cambridge University Press.

Read, J. (2009). A genealogy of homo-economicus: Neoliberalism and the production of subjectivity. *Foucault Studies, 6*, 25–36.

Read, J., Kirsch, I. & McGrath, L. (2019). Electroconvulsive therapy for depression: A review of the quality of ECT vs sham ECT trials and meta-analyses. *Ethical Human Psychiatry and Psychology, 21*, 64–103.

Reddy, M.S. & Starlin Vijay, M. (2017). Empirical reality of dialectical behavioral therapy in borderline personality. *Indian Journal of Psychological Medicine, 39*(2), 105–108.

Redley, R. (2008). Understanding the social exclusion and stalled welfare of people with learning disabilities. *Disability and Society, 24*(4), 489–501.

Reeve, D. (2000). Oppression in the counselling room. *Disability and Society, 15*(4), 669–682.

Repper, J. & Perkins, R. (2003). *Social inclusion and recovery: A model for mental health practice*. Bailliere Tindall.

Rizq, R. (2012). The perversion of care: Psychological therapies in a time of IAPT. *Psychodynamic Practice, 18*(1), 7–24.

Roberts, R. (2015). *Psychology and capitalism*. Zero Books.

Robertson, D. (2010). *The philosophy of Cognitive-Behavioural Therapy (CBT): Stoic philosophy as rational and cognitive psychotherapy*. Karnac Books.

Robins, D. (1993). *Tarnished visions*. Oxford University Press.

Rogers, A. & Pilgrim, D. (2003). *Mental health and inequality*. Palgrave Macmillan.

Rogers, A. & Pilgrim, D. (2005). *A sociology of mental health and illness* (3rd ed.). Open University Press.

Rogers, A. & Pilgrim, D. (2015). *A sociology of mental health and illness* (4th ed.). Open University Press.

Rosa, S.K. (2020, March 20). With 1,500 mutual aid groups set up in a matter of days, will things ever be the same again? *Novara Media*. https://novaramedia.com/2020/03/20/with-1500-mutual-aid-groups-set-up-in-a-matter-of-days-things-will-never-be-the-same-again/

Rose, N. (1985). *The psychological complex*. Routledge.

Rose, N. (1996). *Inventing our selves: Psychology, power and personhood*. Cambridge University Press.

Rose, N. (1999). *Governing the soul: The shaping of the private self*. Free Association Books.

Rose, N. (2007). *The politics of life itself: Biomedicine, power, and subjectivity in the twenty-first century*. Princeton University Press.

Roser, M. & Ortiz-Ospina, E. (2013). *Global extreme poverty* (revised 2017/2019). Our World in Data. https://ourworldindata.org/extreme-poverty

Roth, A. & Fonagy, P. (2005). *What works for whom? A critical review of psychotherapy research*. Guilford Press.

Rothbaum, B.O. (1997). A controlled study of eye movement desensitization and reprocessing in the treatment of posttraumatic stress disordered sexual assault victims. *Bulletin of the Menninger Clinic, 61*, 317–334.

Rothschild, B. (2000). *The body remembers: The psychophysiology of trauma and trauma treatment*. W.W. Norton & Co.

Rousmaniere, T. (2016). *Deliberate practice for psychotherapists: A guide to improving clinical effectiveness*. Routledge.

Rousmaniere T., & Wolpert, M. (2017). Talking failure in therapy and beyond: A conversation across the Atlantic, between Dr Tony Rousmaniere and Professor Miranda Wolpert. *The Psychologist Magazine, 30*, 40–43.

Royal College of Psychiatrists. (2014). *Report of the second round of the national audit of schizophrenia*. Royal College of Psychiatrists.

Rutherford, J. (2008). The culture of capitalism. *Soundings, 38*, 8–18.

Rutherford, T. (2013). *Historical rates of social security benefits*. House of Commons Library. http://researchbriefings.files.parliament.uk/documents/SN06762/SN06762.pdf

Ryan, F. (2017, May 4). Pushing people to the brink of suicide: the reality of benefit assessments. *The Guardian*. www.theguardian.com/commentisfree/2017/may/04/benefits-assessments-damaging-lives-hardworking-britain

Ryan, F. (2019). *Crippled: Austerity and the demonization of disabled people*. Verso.

Sampson, E.E. (1981). Cognitive psychology as ideology. *American Psychologist, 36*(7), 730–743.

Sands, A. (2000). *Falling for therapy: Psychotherapy from a client's point of view*. Macmillan.

Sapolsky, R.M. (2004). *Why zebras don't get ulcers*. Holt Paperbacks.

Sarachild, K. (1973). Consciousness-raising: A radical weapon. Reprinted in Redstockings (Eds.). (1975/1978). *Feminist Revolution: An abridged edition with additional writings*. (pp.144–150). Random House.

Saunders, P. & Harris, C. (1990). Privatization and the consumer. *Sociology, 24*(1), 57–75.

Savage, M. (2018, April 22). 'If you create a hostile environment, you shouldn't be surprised that it's hostile.' *The Guardian*. www.theguardian.com/uk-news/2018/apr/22/hostile-environment-landlords-check-immigration-status-under-coalition-government

Savage, M. (2000). *Class analysis and social transformation*. Open University Press.

Sayer, A. (2000). *Realism and social science*. Sage.

Sayer, A. (2005). *The moral significance of class*. Cambridge University Press.

Scheff, T.J. & Fearon, D.S. (2004). Cognition and emotion? The dead end in self-esteem research. *Journal for the Theory of Social Behaviour, 34*(1), 73–90.

Schilling, C. (2003). *The body and social theory* (2nd ed). Sage.

Schofield, W. (1986). *Psychotherapy: The purchase of friendship*. Routledge.

Schwartz, B. (2005). *The paradox of choice: Why more is less*. Harper Perennial.

Scott, M.J. (2018). Improving access to psychological therapies (IAPT) – The need for radical reform. *Journal of Health Psychology, 23*(9), 1136–1147.

Segal, Z., Teasdale, J. & Williams, M. (2002). *Mindfulness-based cognitive therapy for depression*. Guilford Press.

Sennett, R. (1998). *The corrosion of character: The personal consequences of work in the new capitalism*. W.W. Norton & Co.

Sennett, R. (2006). *The culture of new capitalism*. Yale University Press.

Shakespeare, T. (2018). *Disability: The basics*. Routledge.

Shapiro, F. (1995). *Eye movement desensitization and reprocessing*. Guilford Press.

Shedler, J. (2015). Where is the evidence for 'evidence-based' therapy? *The Journal of Psychological Therapies in Primary Care, 4*, 47–59.

Sherman, J.J. (1998). Effects of psychotherapeutic treatments for PTSD: A meta-analysis of controlled clinical trials. *Journal of Traumatic Stress, 11*(3), 413–435.

Shotter, J. (1993a). *Cultural politics of everyday life*. Open University Press.

Shotter, J. (1993b). Bakhtin and Vygotsky: Internalisation as a boundary phenomenon. *New Ideas in Psychology, 11*, 379–390.

Shusterman, R. (Ed.). (1999). *Bourdieu: A critical reader*. Blackwell.

Shweder, R.A. (2004). Deconstructing the emotions for the sake of comparative research. In A. Manstead, N. Frijda & A. Fischer, *Feelings and emotions: The Amsterdam symposium* (pp.81–97). Cambridge University Press.

Sims, P., Brooke, C., Newling, D. & Hull, L. (2008, March 17). The suffering of Shannon Matthews: Why police now fear the worst about her 24-day ordeal. *Daily Mail*. www.dailymail.co.uk/news/article-536488/The-suffering-Shannon-Matthews-Why-police-fear-worst-24-day-ordeal.html

Sinclair, U. (1935). *I, candidate for Governor: And how I got licked*. University of California Press.

Slater, T. (2012). The myth of 'Broken Britain': Welfare reform and the production of ignorance. *Antipode 46*(4), 948–969. https://doi.org/10.1111/anti.12002

Slobodian, Q. (2020, June 1). How the libertarian right plans to profit from the pandemic. *The Guardian*. www.theguardian.comcommentisfree/2020/jun/01/coronavirus-libertarian-right-profit-coronavirus-pandemic

Smail, D. (1978). *Psychotherapy: A personal approach*. Dent.

Smail, D. (1983). Psychotherapy and 'change': Some ethical considerations. In Fairbairn, S. & Fairbairn, G. (Eds.), *Psychology, ethics and change* (pp.31–43). Routledge & Kegan Paul.

Smail, D. (1993). *The origins of unhappiness: A new understanding of personal distress*. Harper Collins.

Smail, D. (2005). *Power, interest and psychology: Elements of a social-materialist understanding of distress*. PCCS Books.

Smail, D. (2006). Is clinical psychology selling its soul (again)? *Clinical Psychology Forum, 168*, 17–20.

Smith, C. (2007). Why Christianity works: An emotions-focused phenomenological account. *Sociology of Religion, 68*(2), 165–178.

Smith, D. (2004). The uses and abuses of positivism. In Mair, G. (Ed.), *What matters in probation* (pp.34–52). Willan Publishing.

Smith, M.L. & Glass, G.V. (1977). Meta-analysis of psychotherapy outcome studies. *American Psychologist, 32*(9), 3752–3760.

Smith, M.L., Glass, G.V. & Miller, T.I. (1980). *The benefits of psychotherapy.* The John Hopkins University Press.

Sontag, S. (1978). *Illness as metaphor and AIDS and its metaphors.* Picador USA.

Spellman, B.A. (2015). A short (personal) future history of revolution 2.0. *Perspectives on Psychological Science, 10*(6), 886–-899.

Srnicek, N. (2016). *Platform capitalism.* Polity Press.

Staddon, J. (2017). *Scientific method: How science works, fails to work or pretends to work.* Taylor & Francis.

Stanley, S. (2012). Mindfulness: Towards a critical-relational perspective. *Personality and Social Psychology Compass, 6*(9), 631–641.

Stegenga, J. (2018). *Medical nihilism.* Oxford University Press.

Stein, B. (2006, November 26). In class warfare, guess which class is winning. *New York Times.* www.nytimes.com/2006/11/26/business/yourmoney/26every.html

Stenfert Kroese, B. & Holmes, G. (2000). I've never said 'no' to anyone in my life. In C. Newnes, C. Dunne & G. Holmes (Eds.), *This is madness too: A critical look at the mental health treatment system* (pp.71–80). PCCS Books.

Stewart, H. (2017, March 9). Women bearing 86% of austerity burden, Commons figures reveal. *The Guardian.* www.theguardian.com/world/2017/mar/09/women-bearing-86-of-austerity-burden-labour-research-reveals

Stiglitz, J.E. (2002). *Globalization and its discontents.* Penguin.

Stiglitz, J.E. (2013). *The price of inequality.* Penguin.

Stivers, R. (2004). *Shades of loneliness: Pathologies of a technological society.* Rowan & Littlefield.

Stoffers-Winterling, J.M., Völlm, B.A., Rücker, G., Timmer, A., Huband, N. & Lieb, K. (2012). Psychological therapies for borderline personality disorder. *Cochrane Database of Systematic Reviews, 8.*

Strupp, H.H., & Hadley, S.W. (1979). Specific vs nonspecific factors in psychotherapy: A controlled study of outcome. *Archives of General Psychiatry, 36*(10), 1125–1136.

Stuckler, D. & Basu, S. (2013). *The body economic: Why austerity kills.* Allen Lane.

Sturge, G. (2019, July 23). *UK prison population statistics.* House of Commons Library Briefing Paper. CBP-04334.

Sue, D. & Sue, D.W. (2012). *Counseling the culturally different: Theory and practice.* John Wiley & Sons.

Sweeney, A., Clement, S., Filson, B. & Kennedy, A. (2016). Trauma informed mental healthcare in the UK: What is it and how can we further its development? *Mental Health Review Journal, 21*(3), 174–192.

Sykes, M.W. (2003). Why is this man smiling? A self described grouch is trying to turn happiness into a science. *Psychotherapy Networker,* Jan/Feb, pp.46–53.

Tajfel, H. (1982). Social psychology of intergroup relations. *Annual Review of Psychology, 33,* 1–39.

Tallman, K. & Bohart, A. (1999). *How clients make therapy work: The process of active self-healing.* American Psychological Association.

Tarrier, N., Pilgrim, H., Sommerfield, C., Fragher, B., Reynolds, M., Graham, E. & Barrowclough, C. (1999). A randomized trial of cognitive therapy and imaginal exposure in the treatment of chronic post-traumatic stress disorder. *Journal of Clinical and Consulting Psychology, 67*(1), 13–18.

Tavris, C. & Aronson, E. (2007). *Mistakes were made (but not by me): Why we justify foolish beliefs, bad decisions, and hurtful acts.* Houghton Mifflin.

Taylor, D. (2019, October 29). Prisoner rehabilitation does not work, says former prison boss. *The Guardian*. www.theguardian.com/society/2019/oct/29/prisoner-rehabilitation-does-not-work-says-former-prisons-boss

Throop, A. (2008). *Psychotherapy, American culture, and social policy: Immoral individualism*. Palgrave Macmillan.

Timimi, S. (2020). *Insane medicine: How the mental health industry creates damaging treatment traps and how you can escape them*. Sami Timimi.

Timmins, N. (1995). *The five giants: A biography of the welfare state*. HarperCollins.

Timms, K. (2015). *Staff training and challenging behaviour: An analysis of social relations in services to people with intellectual disabilities*. PhD Thesis. University of Birmingham.

Tolin, D. (2007). Is cognitive-behavioral therapy more effective than other therapies? A meta-analytic review. *Clinical Psychology Review, 30*(6), 710–720.

Tolman, C. (1994). *Psychology, society, subjectivity: An introduction to German critical psychology*. Routledge.

Torado, L. (2014). *Hand to mouth: Living in bootstrap America*. Berkeley Books.

Townsend, P. & Davidson, N. (1982). *Inequalities in health: The Black report*. Penguin.

TUC. (2012). *Support for benefit cuts dependent on ignorance, TUC-commissioned poll finds*. TUC. www.tuc.org.uk/news/support-benefit-cuts-dependent-ignorance-tuc-commissioned-poll-finds

Tyrer, P. & Tyrer, H. (2018). *Nidotherapy: Harmonising the environment with the patient*. Cambridge University Press.

United Nations General Assembly: Human Rights Council (2018). *Visit to the United Kingdom of Great Britain and Northern Ireland. Report of the special rapporteur on extreme poverty and human rights*. United Nations. https://undocs.org/A/HRC/41/39/Add.1

Vale, P. (2013, September 10). Michael Gove: 'Families turn to food banks because of poor financial management'. *Huffington Post*. www.huffingtonpost.co.uk/2013/09/10/michael-gove-families-tur_n_3901443.html

Valentine, G. & Harris, C. (2014). Strivers vs skivers: Class prejudice and the demonisation of dependency in everyday life. *Geoforum, 53*, 84–92.

Van Dam, N.T., van Vugt, M.K., Vago, D.R., Schmalzl, L., Saron, C.D., Olendzki, A., Meissner, T., Lazar, S.W., Kerr, C.E., Gorchov, J., Fox, K.C.R., Field, B.A., Britton, W.B., Brefczynski-Lewis, J.A. & Meyer, D.E. (2018). Mind the hype: A critical evaluation and prescriptive agenda for research on Mindfulness and Meditation. *Perspectives in Psychological Science, 13*(1), 36–61.

Verhaeghe, P. (2014). *What about me? The struggle for identity in a market based society*. Scribe Publications.

Vygotsky, L.S. (1962). *Thought and language*. MIT Press.

Wain, M. (1998). *Freud's answer*. Ivan R. Dee.

Wallace T., Foy, S. & Burden, L. (2020, May 13). Furlough scheme extended to October at cost of up to £100 bn. *The Telegraph*. www.telegraph.co.uk/business/2020/05/12/mervyn-king-calls-government-keep-furlough-open-ended/

Walsh, G., Dahling, J.J., Schaarschmidt, M. & Brach, S. (2016). Surface-acting outcomes among service employees with two jobs. *Journal of Service Management, 27*(4), 534–562.

Wampold, B.E. (2001). *The great psychotherapy debate: Model, methods and findings*. Erlbaum.

Wampold, B.E. & Imel, Z.E. (2015). *The great psychotherapy debate: The evidence for what makes therapy work* (2nd ed.). Routledge.

Wampold, B.E., Flückiger, C., Del Re, A.C., Yulish, N.E., Frost, N.D., Pace, B.T., Goldberg, S.B., Miller, D., Baardseth, T.P., Laska K.M. & Hilsenroth, M.J. (2017). In pursuit of truth: A critical examination of meta-analyses of cognitive behavior therapy, *Psychotherapy Research*, 27(1), 14–32.

Wampold, B.E., Mondin, G.W., Moody, M., Stich, F., Benson, K. & Ahn, H. (1997). A meta-analysis of outcome studies comparing bona fide psychotherapies: Empirically, 'All must have prizes.' *Psychological Bulletin*, 122(3), 203–215.

Watkins, C.E. (2011). Does psychotherapy supervision contribute to patient outcomes? Considering thirty years of research. *Clinical Supervisor*, 30(2), 235–256.

Watters, E. (2010). *Crazy like us: The globalization of the American psyche*. The Free Press.

Westen, D., Novotny, C.M. & Thompson-Brenner, H. (2004). The empirical status of empirically supported psychotherapies: Assumptions, findings, and reporting in controlled clinical trials. *Psychological Bulletin*, 131(3), 427–433.

Wetherell, M. (2012). *Affect and emotion: A new social science understanding*. Sage.

Whelan, J. & Layte, R. (2007). Opportunities for all in the new Ireland. In T. Fahey, H. Russell & C.T. Whelan (Eds.), *Best of times? The social impact of the Celtic Tiger* (pp.67–85). Institute of Public Administration.

White, M. (2010, August 12). Clicktivism is ruining leftist activism. *The Guardian*. www.theguardian.com/commentisfree/2010/aug/12/clicktivism-ruining-leftist-activism

Whittock, D. (2016). It made me realize that's how I was: Identity management by people with diagnoses of 'learning disability' and 'mental illness'. In E. Speed, J. Moncrief, & M. Rapley (Eds.), *De-medicalising misery II: Society, politics, and the mental health industry* (pp.120–135). Palgrave Macmillan.

Wilderson, F. (2008). *Biko and the problematic of presence*. In A. Mngxitama, A. Alexander & N.C. Gibson, *Biko lives! Contesting the legacies of Steve Biko* (pp.95–113). Palgrave Macmillan.

Wilkinson, R.G. (2005). *The impact of inequality: How to make sick societies healthier*. Routledge.

Wilkinson, R.G. & Pickett, K. (2010). *The spirit level: Why equality is better for everyone*. Penguin.

Wilkinson, R. & Pickett, K. (2018). *The inner level*. Penguin.

Wilkinson, R. & Pickett, K. (2020, May 4). Why coronavirus might just create a more equal society in Britain. *The Guardian*. www.theguardian.com/commentisfree/2020/may/04/coronavirus-equal-society-britain-wellbeing-economic-growth

Williams, J. & Watson, G. (1996). Mental health services that empower women. In T. Heller, J. Reynold, R. Gomm, R. Muston, & S. Pattison (Eds.), *Mental health matters: A reader* (pp.242–251). Macmillan/Open University.

Willig, C. (2001). *Introducing qualitative research in psychology*. Open University Press.

Willis, M. & Cromby, J. (2020). Bodies, representations, situations, practices: Qualitative research on affect, emotion and feeling. *Qualitative Research in Psychology*, 17(1), 1–12.

Willner, P., Rose, J., Stenfert Kroese, B., Murphy, G.H., Langdon, P.E., Clifford, C., Hutchings, H., Watkins, A., Hiles, S. & Cooper, V. (2020). Effect of the COVID-19 pandemic on the mental health of carers of people with intellectual disabilities. *Journal of Applied Research in Intellectual Disabilities*, 33(6), 1523–1533. doi: 10.1111/jar.12811.

Wilton, J. & Williams, A. (2019). *Engaging with complexity: Providing effective trauma-informed care for women*. Centre for Mental Health/Mental Health Foundation. www.mentalhealth.org.uk/publications/engaging-complexity-providing-effective-trauma-informed-care-women

Wintour, P. (2015, July 15). Biggest crackdown on trade unions for 30 years launched by Conservatives. *The Guardian*. www.theguardian.com/politics/2015/jul/15/trade-unions-conservative-offensive-decades-strikes-labour

Wodak, R. (2015). *The politics of fear: What right-wing populist discourses mean.* Sage Publications.

Wright, E.O. (2010). *Envisioning real utopias.* Verso.

Young, I.M. (1990). *'Throwing like a girl' and other essays in feminist philosophy and social theory.* Indiana University Press.

Younge, G. (2017, June 17). A shock to the system: How Corbyn changed the rules British politics. *The Guardian.* www.theguardian.com/politics/2017/jun/16/a-shock-to-the-system-how-jeremy-corbyn-changed-the-rules-of-british-politics

Zilbegeld, B. (1982). *The shrinking of America. Myths of psychological change.* Little, Brown & Company.

Zuboff, S. (2019). *The age of surveillance capitalism: The fight for a human future at the new frontier of power.* Profile Books.

Name index

A
Adair-Stantiall, A. 144, 145
Adams, G. 41
Ahn, H. 66
Akala 176
Allagui, I. 29
Allen, K. 113, 114
American Psychiatric Association (APA) 154
American Psychological Association 67
American Society of Clinical Psychology 67
Ameripour, M. 118
Anderson, M. 128
Anderson, T. 71
Angell, M. 200
Anonymous 29
Arab Spring 29
Archer, M. 199
Armstrong, S. 150
Aronson, E. 128
A Service User 162
Athanasiou, A. 124
Atkinson, P. 76
Atkinson, R. 182–183
Aubrecht, K. 53

B
Baldwin, P. 4
Ball, S.J. 53–54
Bangor Centre for Mindfulness Research and Practice 83
Barker, G. 119
Barlow, D.H. 70
Barr, B. 116
Barr, N. 22

Bartley, M. 132
Basu, S. 116
Bates, Y. 70
Bausell, R.B. 64
BBC News 6, 116
Beck, A. 56, 95
Beck, J.S. 56
Becker, D. 53, 54
Behavioral Tech 87
Bell, E.C. 66
Benefits Street 33
Benish, S. 69
Bennett, T. 129
Bentall, R. 196,
Berger, P. 126
Bergin, A.E. 64
Berman, J.S. 65
Bhaskar, R. 50
Biko, S. 136
Bilet, T. 76
Billig, M. 49, 76
Bisson, J. 93
Bite Size 157–158
Black Lives Matter 176, 177
Blackman, L. 21
Blair, T. 25
Bodhi, B. 83, 85
Bohart, A.C. 65, 78
Bostock, J. 174
Bowcott, O. 31
Bowers, J. 112, 197
Boydell, J. 193
Boyle, M. 7, 96, 135, 142, 154, 196
Bourdieu, P. 131, 135, 191, 198

Bracken, P. 157
Bradley, B. 198
Brady, E. 196
Breggin, P. 200
Bregman, P. 16, 119
Brewer, C. 143
Britain on the Fiddle 33
British Psychology Society (BPS) 42, 154, 156
  Division of Clinical Psychology (DCP) 150
Broadbent, A. 81
Brown, N. 183
Brown, P. 145
Brown, S. 109, 128, 129
Brown, S.D. 55, 123
Brown, W. 3, 14, 30
Bruce, M.L. 56
Buddhism 83
Buffet, W. 23
Bulmer, D. 174, 175
Burkeman, O. 57
Burnett, R. 144
Burnham, J. 170
Burr, V. 126
Burstow, B. 73, 157
Burton, M. 150, 172, 175
Busfield, J. 200
Butler, P. 6, 19, 32
Butt, R. 21

C

Caldini, R. 198
Cambridge Analytica 29
Cameron, D. 114, 119
Canguilhem, G. 46
Cardemil, E. 71, 166
Care Quality Commission 137, 148
Carver, C.S. 55
Cederstrom, C. 101, 109
CEP Mental Health Policy Group 84, 161
Chaiklin, H. 175
Chakelian, A. 6
Chan, A.-W. 74
Chapman, S. 6
Charlton, B. 47, 64
Chassin, L. 195
Cheetham, T.D. 6
Cherry, F. 44
Chomsky, N. 107, 111

Churchill, C. 163
Churchill, W. 5
Cialdini, R. 79
Clarke, J. 31, 114
Climate Action 28
Cloud, D. 119
Clough, P. 124
Cobain, I. 139–140
Cocker, J. 115, 119
Cohen, B.M.Z. 154
Coles, S. 152, 159, 179
Collini, S. 34
Cooke, B. 175
Cooper, M. 62
Corbyn, J. 186
Corralejo, S.M. 77
Courea, E. 119
Crass 26–27
Crick, F. 47
Critical Psychiatry Network 59
Cromby, J. 52, 57, 59, 115, 123, 124, 125, 126, 141, 195, 196
Crook, J. 83
Crowley, M. 31
Csordas, T. 191
Cuijpers, P. 73, 75
Curran, J. 70
Curt, B. 191
Cygnet Healthcare 136–137, 148

D

Daguerre, A. 31
Dahlstedt, M. 99
Dalal, F. 69, 74, 76
Dallos, R. 48, 152, 153
Damasio, A.R. 124, 191, 198
Dardot, P. 35, 114
Das Nair, R. 158
Davidson, N. 4
Davies, D. 71, 81
Davies, W. 62, 182, 184, 201
Davis, M. 175
Deleuze 123
Diamond, B. 157, 158, 174, 179
Diamond, R. 174
Dickens, C. 160
Dineen, T. 76
Dixon, T. 124
Doherty, A. 183

Dohrenwend, B.P. 193
Donnison, D. 135, 201
Donovan, M. 32
Dorling, D. 2, 23, 38, 154
Double, D. 59, 152
Dragioti, E. 72
Driessen, E. 73
Dryden, W. 164
Duffy, S. 116
Dunford. J. 182
Dunne, E. 197
Dunner, D.L. 196
Durham, R.C. 96
Durlak, J.A. 65

E

Eagleton, T. 33, 102
Earle, S. 184
Earnshaw, M. 175
Edge, I. 174
Edwards, D. 126, 128
Ehrenreich, B. 108
Elias, N. 191
Elkin, I. 75
Elkin, L. 47
Elliott, L. 113, 114, 119
Ellis, D. 29
Ellsberg, M. 193
Eltantawy, N. 29
Epstein, W.M. 49, 53, 64, 66, 75, 77, 79, 80, 143, 149, 175, 200
Etherington, D. 31
European Association for Experimental Social Psychology 112
European Central Bank 114
European Commission 114
European Union 113
Evaldsson, A.-C. 131
Evans, S. 124
Evans, T.M. 142
Extinction Rebellion 121

F

Fagan, R. 174
Fairbank, S. 158
Falkai, P. 196
Fals-Borda, O. 174
Fancher, R. 197
Farias, M. 70, 85

Farina, A. 195
Farlow, A. 113
Fearon, D.S. 52, 141
Federal Ministry for Economic Affairs 28
Fenichel, O. 143
Fenney, D. 152
Ferguson, D. 138
Ferguson, I. 99
Ferneyhough, C. 141
Fine, M. 35, 191
Finley, K. 30
Fisher, M. 103, 104, 109, 115, 119–120, 142, 155, 176
Fisher, S. 78
Fonagy, P. 64
Ford, M. 30
Forde, R.A. 144
Fordism 25–27, 106, 107, 115
Foti, A. 37
Foucault, M. 46, 47, 82, 100, 135
Fox, C. 52
Fox, D. 44
Frank, J.D. 63
Franklin, R. 47
Free Association, The 191
Freedland, J. 198
Freire, P. 173–174
Freud Archives 70
Freud, Lord 6
Freud, S. 98, 133, 134, 140
Friedli, L. 4, 53, 55, 56, 84, 118
Frost, N.D. 67
Fryer, D. 113, 117, 174
Fryers, T. 194
Fuchs, T. 153
Fukayama, F. 104
Furedi, F. 47, 100

G

Garcia-Moreno, C. 193
Garland, D. 144
Garthwaite, K. 6
Gayle, D. 146
Gergen, K.J. 126
Gigerenzer, G. 76
Gilbert, J. 24–27
Gilbert, P. 37
Glass, G.V. 64
Glazebrook, C. 193

Gleitman, H. 42, 43, 47, 49
Godsi, E. 143
Goldacre, B. 74
Goldberg, S. 65
Goodman, L.A. 56
Gould, S.J. 46
Gove, M. 6
Graeber, D. 106
Greenberg, G. 78
Gregg, M. 124
Grierson, J. 145
Guatama Buddha 83
Gunnell, D. 142, 193

H
Hadley, S.W. 65
Hagan, T. 135, 201
Hakim, C. 165
Hallam, R. 70, 152
Halley, J. 124
Han, B.-C. 110
Hanley, B. 175
Hanley L. 24, 32–33
Harper, D. 53, 196
Harré, R. 15, 52, 194, 199
Harris, C. 27, 31, 117, 174
Harrison, G. 193
Harvey, D. 22, 23, 103, 107
Hassiotis, A. 149
Hattie, J.A. 65
Haug, F. 177
Healy, D. 73
Hearn, A. 31
Heenan, M. 164
Heise, L. 193
Herman, E.S. 107
Hern, A. 182
Hillbrecht, M. 30
HM Inspectorate of Prisons 144
Hobfall, S.E. 55
Hochschild, A.R. 106
Hoffart, A. 76
Holland, S. 174, 177
Holmes, G. 77, 152, 171, 174, 175
Home, S. 191
Homeless Link 5
Hook, D. 135
Houghton, P. 158, 159
Howard, A. 65

Hróbjartsson, A. 80
Hunt, J. 119

I
Iacobucci, G. 5
Illich, I. 158, 175
Iliffe, S. 62
Illouz, E. 79, 200
Imel, Z.E. 62, 64, 65, 66, 67, 69, 71
Improving Access to Psychological
 Therapies (IAPT) 84, 99, 118, 159, 164, 200
Independent Living 118
Inequality.org 23
Ingleby, D. 107, 151
International Monetary Fund (IMF) 113, 114, 119

J
Jackson, C. 62, 81
Jacobson, N. 49
James, O. 23, 35, 38, 113, 115
Jameson, F. 103
Jansen, H.A.F.M. 193
Jenkin, Lady 6
Jenkins, R. 194
Jensen, J.A. 93
Jensen, S.A. 77
Jensen, T. 33
Jessop, B. 31
Johnson, J.G. 193
Johnson, M. 125, 190
Johnstone, L. 7, 48, 135, 142, 152, 153, 154, 157
Jones, G. 116
Jones, L. 145
Jones, O. 32, 198
Jonsson, U. 71
Jopling, D. 78
Joseph, J. 195
Judt, T. 16, 39

K
Kabat-Zinn, J. 83
Kagan, C. 150, 156, 172, 174, 175
Kagan, J. 165, 174, 198
Kahneman, D. 197
Kazmi, A. 29
Kearney, A. 166
Kebler, J. 29

Keenan, S 159
Kelly, A.E. 79
Kendall, P. 196
Kendler, K. 194
Khazan, O. 182
Kim, S. 71, 166
Kings Fund 116
Kirsch, I. 80, 200
Klein, N. 106, 184–185
Kleinman, A. 197
Kothari, U. 175
Kotter, J.P. 13
Kubler-Ross, E. 13
Kupfer, D. 154, 155
Kwiecinski, R. 193

L

Labour Party 29, 120
Laing, R.D. 151
Lait, J. 143
Lambert, M.J. 64
Landin-Romero, R. 92
Langer, S. 123, 125, 191
Langlois, J. 195
Laval, C. 35, 114
Layard, R. 84
Layte, R. 23
Lazzarato, M. 114
Lecrubier, Y. 196
Le Doux, J. 198
Lehrhaupt, L. 83
Lewin, K. 9
Lewis, S. 146
Lilienfeld, S.O. 70, 94
Lilly, R.S. 55
Linehan, M. 87
Loach, K. 118
Loewenthal, D. 62
London School of Economics 84
Longmore, R. 66
Lordon, F. 106
Lovett, H. 146, 148
Luber, M. 91
Luckmann, T. 126
Lynch, T. 197

M

Machin, S. 185
Mahayana Buddhism 83

Maier, W. 196
Mair, G. 144
Mair, K. 202
Major, L.E. 185
Malinowski, P. 86
Malli, M.A. 150
Marmot, M. 56
Martin, E. 109
Martin, L. 100
Martin-Baro, I. 172–174
Marx, K. 104, 105
Mason, P. 24–25, 26
Masson, J. 70, 133
Massumi, B. 124
Matthews, K. 32–33
Matthews, S. 32
May, R. 65
May, T. 6
McCranie, A. 160
McGarvey, D. 161
McGrath, L. 159, 160
McKenzie, L. 108, 175
McLean, S. 175
McNamee, S. 126
McVeigh, K. 2
Meditation Research Lab, Liverpool John
    Moores University 86
Meeks, J. 22
Meibert, P. 83
Melluish, S. 174, 175
Meltzer, H. 36
Mental Elf 163
Mental Health Foundation 161
Merleau-Ponty, M. 191
#MeToo 177
Mews, A. 145
Middleton, D. 128, 129
Midlands Psychology Group xii, 179–180,
    206
Milburn, K. 120–121, 186
Mindfulness All-Party Parliamentary Group
    (MAPPG) 84, 85
Mindfulness in Schools Project 87
Ministry of Justice 145
Mishra, P. 83
Mollon, P. 75
Moloney, P. 53, 62, 81, 85, 144, 175
Momentum 121
Monbiot, G. 1, 3, 107

Moncrieff, J. 73, 95, 152, 200, 201
Montero, M. 172, 174
Moore, P. 30
Moore, T. 184
Morgan, A. 77
Morris, N. 6
Morrison, A.P. 193
Morrison, K. 200
Muhammad, S. 182
Munder, T. 72
Mutch, A. 131
Mute 37
Myrdal, G. 45

N

Nafstad, H.E. 108
Napoleon, T. 195
National Collaborating Centre for Mental Health 86, 88–90, 96–97
National Health Service (NHS) 5, 15, 58, 59, 83, 84, 116, 118, 136, 148, 152, 156, 174, 182, 184
National Hearing Voices Network 157
National Institute for Health and Care Excellence (NICE) 64, 75, 86–87, 88, 92–93, 96–97, 148
National Institute of Health (NIH) 73
National Institute of Mental Health Collaborative Research Program (MHCRP) 75
Needs, A. 144, 145
Nelson, F. 6
New Labour 25
Newman, J. 31, 114
Newnes, C. 189
New Optimists 57
Newton, T. 195
New York Times 23
Nightingale, D.J. 126
Norcross, J.C. 71, 202
Nordt, C. 115
Norton, N.C. 65
Norton, P.J. 69
Nottingham Mental Health Alliance 178–179
Nylander, P.-A. 146

O

O'Brien, J. 123
O'Boyle 114

Occupy 29, 121
O'Grady, K. 195
O'Hara, M. 116
Oliver, M. 150
Olson, G. 139
O'Mahony, S. 81
Open Democracy UK 24, 116
Open Science Collaboration 49
Orban, V. 184
Orford, J. 156, 172
Orlinksy, D. 63
Orne, M.T. 79
Ortiz-Ospina, E. 57
Osborne, G. 114
Oxford Mindfulness Centre 87

P

Page, K. 193
Papadopoulos, D. 123, 198
Parker, I. 111, 126, 200
Pearce, S.H.S. 6
Peck, T. 6
Peev, G. 119
Perkins, R. 56
Peterson, J. 10
Pickett, K. 2, 37, 38, 56, 59, 154, 182, 194
Pilgrim, D. 36, 37, 46, 47, 48, 49, 51, 53, 62, 64, 118, 151, 160, 196, 201
Plan C 177
Plomin, J. 137
Potter, J. 126
Power, K. 95
Power, M. 35
Price, E.C. 69
Prilleltensky, I. 111, 172
Prinz, J. 153
Proctor, G. 62
Psychologists Against Austerity 117, 159
Psychologists for Social Change 159
Purser, R. 85

R

Rapley, M. 77, 146, 148
Read, J. 30, 152, 193
Reavey, P. 128, 129
Reddy, M.S. 90
Redley, R. 150
Rees-Mogg, J. 6
Reeve, D. 71

Reeves, J. xii
Repper, J. 56
Ritsher, J.E.B. 193
Rizq, R. 62, 81, 99
Roberts, C. 144
Roberts, R. 105, 110
Robertson, D. 113
Robins, D. 175
Robinson, A. 30
Rogers, A. 36, 37, 64, 196
Rogers, C.R. 63, 65
Romano, Z. 37
Rosa, S.K. 182
Rose, N. 44, 60, 79, 99, 108
Rose, S. 195
Roser, M. 57
Ross, C.A. 145, 193
Roth, A. 64
Rothbaum, B.O. 93
Rothschild, B. 128
Rousmaniere, T. 65, 67, 79
Roxer, M. 57
Royal College of Psychiatrists 97
Rutherford, J. 23
Rutherford, T. 31
Ryan, F. 31, 116, 118

S

Sampson, E.E. 43, 112, 197
Sands, A. 78
Sapolsky, R.M. 37
Sarachild, K. 177
Sartorious, N. 196
Saunders, P. 27
Savage, M. 36, 114
Sayer, A. 50
Scheff, T.J. 52, 141
Schilling, C. 165
Schmidt, E. 184
Schofield, W. 165
Schore, A. 191, 195
Scott, M.J. 76
Schutz, A. 191
Schwartz, B. 34
Schwitzgebel, E. 197
Segal, Z. 83
Seigworth, G. 124
Seligman, M. 81
Sennett, R. 39

Sex Offender Treatment Programme (SOTP) 145
Shakespeare, T. 148, 149
Shallice, T. 197
Shapiro, F. 91–92, 93, 94
Shedler, J. 74, 75
Sherman, J.J. 67
Shoplifters and Proud 33
Shotter, J. 126, 127, 142, 199
Shusterman, R. 131
Shweder, R.A. 124, 125
Sims, P. 32
Sinclair, U. 132–133
Slater, T. 33
Slobodian, Q. 185
Smail, D. x, xii, 10, 16, 17, 36, 52, 62, 77, 107, 109, 126, 132–135, 137–139, 180, 189, 192, 199, 201, 206–207
Smith, C. 141
Smith, D. 144
Smith, M.L. 64
Sonn, C.S. 172, 174
Sontag, S. 109
Speed, E. 53
Spellman, B.A. 49
Spicer, A. 101, 109
Srnicek, N. 29
Staddon, J. 73, 79
Stambe, R. 113, 117
Stanley, S. 83
Starlin Vijay, M. 90
Stearn, R. 4, 84, 118
Stegenga, J. 81
Stein, B. 23
Stenfert Kroese, B. 77
Stenner, P. 123
Stephenson, N. 198
Stewart, H. 115
Stiglitz, J.E. 23
Stivers, R. 78
Stoffers-Winterling, J.M. 90
Strupp, H.H. 65
Stuckler, D. 116
Sturge, G. 144
Sue, D. 166
Sue, D.W. 166
Sweeney, A. 9
Sykes, M.W. 81

T

Tajfel, H. 44, 112
Tallman, K. 65, 78
Tarrier, N. 66
Tavris, C. 128
Taylor, D. 145
Thatcher, M. 4, 21, 23–28, 33, 38, 40, 58, 107, 119
Theravada Buddhism 83
Throop, A. 153
Tienari, P. 195
Timimi, S. 76, 196
Timmins, N. 186
Timms, K. 149
Tolin, D. 71
Tolman, C. 123, 190
Torado, L. 109
Townsend, P. 4
Treacher 62, 151
Truax, P. 49
Trump, D. 14–15, 59, 120, 184
TUC 32
Tversky, A. 197
Tyrer, H. 80
Tyrer, P. 80

U

UK Uncut 29, 121
United Nations General Assembly Human Rights Council 150
University of Massachusetts Center for Mindfulness 87
Uston, T.B. 196

V

Vale, P. 6
Valentine, G. 31
Van Dam, N.T. 86
van Os, J. 193, 196
Verhaeghe, P. 23, 36
Vonnegut, K. x
Vygotsky, L.S. xi, 126, 190, 191

W

Wain, M. 98
Wallace, T. 185
Walsh, G. 31
Wampold, B.E. 62, 64, 65, 66, 67, 69, 71, 72
Warner, V. 193

Watkins, C.E. 65
Watson, J. 47, 56
Watters, E. 153, 154, 197
Watts, C. 193
Weishaar, A.T. 56
We Pay Your Benefits 33
Westen, D. 72, 76, 200
Wetherell, M. 124
Whelan, J. 23
Whitaker, R. 200
White, M. 29
Whittock, D. 149
Whorlton Hall, Co. Durham 136
Wiest, J.B. 29
Wikholm, C. 70, 85
WikiLeaks 29
Wilderson, F. 136
Wilkinson, R.G. 2, 37, 38, 56, 59, 154, 182, 194
Williams, J. 56, 152
Willig, C. 177
Willis, M. 124
Willner, P. 150
Wilson, T. 197
Wilton, J. 152
Winterbourne View 149
Wintour, P. 31, 113, 114
Wittchen, H.U. 196
Wodak, R. 184
Wolpert, M. 79
Wood, M. 116
World Bank 113
World Economic Forum 119
World Health Organisation (WHO) 55
Worrell, M. 66
Wright, E.O. 36, 37

Y

Young, I.M. 131, 191, 198
Young, R. 195
Younge, G. 37, 118

Z

Zilbegeld, B. 77, 79
Zizek, S. 103
Zuboff, S 29

Subject index

A

affective turn 124
alienation 105, 106, 170
antipsychotic drugs 95
anxiety 35, 36, 48, 78, 141, (*see also* CBT, depression, EMDR, MBSR)
    CBT for, 66, 69, 95
    as diagnosis 141, 194
    and EMDR 92-93
    MBSR for, 85-86
    and neoliberalism 36, 97, 117
    in response to therapy 70, 101
    social, 36
    and social status 37
    therapies for, 69, 76, 83, 89
    and women 193
austerity 34, 113-117
    and Covid-19 181
    impact
        on equalities 119
        on mental health 142
        on people with learning disabilities 150
    psychologists' responses to, 117-118, 159-161

B

Beck's Depression Inventory 66n, 77n
Behavioral Tech 87
behavioural economics 186
Beveridge report 4, 186
bilateral stimulation 92
biomedical psychiatry 95, 151
borderline personality disorder 87, 88, 90
    diagnostic criteria for, 88

C

capitalist realism 103-105, 115
challenging behaviour 135, 146-147, 149
client deterioration 70-71
clinical significance 49, 77, 95
coercion 134
    neoliberalism and, 28, 39, 105, 107,
cognitive behavioural therapy (CBT) 48, 56-57
    as 'coercive bullying tactic' 164
    effectiveness, studies of, 66-67, 69-70, 75, 80, 93, 97, 99
    as mechanised form of treatment 62
    and mindfulness 84
    negative effects of, 70
    as neoliberal tool 53, 164
    with offenders 144-145
    for psychosis/schizophrenia (CBTp) 16, 95-97
community
    activism and Covid-19 182
    care 95
    neoliberal attacks on, 26, 34, 37-39, 58-59, 104, 117
    in non-Western cultures 153
    psychology/ists xi, 11, 41-42n, 156, 172-176, 177
    therapeutic movement 95, 151-152
    treatment orders 159
compassion 5, 11, 34, 101, 145, 148
    Covid-19 and, 182
    in therapy 99, 101
'compassionate solidarity' 176
compliance
    in Fordism 106

habits as, 131
'compliant environment' (immigration) 114–115
component studies 65–66
consciousness raising 177–190, 208
consumerism 5, 20, 25
    neoliberalism and, 34, 105, 108, 110
Covid-19 1, 20–21, 29, 57, 150, 181–187
    and under-25s 185–186
    and zenophobia 184
critical consciousness 121,
critical realism 45, 50–51, 123n
culture(al)
    change 28
        of neoliberalism 35–39
        in public expectations 31–32
        contexts/forces/norms 10, 43, 46, 50, 113, 120, 122–123, 129, 134, 138, 140, 172, 186
    differences 24, 165
    gurus 10
    of individualism 51, 100
    non-Western, 153, 197
    psychology 41
    studies 22
    therapy, 20, 82
    warfare 33
    Western, 8
    working-class, 24–26, 27, 33, 34, 35

D

democracy 14
depression (*see also* anxiety) 13, 36
    Black Dog group 171
    and inequality 36
    therapy outcome studies 73, 75, 89
        for CBT 66, 97
        for DBT 87
        for EMDR 93
        for MBSR 83, 85–87
    and serotonin hypothesis 115
    and unemployment/adversity 117, 141, 193
Depression Report, The 84
depressive hedonia 115
diagnosis (psychiatric) 51, 139, 152, 154, 156, 157, 158, 162
    'demi-regularities' in, 51
Diagnostic and Statistical Manual of Mental Disorders (DSM) 154

digital revolution 28–29, 30, 33
dialectical behaviour therapy (DBT) 20, 82, 87–91
dissent 14, 138
distress
    alternative accounts of, 158–159
    and austerity 116
    competition and, 35–36
    eating, 74, 76
    as internal/individualised process 10, 56, 95–96, 99, 100, 101, 164
    neoliberalism and, 35–39
    prevention of, 172–176
    psychiatric categorisation of, 69, 136, 139, 143–144, 151, 154
    psychology therapies and, 61–62, 63, 71–74
    social materialist influences 26, 50, 53–54, 56, 100, 101, 113, 115, 169
    studies of, 50, 77
    terminology 17–18
    tolerance 87, 89–90
evidence-based therapy 64, 76
efficacy
    of art therapies 96
    of CBT 99, 159
    of DBT 87
    of psychological therapies 20, 62, 69, 72, 81, 82, 86, 98, 100, 101
emotional labour 106
empowerment 158
    of disabled people 150n
Erhard seminars training (est) 100
ethics 3, 8, 14, 51, 90, 98, 127, 145n, 148, 159
    (*see also* moral, political)
    of IAPT roll-out 159
eye movement desensitisation and reprocessing (EMDR) 66, 82, 91–95

F

feeling 18, 20, 47, 95, 122, 123n, 124–125, 126, 130, 138, 140–142, 155, 160, 184
    as material 124
formulation 47–48, 152–153

H

habit 18, 20, 122, 129–132, 140–141, 142, 175n

I

individualism 2, 19, 28, 51–58, 59, 112–113, 115, 122, 162, 172 (*see also* subjectivism)
    ideology of, 103n, 141, 185–186
inequality 20, 36–37
    austerity and, 116
    and capitalism 27, 186
    and Covid-19 183
    and neoliberalism 21, 53, 104, 119
    psychotherapy and, 102
    social 35, 37, 56, 99
institutional abuse (learning disabilities) 148
interests 134–135, 136, 140
    of business 108, 109
    client *vs.* clinician 77
    of psychology/ists xiii, 8, 9, 10, 10n, 11, 45, 58, 133, 142, 166–168
    of the rich and powerful 33, 54, 104, 105, 107, 113, 121, 140, 186
    shared, of communities 35, 171

L

language
    as concept 18, 20, 122, 123n, 125–128, 129, 140–141, 142, 186–187
    conceptual, 66n
    learning, 111
    terminology, 6, 17–18, 33, 116, 125, 166

M

mainstream psychology 41–44
    alignment with neoliberalism 58–60, 102–103, 108
    and the body 124–125
    challenges to, 44–51
    contrast with community psychology 172–173
    and habit 129
    individualism in, 52–58, 162
    and 'persuasion' 107
    positivism in, 42–47
    'victim-blaming' 109
material influences (*see also* power, YAVIS)
    adverse environment/circumstances 2, 10, 15, 27, 39, 43, 52, 109, 113, 162
    and imagining 141
    vs. private, individual 57, 100, 113
    and trauma 55, 94
    and the body 122, 123, 1243
    and Covid-19 185, 186
    habit 129–130, 142
    and neoliberalism 107
    outsight and, 21
    resources, lack of/access to 15, 51, 55, 56, 62n, 101, 136, 150n
        digital 28–29
        of the media 136
    and social structures 33n, 102n, 108
    and subjectivities 59, 102, 113, 122
    on working class culture 34
    and YAVIS 165–166
    on younger people 165
materialism, 'new' 123n
materialist (definition) 17
memory 4, 18, 20, 52, 128–129, 140–142
    and EMDR 92
'memory work' 177
meta-analysis 64, 65, 69, 71, 72, 73, 85, 85n, 86, 93, 96
Mindful Nation UK 84–85
mindfulness 83–87
mindfulness-based stress reduction (MBSR) 83–87
moral 3, 37, 51, 98, 108

N

neoliberal
    core values 35
    culture 23–28, 139–140, 168–170
    squid 105–107
neoliberalism 21–23, 29, 30, 31, 34, 62, 62n, 85n, 97, 99, 101, 104, 104n, 108, 112–113, 115, 120, 134, 185
    alternatives to, 176–178
    and CBT 99
    and Covid-19 181–183
    and distress 35–39, 142, 154
    and empathy 139
    and psychology 52–58
    and psycho-compulsion 117–118
NICE guidelines
    critique of, 75n
    for depression 88–89
    for EMDR 93
    for schizophrenia 96

O

optimism 55–58, 102
    New, 57

P

paraprofessionals 64–65
positive behavioural support (PBS) 80n, 147–149, 149n, 161
philanthrocapitalism 119
placebo effects 63, 67, 78, 81, 85
political 43, 51, 98, 100, 103, 112, 159, 172
positive psychology 55, 108n, 118
post-traumatic stress disorder (PTSD) 55, 66–67, 69 (see also EMDR)
    complex, 83
positivism 42, 45, 45n, 47, 50, 51, 111, 122, 172
poverty 6,
    and inequality 53, 99
    and mental distress 55, 56, 109, 113, 116, 193
    neoliberalism and, 36, 37
    'poverty porn' 33
    rates of, 150n, 154
power 18, 20, 135–137, 140–141
    collective, 178, 180
    and depression/anxiety 141
    distal and proximal, 137–138, 161
    and distress 142–143, 155–156
    and eating disorders 141
    and empowerment 149
    Foucault and, 46, 82
    Freire and, 173
    horizon 138–139
    ideological, and psychology 107–113
    and interests 122–123, 134–135, 141, 179, 186
    interpersonal, 167–170
    'softcop', 170
    of therapies 66, 67, 73, 75, 75n, 78, 81
    of therapists/psychologists 53, 65, 99
        commitment to devolving, 172
    and trauma 145
Power Threat Meaning Framework (PTMF) 154–156, 161–162
privatisation 4, 19, 27n, 35, 37, 59, 186
psycho-compulsion 117, 118
publication bias 72, 73, 81n

R

randomised controlled trials (RCTs) 63–64, 66 (see also efficacy)
    blinding in, 80
    validity of, 72
reification 127
replication 65
    crisis 49–50
Research Excellence Framework 8
researcher allegiance/bias 64, 72, 73, 144, 144n
resilience 3, 21, 33, 52–55, 57, 110, 145
rethinking mental illness 153–156

S

schizophrenia (see also CBT, NICE guidelines) 136, 153, 159
seduction, as government tactic 22, 28, 39, 105, 107 (see also neoliberal squid)
selfish capitalism 35
social
    class 130–131, 138
    constructionism 125, 126n
    materialism 165–166, 178
    unconscious 139–140
socio-economic
    policies and structures, effects of 10
    status 55, 56
statistical significance 49, 64, 69, 72, 76n
stress 52–55 (see also MBSR, PTSD)
    management 109
    and social inequality 37
subjectivism 43, 44, 112–113, 122, 162, 173 (see also individualism)
subjectivity 21, 21n, 43, 59, 60, 107, 131, 140, 141–142, 190
suicide 2. 70, 115n, 116
    in prisons 144, 145

T

technologies
    information/new, 28–30, 98
    neurological, 154, 194
    psychological, 118
    of the self/subjectivities 82, 100, 100n
        psychotherapies as, 202
techniques
    behavioural, 149, 186
    therapeutic, 61–63, 65–69, 78n, 100, 101

(*see also* CBT, CBTp, DBT, MBSR, positive psychology)
trauma (*see also* CBT, DBT, EMDR)
  and abuse 4, 143
  childhood, 51
  combat, 93
  and offenders 145
trauma-informed
  mental health services 9, 125
  therapeutic approaches 67, 70
    and memory 128, 141
    so-called, 125
trauma-focused CBT (TFCBT) 93
treatment fidelity 67
treatment as usual 69, 76

V

values
  communication of, 130, 138
  of community psychology 175–176
  of community and trust 24–28
    effects of neoliberalism on, 37–39
  corporate, 106
    psychology as reinforcing, 58–59
  dominant present-day/neoliberal, 12–14, 103, 120, 168
    CBT and, 53
  extrinsic *vs.* intrinsic, 106–107
  humanistic, of social work 156
  interplay with interests and power 10, 46–47
  of psychology/ists 9, 60, 159, 161
  of recovery 53
variable(s) 50, 55, 56
  dependent 82, 88
  independent 82, 86, 87, 88, 92, 97
victim-blaming 109

W

woke 176–177
working class (*see also* culture)
  children and education 138
  clients 166n
  politics 25
  workers' rights 149

Y

YAVIS 165–166